Mac OS X LEOPARD

KILLER TIPS

Scott Kelby
Dave Gales

KU-443-963

MAC OS X LEOPARD KILLER TIPS

**The Mac OS X Leopard
Killer Tips Team**

COPY EDITORS
Kim Doty
Cindy Snyder

COVER DESIGN AND
CREATIVE CONCEPTS
Jessica Maldonado

PUBLISHED BY
New Riders

Copyright © 2009 by Scott Kelby

First edition: December 2008

All rights reserved. No part of this book may be reproduced or transmitted in any form, by any means, electronic or mechanical, including photocopying, recording, or by any information storage and retrieval system, without written permission from the publisher, except for inclusion of brief quotations in a review.

Composed in Myriad Pro by Kelby Media Group, Inc.

Trademarks
All terms mentioned in this book that are known to be trademarks or service marks have been appropriately capitalized. New Riders cannot attest to the accuracy of this information. Use of a term in the book should not be regarded as affecting the validity of any trademark or service mark.

Macintosh and Mac are registered trademarks of Apple Inc.
Windows is a registered trademark of Microsoft Corporation.

Warning and Disclaimer
This book is designed to provide information about Mac OS X tips. Every effort has been made to make this book as complete and as accurate as possible, but no warranty of fitness is implied.

The information is provided on an as-is basis. The authors and New Riders shall have neither liability nor responsibility to any person or entity with respect to any loss or damages arising from the information contained in this book or from the use of the discs or programs that may accompany it.

ISBN 10:   0-321-50193-4
ISBN 13: 978-0-321-50193-6

9 8 7 6 5 4 3 2 1

Printed in the United States of America

www.newriders.com
www.kelbytraining.com

For my longtime friend, and total Mac-head, Jim Workman.

—Scott Kelby

For my high school sweetheart, confidant, counselor, voice of reason, best friend, and wife of 31 years—Kathy. The secret history we are building together is my most valuable possession and greatest accomplishment.

"A wife of noble character is her husband's crown." — Proverbs 12:4

—Dave Gales

ACKNOWLEDGMENTS SCOTT KELBY

I learned the only downside of co-authoring a book long ago—you only get half as much space to thank the large army of people without whose help, dedication, and tireless efforts, there wouldn't be a book, and to them I'm greatly indebted.

First, I want to thank absolutely just the coolest person I've ever met—my wife, Kalebra. I don't know how I ever got lucky enough to marry her 19 years ago, but it was without a doubt the smartest thing I've ever done, and the greatest blessing God's ever given me. She just flat-out rocks, and at this point, I can't imagine that the crush I've had on her since the first time I met her will ever go away. I love you, Sweetie!

Secondly, I want to thank my son, Jordan. Little Buddy, there's so much of your mom in you, in particular her kind, loving heart, and that's about the best head start anyone could ask for in life. You're the greatest little guy in the world, and such a wonderful, caring role model for your little sister.

Thanks to my little blessing from above, my daughter Kira. You're a little clone of your mom, and that's the best compliment I could give anyone. You're a very lucky little girl, and I'm a very blessed man to be your dad.

I owe a huge debt of gratitude to my good friend, mentor, and this book's co-author, Dave Gales. Over the years Dave has taught me so much, and made such a difference in my life, that just saying "Thanks" is woefully inadequate. Dave is the person who gave me my first Bible, which I still have to this day, and which is dog-eared from being read cover to cover many times. Thanks, my friend, and may God's blessings continue to pour upon you and your family.

I want to thank my team at Kelby Media Group, including my friend and genius guy Creative Director Felix Nelson, my awesome book designer Jessica Maldonado, my incredible world-class editor Kim Doty, my amazing layout master Dave Damstra, my tech editor extraordinaire Cindy Snyder, and my Traffic Director Kim Gabriel. They're a unique group of people, with limitless energy and amazing talent, and I'm honored to get to work with such a gifted team.

As always, a special thanks goes to my very good friend Dave Moser for always looking out for me, and for making sure that everything we do is better than we did before.

I owe a big, big thanks to my good friend Terry White for helping with the development of this book. He was kind enough to share so many of his cool tips and amazing tricks with me, and this book is far better than it would have been without his help.

I want to thank my friend and business partner Jean A. Kendra for her support and enthusiasm for all my writing projects, and of course, I couldn't do any of it without the help of my wonderful "Italian Confidential Secretary" Kathy Siler.

Thanks to Nancy Aldrich-Ruenzel, Scott Cowlin, and everyone at New Riders and Peachpit for their ongoing commitment to excellence, and for the honor of letting me be one of their "Voices That Matter."

And most importantly, an extra special thanks to God and His son Jesus Christ for always hearing my prayers, for always being there when I need Him, and for blessing me with a wonderful life I truly love, and such a warm, loving family to share it with.

ACKNOWLEDGMENTS DAVE GALES

First, I want to thank my wife, Kathy. Many years ago, she looked at a skinny, long-haired hippie and saw someone to love. Ever since, the Lord has taken us on an adventure that has mostly amazed, but sometimes terrified, us. She has cheered my successes, stood with me when I've stepped out of the boat, reassured me when I've failed, and encouraged me to not stop dreaming. I'm not skinny anymore (thanks to her love of baking coupled with my lack of self control), but I'm a much better man than I would have ever been without her. Thanks, as well, sweetie, for keeping me supplied with plenty of chocolate chip cookies, boiled oatmeal cookies, chocolate chewy cookies, and brownies (see why I'm not skinny any more?) to keep me going during late-night writing sessions.

Next, I want to thank my children: Megan, Jon, and Josh. It's amazing that children from the same gene pool can be so different. It's truly a delight to watch each of them discover and develop their gifts and talents. I couldn't love them more or be more proud of each of them. The same sentiments also apply to Autumn, a loud extrovert who joined a family of quiet introverts ten years ago. At last, someone who shares my love of country music—she just won't admit it.

Of course, I want to thank my long-time friend, Scott Kelby, for the privilege of co-authoring this book. I knew Scott way before his bio was filled with mentions of dozens of prestigious awards and stellar accomplishments. Other than the fact that I have to get in the queue outside his office door to see him these days, he's still the same Scott I've known for all these years. It's been a blast watching him develop his skills, unleash his talents, and achieve the level of influence he now has in his field. But, more importantly, it's been a source of deep satisfaction to see him keep his priorities straight and stay focused on those things that matter most in life. God has begun a very good work in your life, my friend, but the best is yet to come!

I want to thank Dave Moser for the influence he has had on my life. He mentored me during the period I was transitioning from pastoring to working in the "real world." He took me under his wing and providing many insights and practical wisdom that helped me preserve my job and some measure of sanity. Thanks, Dave, for pushing me to be a better soldier.

Thanks to my boss, Kleber Stephenson, who is the best boss a person could ever dream of having. (Man, I hope he's reading this). Kleber generously welcomed me back to the seminar team after I took a year off to deliver rice halfway around the world. Thanks for letting me be a part of the wildly successful training network you are building.

Thanks to my Kelby Training Seminars team: Rosemarie "Ro Ro" Ales, Jamie Camanse, Phyllis DeFreece, Jeff Leimbaugh, Jackie Prince, and Debbie Stephenson. You guys are like family (there are some months I see you more than I see my real family!) and there's nobody I'd rather share the "glamour" of traveling all over the country with. Now that the book is done, I'm looking forward to unchaining myself from my laptop and getting out of the hotel for some fun! Who knows? I might even go to the mall with you!

Thanks to Ted Waitt and the team at Peachpit for walking me through the process of writing this book. Ted's continued reassurance that it would get done kept me going.

Thanks to Auto!Automatic!! for the music that kept me charged up and focused on many late nights.

Thanks to God, the author of creativity and the ultimate designer, for surrounding us with such incredible beauty. Your creation overwhelms every one of our senses and is a reflection of your majesty, power, love, and mercy. Your grace showered on me makes life possible. To Jesus Christ, who is crazy enough to love me. To the Holy Spirit, who continually reminds me of who I am in Christ, and lets me know when I'm getting off course.

One last thing: Any references in this book to ADD, OCD, or other conditions with initials, apply to me, not Scott. I'm the one with all the issues.

OTHER BOOKS BY SCOTT KELBY

The iPod Book

The iPhone Book

The Mac OS X Leopard Book

Scott Kelby's 7-Point System For Adobe Photoshop CS3

The Adobe Photoshop Lightroom 2 Book for Digital Photographers

The Digital Photography Book

The Digital Photography Book, volume 2

The Adobe Photoshop CS4 Book for Digital Photographers

The Photoshop Channels Book

Photoshop Down & Dirty Tricks

Photoshop Killer Tips

Photoshop Classic Effects

InDesign Killer Tips

The Photoshop Elements Book for Digital Photographers

Scott Kelby

Scott is Editor and Publisher of *Photoshop User* magazine, and Editor-in-Chief and Publisher of *Layers* magazine. He is President and co-founder of the National Association of Photoshop Professionals (NAPP), the trade association for Adobe® Photoshop® users, and President of the software, education, and publishing firm Kelby Media Group.

Scott is a photographer, designer, and award-winning author of more than 50 books on technology and digital imaging, including the best-selling books: *The iPod Book, The Digital Photography Book, The iPhone Book, Scott Kelby's 7-Point System for Adobe® Photoshop CS3,* and *The Adobe Photoshop Book for Digital Photographers.* Scott has authored several best-selling Macintosh books, including *Mac OS X Killer Tips, Getting Started with Your Mac and OS X,* and the award-winning *Macintosh: The Naked Truth,* all from New Riders and Peachpit Press.

His books have been translated into dozens of different languages, including Russian, Chinese, French, German, Spanish, Korean, Greek, Turkish, Japanese, Dutch, and Taiwanese, among others. For four years straight, Scott has been awarded the distinction of being the world's #1 best-selling author of all computer and technology books, across all categories.

Scott is Training Director for the Adobe Photoshop Seminar Tour, Conference Technical Chair for the Photoshop World Conference & Expo, and is a speaker at trade shows and events around the world. He is also featured in a series of training DVDs, and has been training creative professionals since 1993.

For more background info on Scott, visit his daily blog, *Adobe Photoshop Insider,* at www.scottkelby.com.

Dave Gales

A continuous owner and fan of Apple computers and products, beginning with the Apple IIe in 1983, Dave Gales has used every Mac operating system ever produced. Any Apple update always has his immediate and undivided attention. With a well-documented weakness for gizmos and gadgets, he takes staying on the cutting edge of the latest Apple technology as a personal challenge.

As much as he loves his Mac, Dave's real passion is making a difference in the lives of people. A pastor for 20 years, he has had the opportunity to be present for diverse crisis situations in order to give a helping hand. He has pitched his tent on a tiny Indonesian island after a major earthquake, and he has camped out in a K-Mart parking lot of a Gulf Coast town devastated by Hurricane Katrina. Working out the logistics to get donated supplies into the hands of those most needing the help has been a source of great satisfaction.

Dave has collaborated on several of Scott Kelby's books over the last seven years and was the contributing author of the *Mac OS X Conversion Kit* book. He is currently a member of the Kelby Training Seminar team that conducts one-day seminars on Photoshop, Lightroom, and InDesign in cities across the United States and Canada.

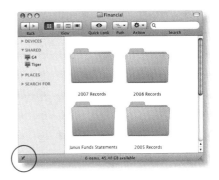
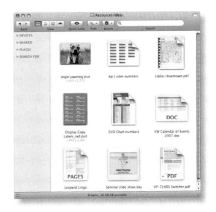

TABLE OF CONTENTS

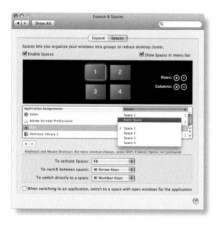

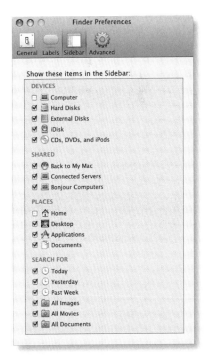

TABLE OF CONTENTS

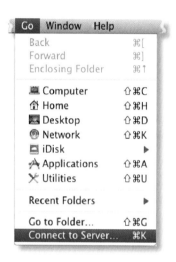

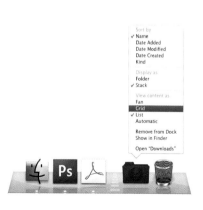

TABLE OF CONTENTS

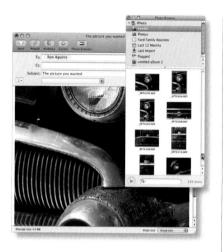

TABLE OF CONTENTS

TABLE OF CONTENTS

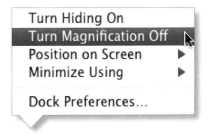

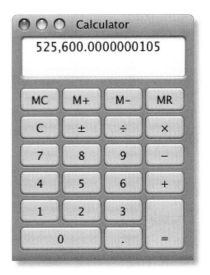

TABLE OF CONTENTS

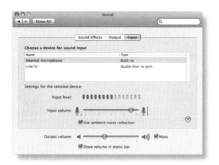

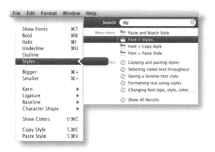

TABLE OF CONTENTS

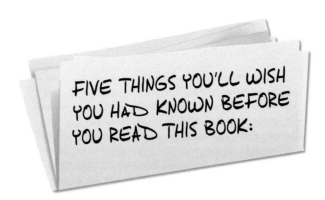

FIVE THINGS YOU'LL WISH YOU HAD KNOWN BEFORE YOU READ THIS BOOK:

(1) Why a book of just tips?

Think about it, if you were writing a book and you found some really great undocumented keyboard shortcut, or maybe a closely-guarded inside secret that you wanted to share with your readers, you'd want it to stand out, right? You'd want to do something that would grab the reader's attention and say, "Hey, look over here—there's something very cool, or important, or special." Right? Right.

So, for years, authors have been creating these little tips in the margins of their books (like the one shown here, at left). That's a pretty standard look for a sidebar tip—it has a bold title, a tint behind the text, and it's off by itself, so it draws the reader's attention.

These "sidebar tip" boxes really work. Well, they work on me anyway, because anytime I buy a computer book and see a sidebar tip box, I usually read it first, because I know it's going to have something like an undocumented keyboard shortcut, or an insider secret that's going to help me.

But there are two problems with your average sidebar tips:

> (1) They usually don't include a graphic or photo;
> (2) And more importantly, there are just not enough of 'em!

So I got to thinkin': Wouldn't it be cool if there was a book where the whole book, cover to cover, was nothing but those little sidebar tips, but with graphics? No long paragraphs explaining the Hierarchical File System. No detailed descriptions of how to configure a LAN, or 16 ways to partition your hard drive—just the fun stuff, just the tips. Well, that's exactly what you're holding— a book of nothin' but killer sidebar tips, but without the sidebars.

(2) So what exactly is a "Killer Tip"?

"Double-click on a folder to open it" may be a tip, but it's a boringly obvious tip, so it's definitely not a Killer Tip. If it's a Killer Tip, it makes you nod and smile when you read it, and you'll be nodding and smiling so much in this book, you're going to look like a bobbing dog in the rear window of a Buick Park Avenue (if they still even make that car). The goal here is to give you tips that are so cool that after reading just a few you have to pick up the phone, call your Mac buddies, and totally tune them up with your newfound Mac OS X power.

TIP

This is a sidebar tip. Every great Mac book has a few of them. But this book is nothing <u>but</u> them. A whole book of cool sidebar tips. Without the sidebars.

(3) This book is not really for beginners, but...

Now, I have to tell you, the tips in this book are designed for people who are already somewhat familiar with Mac OS X, so there's not much stuff here for people who are brand new to the Mac. However, if you are a Mac beginner, I have a special bonus for you—a secret special download-able chapter of beginner tips that I put together just for you. So technically the tips in this downloadable beginners' chapter are not Killer Tips, they're Mac OS X beginners' tips written in a Killer Tips style, but hey—they're free, I made them especially for you, and all you have to do is download the PDF chapter from www.kelbytraining.com/books/leopardtips.

(4) Should you read the intro page at the beginning of each chapter?

That depends. The intro page at the beginning of each chapter is designed to give you a quick mental break, and honestly, they have little to do with the chapter. In fact, they have little to do with anything, but writing these off-the-wall chapter intros is kind of a tradition of mine (I do this in all my books), so if you're one of those really "serious" types, you can skip them because they'll just get on your nerves.

(5) Where should I start?

You can start in any chapter and immediately try the tips that interest you the most. My books aren't set up like a novel—you can jump in anywhere and start on any page. Well, with this book you don't have to start at Chapter 1 and read your way through to the back (although there's nothing wrong with that).

Okay, bunky—you're ready to rip into it, and now you know what to expect, how to use the book, whether you should avoid the intros or not, and you found out about the bonus beginner's chapter to boot. See, I thought you'd want to know this stuff before you read the book.

—Scott Kelby

TIP

When you see a gray tinted box hanging out in the sidebar like this, you can't help but read it, right? They're intoxicating— you're drawn to them. Okay, here's a real tip: If you like sidebar tips, buy this book.

Chapter 1

Window Wonderland

Cool Window Tips

I have to be honest with you. I have some major concerns about the subhead for this chapter: "Cool Window Tips." My fear is that you

Window Wonderland

cool window tips

might give it a quick glance and accidentally read it as "Cool Windows Tips" which this chapter, in a Mac OS X book, clearly is not. In fact, this couldn't be a chapter on Microsoft Windows, primarily because I don't know Windows. Well, I know where the Start menu is, and I can launch an application (if it's fairly easy to find), but that's as much as I'm willing to admit (at least without a Congressional subpoena). Besides, how could there be anything cool about Windows? So what is this chapter really about? I was hoping you would know. Hmmmm. This is kind of embarrassing. Okay, I'll take a stab at it—it sounds like it's probably filled with tips on using Finder windows, managing your files within them, and other cool window tips that will amuse your friends and absolutely captivate small children and family pets (except, of course, for fish, who are waiting patiently for you to overfeed them).

3

   SET YOUR OWN PICTURE AS THE DEFAULT DESKTOP

Leopard's default desktop picture was taken from the bridge of the Enterprise during its inter-galactic travels. If you want to personalize your desktop, you can use one of your own photos. Just Control-click anywhere on the desktop to open the Desktop & Screen Saver preference pane, then choose Change Desktop Background. When it opens, you'll see a list of items you can use to replace the default image. If the picture or graphic you want to use isn't in the list, click the plus sign (+) button below the list and navigate to its location. Then just click once on the image you want to use and press the Choose button in the lower-right corner.

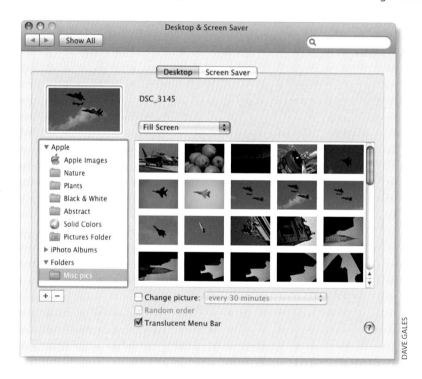

   UNCOMFORTABLE WITH THE SEE-THROUGH MENU BAR?

One of the new features introduced in Leopard that people either love or hate is the transparency—especially in the menu bar. Even before Apple released it, word had leaked out and people were huffing and puffing about how much they hated it (never mind that most of them had never seen it), and how it made the items on the menu bar unreadable. Well, Apple heard the cries of the masses and responded by including a way to turn off the transparent menu bar when they released the Leopard 5.2 update. Personally, I love the transparency. I think it looks elegant when it takes on the color of whatever is behind it. But if you disagree with me, go to the Apple menu, select System Preferences, and click on the Desktop & Screen Saver icon. At the bottom of the Desktop preference pane is the Translucent Menu Bar option. Just turn off the checkbox and you'll never have to see another translucent menu bar again—unless you look at my screen, that is.

OPEN FOLDERS IN NEW WINDOWS

By default, if you double-click on a folder (in Icon or List view), it will open in the same window, which means if you want to see the contents of the original window, you need to click the Back button. Well, if you're like me and you'd like these folders to open in their own separate windows so you can still see the original one, go to the Finder menu at the top of your screen, and choose Preferences. Now click on the General icon up top and turn on the Always Open Folders in a New Window checkbox. Ahhh, that's better!

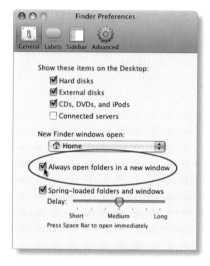

TEMPORARILY OVERRIDE THE OPEN FOLDERS PREFERENCE

Whether you prefer the "everything opens in the same window" or the "give me a new window" scheme, occasionally you may want to get crazy and open a new window the other way. You can override the preference you've set by pressing the Command key when you double-click on a folder. If you want to get really crazy, Option-double-click on a folder or document, and the folder (or document) will open and the old window will close automatically.

 HIDE THE BARS

If you're one of those people who likes to work without a toolbar and sidebar (kind of like working without a net, but not quite as dangerous), just click the button in the top-right corner of any Finder window and they will disappear. If you decide you want them back, just click the button again. But here's another neat thing: if you open a folder located inside a "bar-less" window, it will open the same way.

 HOW TO SEE IF YOU CAN WRITE TO A FOLDER

Mac OS X has various levels of security to control who has permission to mess with certain folders or files. If a network administrator set up your Mac, chances are pretty good that you're locked out of some folders. When you try to drop a file into one of these locked folders, you get a "Just who do you think you are, Jack?" message. (If you listen closely, you can sometimes hear the network overlord snickering.) To avoid the humiliation of being reminded of your powerlessness, look in the bottom-left corner of the Finder window. If you see a little pencil with a line through it (as shown here), forget it—you don't have permission to make any changes to this folder. This is why so many network administrators one day wind up having an "accident."

GO WITH THE FLOW (ALL THE COOL PEOPLE DO)

Apple's System 1 introduced the world to viewing folders as icons. System 7 gave us List view. When OS X added the option to view your files in Column view, the geeks couldn't have been more ecstatic (unless they actually got a date with a real, live female who wasn't a sister, cousin, or prom queen who lost a bet). Well, Leopard has added Cover Flow view. You've seen it in iTunes, Front Row, Apple TV, your iPod—basically on everything Apple has done lately— and it's pretty slick. To view your files in Cover Flow view, click the right-most of the four View buttons on the toolbar along the top of any Finder window and enjoy. Seriously, I can waste hours watching all those beautiful icons with their way crazy cool reflections flow by on my screen. It's another one of those things (as if you needed more) to show your PC-using friends and watch them try to hide their envy. But as cool as it is, personally I find it easier to find stuff by picking it out of a list. Easier, but not nearly as much fun.

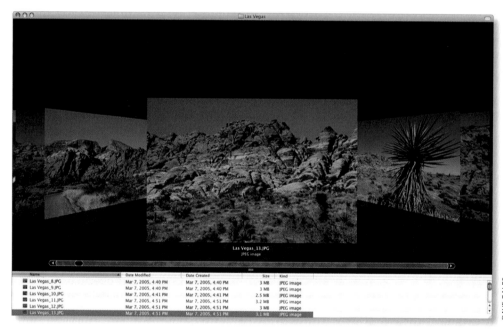

DAVE GALES

   LET IT FLOW, LET IT FLOW, LET IT FLOW

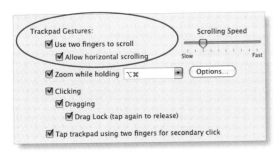

You have several options for moving around in Cover Flow view. If you want to flip through your files one at a time, use the Arrow keys on your keyboard. But that's like getting into a Ferrari and driving in stop-and-go traffic. If you really want to enjoy Cover Flow, press-and-hold the Arrow keys and your files will flow. Ooooooh. Aaaahhhhh. But the ultimate flowing experience uses your laptop's trackpad. To enable two-finger scrolling, go to the Apple menu, select System Preferences, click on the Keyboard & Mouse icon, and then click the Trackpad tab. Under the Trackpad Gestures section, make sure the Use Two Fingers to Scroll and Allow Horizontal Scrolling checkboxes are both turned on. Now when you open a folder in Cover Flow view, put two fingers on the trackpad and move back and forth and watch your files glide across your screen. Now you're flowing, baby.

   REARRANGING THE HEADERS IN LIST VIEW

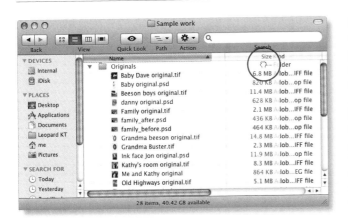

Okay, let's say you're in List view and you decide that you want the Size column to appear right after the Name column. You can make it so. Just click directly on the Size header and drag it horizontally along the bar until it appears right after Name. You can do the same with the other headers—move 'em where you want 'em. There's only one you can't move—the Name header. It's stuck in the first position.

TELL YOUR ICONS WHERE TO GO, TEMPORARILY AT LEAST

If you have selected Icon view for your desktop or a folder, you have several options for keep-ing your icons arranged neatly. To make all the icons line up on an invisible grid, Control-click anywhere inside the window and select Clean Up from the contextual menu. If you select Ar-range By from the contextual menu, not only can you force the icons to line up, but you can also tell them in what order to line up. That'll show 'em! If you only want to line up particular icons, just Control-click them, then select Clean Up Selection from the contextual menu. But here's the thing: this is a quick way to get things cleaned up, but it's temporary. You can drag any icon off the grid or out of order any time you want.

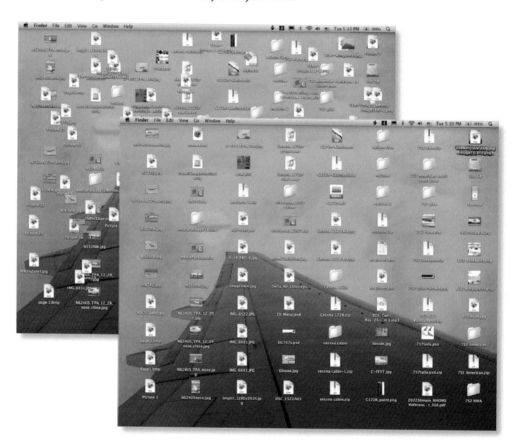

     KEEP YOUR OUT-OF-CONTROL ICONS IN LINE

The previous tip showed how to arrange your icons neatly. The problem is, as soon as you turn your back, they'll crank up some tunes, knock back some cold ones, and get all messed up again. Unacceptable. Open the folder where the messed up icons are hanging out and press Command-J. When the View Options dialog opens, select one of the Arrange By options. Now they're not just lined up on the grid, they're locked to it.

  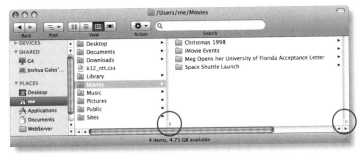   **THE DOUBLE-CLICK FILENAME FIX**

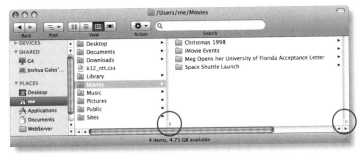

If you're working in a window set to Column view, you're going to run into this all the time—when a file's name is longer than the width of the column, the middle part of the filename is replaced with dots to make it shorter. That's not usually a problem, but if you have one file named "Grandma Ford Final Portrait" and another named "Grandma Ford Un-retouched Portrait," then everything between "Grandma Ford" and "Portrait" is cut out. Luckily, there's a quick fix—just double-click the column resize button (the two little lines) at the bottom of the vertical column divider bar, and the column will expand just enough so you can see even the longest filename of any file in that column. It works the opposite way as well: if you have a column that is way too wide, double-click the resize button and the column will shrink to the perfect size. Pretty darn sweet!

⚫ ⚫ ⚫ SEE A LONG FILENAME WITHOUT WIDENING THE COLUMN

The previous tip showed how you can resize a column with a double-click to be able to read long filenames. If you just need to read one name and don't want to bother resizing the entire column, just hold your cursor over the file's truncated name for a few seconds and eventually its full name will pop up. So what's the problem? The "few seconds" part. Instead, press-and-hold the Option key, then put your cursor over the file's name, and its full name will appear instantly.

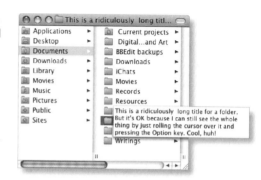

⚫ ⚫ ⚫ GETTING RID OF THE PREVIEW COLUMN

If you've used Mac OS X's Column view, you know that when you click on a file, you'll get a large preview of that file in a new column called the Preview column. Click on a graphic—you see its preview. Large! This "feature" annoys the heck out of some people (you know who you are), so to turn off this special column, just view a window in Column view, then press Command-J to open the Column view options. Turn off the checkbox for Show Preview Column and the Preview column will disappear.

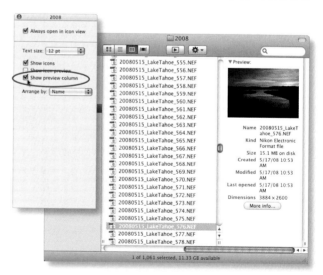

IN LOVE WITH A VIEW? MAKE IT PERMANENT

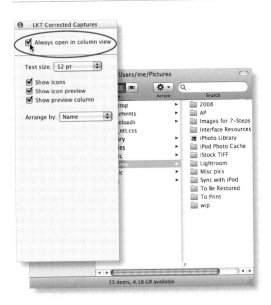

By default, Leopard will open new windows in the last view you selected. So if you had 10 windows open in Column view on the desktop, changed one of them to Cover Flow view, and closed them all, then the next time you open a new window, it will be in Cover Flow view. But I'm a Column view kind of guy and want new windows to always open in Column view. No problem. Click the Finder icon at the left end of the Dock to open a new Finder window and click one of the View buttons on the tool-bar, then press Command-J to open the View Options. If the checkbox at the top is not turned on, click it and the current view will be set as the default. If it's already turned on, click it to clear the previous default, then click it again to set the new one. From now on, new windows will open just the way you like them.

THUMBNAIL PREVIEWS FOR ICONS

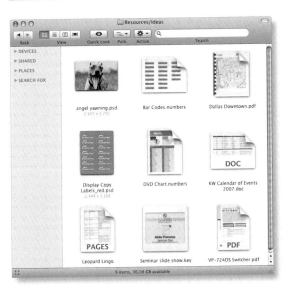

Leopard allows you to replace a file's standard icon with a thumbnail of the document itself. Here's how to do it: From any Finder window, press Command-J (or go under the View menu and choose Show View Options). When the dialog opens, turn on the checkbox next to Show Icon Preview. This works best if you're in Icon view and you've set the icon size to some-thing like 128x128.

DIFFERENT VIEWS FOR DIFFERENT WINDOWS

Column view is my favorite way to look at the stuff in my folders—most of the time. But if I am looking at a folder of images, for instance, Cover Flow view is the way to go, baby. Who wants to look at a tiny list of obscure filenames when you could be looking at big, beautiful previews of the images? Here's how you can set a specific folder to open in a different view mode. For this example, I'm using my Applications folder, but it can be any folder you want. Double-click on whichever folder you want to customize. Once the folder is open, set it to the view mode you want by clicking the buttons on the toolbar, then pressing Command-J to open the View Options dialog. If you had previously set a default view mode (see tip on previous page), the checkbox at the top will be turned on. Simply click it once to turn it off, then click it again to turn it back on and select the current view mode as the default for this folder.

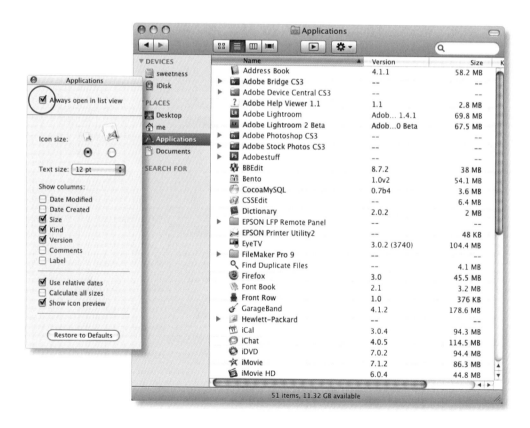

 SCROLL NON-ACTIVE WINDOWS

When you read the title of this tip you probably said, "Yeah, so? Why would I ever want to do that? He's really scraping for tips now." But the first time you use it, you're going to change your tune and think I'm an absolute genius (indulge my fantasy, would you?) because it is something you will use every day. Let's say you're thinking of buying a Lamborghini (now I'll indulge your fantasy), and you're doing some research and putting together a comparison chart of the various models. You have two windows open: a website and your chart. Since only one window can be active at a time, one of them is always partly hidden. You can arrange your windows side by side so you can see the contents of both windows. But when the content you need from the inactive window isn't visible in its window, you have to click on it and scroll up or down, then click back on the other window. In Leopard, you can scroll an inactive window. Here's how: Move your cursor out of the active window and put it over the inactive window you want to scroll, but *don't click on it!* When your cursor is over the window, move the scroll wheel on your mouse (yet another reason to get a fancy mouse) up and down and gasp in wonder as the contents of the inactive window scroll. It still doesn't sound too exciting, but trust me, use it a couple of times and you'll appreciate its coolness.

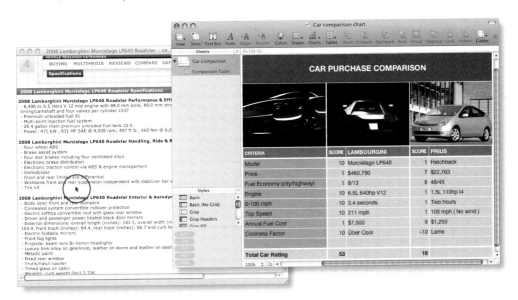

   CLOSE MULTIPLE WINDOWS WITH ONE CLICK

When you're working away on some project, it's easy to wind up with the desktop piled up with windows. When you're done working and want to close all the windows, it can be an annoying process. But if you Option-click the Close button (the round red button in the top-left corner) of any one of the open windows, by the time you blink, they're all gone.

   MINIMIZING MULTIPLE WINDOWS AT ONCE

If you have three or four open windows in the same application and want to minimize them all to the Dock at once, just press-and-hold the Option key and double-click on the title bar of any one of them, and all open windows will go to the Dock. In previous versions of OS X, if you didn't realize you had 50 open windows and used this trick to send them all to the Dock, you had to either quit the application or click each of the icons on the Dock one at a time to undock them. Some clever person at Apple decided that was kind of a pain, so in Leopard (for some applications) if you want to take all the items from one application off the Dock, just Option-click on any one of them. You can still pull them off one at a time by just clicking on them. *Note:* The getting-them-all-off-the-Dock-with-one-click thing only works if they are application windows. If they're Finder windows, it's one at a time.

DAVE GALES

INSTANTLY HIDE AN APPLICATION'S OPEN WINDOWS

Let me state right up front that I neither condone nor encourage anyone to engage in activities such as checking the status of an eBay auction, making hotel and plane reservations for an upcoming vacation, researching how many aliens really are being kept at Area 51, or any other activities of a personal nature while at work. However, if you choose to do so, here's a tip that might come in very handy. If you Option-click anywhere on the desktop, all the open windows for the application you are currently using will instantly disappear. They're not hidden behind other open windows, minimized to the Dock, or closed. The truth of the matter is no one really knows where they go. But then again, no one really cares so long as they aren't on the screen when your boss walks in. When you need to see them again, just click the application's icon in the Dock and get back to "work."

  SEE APPLICATION WINDOWS ONE AT A TIME

If you have windows open for several applications, they can be really distracting because you always see them floating around in the background. Well, you can hide all those messy windows without ever leaving your current application. Just Command-Option-click the Dock icon for the application whose windows you want to see. All the windows from the other applications will be instantly hidden from view. Want to see just the windows for another application? Option-click its Dock icon.

DAVE GALES

CUSTOMIZE (AND UN-CUSTOMIZE) THE TOOLBAR

If you want to customize the items in your toolbar, just Command-Option-click the pill-shaped button in the upper-right corner of the Finder window and the Customize Toolbar dialog will open. Now you can just drag any icons you want onto the toolbar and press Return. If you make a total mess of your toolbar, just Command-Option-click the pill-shaped button again, then drag the default set of tools onto your messed-up toolbar and once again you'll have a toolbar you can be proud of.

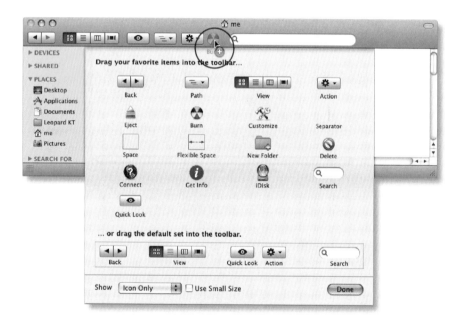

   TOO MANY ICONS ON THE TOOLBAR? SHRINK 'EM

The toolbar icons are fairly large, taking up considerable space both vertically and horizontally. If you add a few extra icons to the toolbar, the additional icons could wind up being hidden from view. What can you do? Well, you can have the toolbar display just the icons, which shrinks the space between the icons by removing the text. To display the toolbar items by icon, rather than by icon and text, Control-click anywhere within the toolbar and choose Icon Only from the contextual menu. If you really want to shrink the toolbar to its bare minimum, try Text Only. For even more space-saving options, Command-click the pill-shaped button in the upper right-hand corner of the Finder window. Each time you click, you get a new space-saving look.

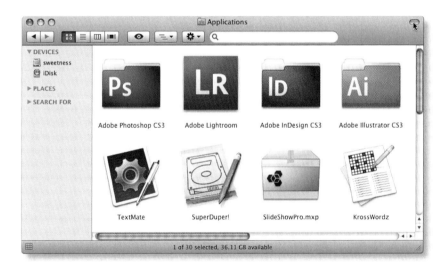

   MAKING TOOLBAR ICONS STICKY

When you shrink a window in an application (like Mail, Safari, TextEdit, etc.), the buttons on the right side of the interface get hidden and wind up in a pop-up menu (if they didn't, they'd just get squashed together). Some of these buttons you probably don't care about, but there are others you might prefer stay visible even when shrinking the window quite a bit (for example,

when I reduce the size of Safari's window, the search field gets hidden almost immediately, but I always want that field to stay visible). But if you Control-click the toolbar icon you want to remain visible and choose Keep Item Visible from the contextual menu, that button will stay visible while others are hidden.

   HOW TO MAKE THE SIDEBAR WORK LIKE THE DOCK

We all love the way you can customize the Dock, but you can also customize the sidebar by adding items that make it even more powerful. For example, if you use Photoshop a lot, just open the window where your Photoshop application resides, click-and-drag the Photoshop icon right over to the sidebar, and the other icons in the sidebar will slide out of the way. Now you can use this sidebar kind of like you would use the Dock—to launch Photoshop, just click its icon in the sidebar. Plus, like the Dock, you can even drag-and-drop images you want to open right onto the sidebar's Photoshop icon. *Note:* The only restriction is you have to put the items you add under the Places section in the sidebar.

   THE SIDEBAR'S SPACE-SAVING ICON VIEW

If you think the sidebar takes up too much room on your screen, just click on its right-hand edge and drag it to the left until it snaps, leaving just enough room to keep the longest filename visible.

   TAKE A QUICK LOOK AT ANY FILE

My hard drive tends to collect files with filenames like "Untitled-1," "Untitled-2," "Untitled-2 copy," etc. It's a pain to have to click on each file and launch an application that will open it, only to find out it's worthless. Leopard has introduced what just might be my favorite new feature—Quick Look. To preview a file, all you have to do is click its icon and hit the Spacebar. A window will open instantly with a preview of the file. And here's the best thing: you never have to launch an application. Yeah, you heard me, a preview without an application. I'm not talking a lousy thumbnail-size preview, it's big. But wait, there's more. If you order before midnight…(kidding). Quick Look will show you previews of most types of files: images (including JPEG, TIF, PSD, and NEF), graphics, PDFs, text documents, spreadsheets, movies, music files, etc. That's huge, at least for people like me who are too lazy to give new files real names and have no clue what "Untitled-17" is.

PREVIEW MULTIPLE ITEMS WITH AN INSTANT SLIDE SHOW

Having Quick Look show a preview of a file is incredibly timesaving. But if you have 50 images you want to preview, opening them one at a time would be mind-numbing. So here's what you do: Open the folder that has the files you want to preview and press Command-A to select all of them. If you don't want to select every file, you can Shift-click on the first and last items to select everything in between, or Command-click on just certain items. Once you have your items selected, press Command-Option-Y and enjoy the show.

SCOTT KELBY

   VIEW THUMBNAILS OF ALL YOUR ITEMS AT ONCE

Instead of viewing a large preview of one item, you can have Quick Look display thumbnails of all the items you have selected by clicking the button with the four squares (officially known as the Index Sheet button) at the bottom of the preview window. You can also just press Command-Return while you're previewing any item. Press the same keys again and you'll go back to individual previews.

SCOTT KELBY

  USE EXPOSÉ TO, WELL, EXPOSE THINGS ON YOUR DESKTOP

You're using Safari to check the amazing, incredible, unbelievable, creative content at www
.photoshopuser.com (how's that for an absolutely shameless plug?), using Mail to check your
email, updating your calendar with iCal, and listening to music with iTunes. Each of these
applications has at least one window open on your desktop, and the one you need is always
buried somewhere at the bottom of the pile. You can get frustrated having to constantly move
windows around to get to the one you want, or you can use Exposé. Press F9 and you'll see
miniature versions of all the open windows on your desktop (as shown here). Press F10 and
only the windows for the application you are currently using will be visible. Pressing F11 will
clear off all open windows so you can see the desktop.

DAVE GALES

⬤ ⬤ ⬤ SEE ALL EXPOSÉ WINDOWS' TITLES AT ONCE

If you have a lot of windows open on your desktop when you activate Exposé, it can be pretty hard to see the titles of the windows because they're so small. But press the Option key, and you will see an overlay with all the windows' titles.

   USE EXPOSÉ WITHOUT PRESSING A BUTTON

If you don't want to use the F9, F10, or F11 button to access Exposé, you can set up "hot corners" that will tell Exposé to "do its thing" whenever you move your cursor there. To tell Exposé which corners to use, go to the Apple menu, select System Preferences, and choose Exposé & Spaces. In the Active Screen Corners section, you'll see a small preview of your screen with a pop-up menu beside each corner. Just click on a menu and choose an Exposé mode (the top three choices) to assign to that corner. Here's a hint that will save you some frustration: when you are assigning a mode to a corner, press-and-hold one of the modifier keys (Shift, Control, Option, or Command) while you have one of the menu options highlighted. Here's why: If you don't, you'll be amazed at how often your cursor ends up in the corner. You'll be triggering Exposé hundreds of times every day. If you assign a modifier key, nothing will happen unless you press that key, then move your cursor into the corner.

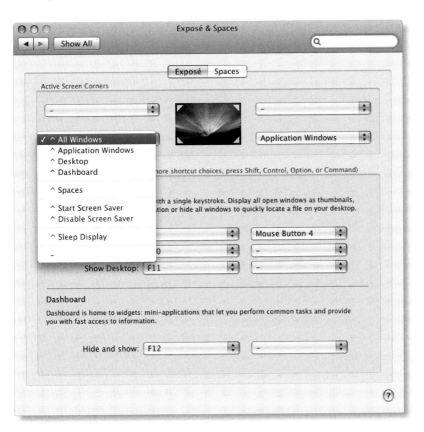

THE TWO-BUTTON MOUSE EXPERIENCE

If you're using a two-button mouse, you can access a new world of Exposé functionality that dare not speak its name because, my friends, you can use the second mouse button to invoke your favorite Exposé mode. Have you got more than two mouse buttons? Four perhaps? Then go to the Apple menu, under System Preferences, and click on Exposé & Spaces. If your multi-button mouse is connected, you'll see that pop-up menus for your mouse buttons have been added. Pick a function and use the pop-up menu to assign it to a button. Now you can use either the keyboard shortcut or your mouse button to make Exposé do its thing.

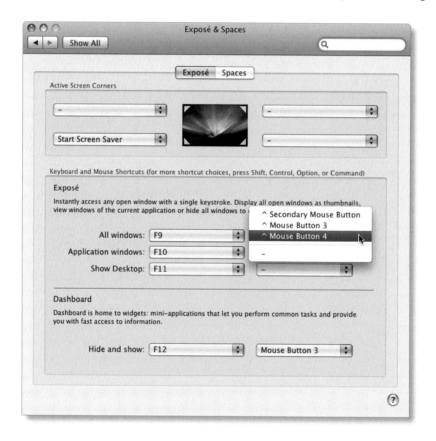

   SWITCHING APPS WITHIN EXPOSÉ

Once you have invoked Exposé by using one of your many mouse buttons (see previous tip) or pressing F9 or F10, you can toggle through the open windows on your desktop by pressing the Tab key. Press the Tab key once and the next open application and its miniaturized windows come to the front. Press Tab again, and the open windows for the next application will highlight. Want the previous app? Press Shift-Tab to drop Exposé into reverse.

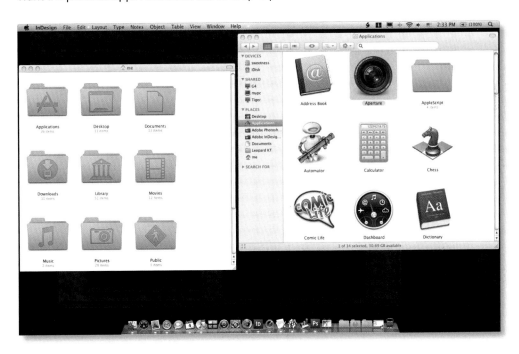

LEOPARD

   EXPOSÉ KEYBOARD TIP

In an earlier tip, I mentioned that you invoke the cool Exposé feature by pressing F9, F10, or F11. But did you know it's how you press those keys that determines how Exposé works? For example, if you press and release the F9 key, Exposé freezes the thumbnails in place, and will continue to freeze them there until you either click on a window or press F9 again. This is ideal for when you're not sure which window you want so you need time to look around. However, if you press-and-hold F9, Exposé only stays active as long as you hold the button down (or until you click a window, whichever comes first), which is perfect for when you just want to look at something quickly, or you know exactly which window you want to jump to.

   EXPOSÉ MOUSE TIP

I mentioned earlier that if you have a multi-button mouse, it opens a new world of Exposé functionality, and I also mentioned (in the previous tip) that Exposé responds to how you press the keys that invoke it. So, here's a cool Exposé tip that lets you switch from one application to another with just one click (rather than two). Click whichever mouse button you assigned to the F9 function (All Windows), then keep holding down the mouse button and release it over the window of the application you want to switch to—it's super fast, 'cause it's just one click.

   EXPAND YOUR DESKTOP WITH SPACES

I love my laptop. When I'm sitting at my desk, I have a nice big external display I plug in and quadruple my screen real estate. I can see all my open windows and switch among them with one click. The problem is, I'm rarely sitting at my desk and, trust me, it's not easy using a 30" display on a plane. Well, Apple has added a new feature in Leopard (it's new to Leopard, but there have been separate applications available that do the same sort of thing) called Spaces, and it lets you create multiple desktops and switch among them easily. To enable Spaces, go to the Apple menu, select System Preferences, click on the Exposé & Spaces icon, then click the Spaces tab at the top. Now simply turn on the Enable Spaces checkbox and you're good to go.

   CHANGE THE KEYBOARD SHORTCUT FOR SPACES

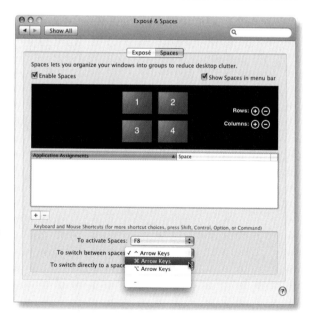

The default keyboard shortcuts for Spaces are F8 to activate it, Control-Arrow keys to switch between spaces you've set up, and Control-Number keys to jump to a particular space. To change these shortcuts, go to the Apple menu, choose Preferences, click on the Exposé & Spaces icon, then click the Spaces tab. Now you can use the pop-up menus at the bottom of the pane to choose new shortcuts (as shown here). If you have a multi-button mouse, select one of your extra mouse buttons to trigger Spaces from the Secondary Mouse Button pop-up menu. *Note:* Don't choose button 2 or you'll be back to pressing Control-click to open contextual menus.

   SET DEFAULT APPLICATIONS FOR SPACES

One of the cool things you can do with Spaces is have particular applications always open in the same space. So if I'm working on a website, for example, I can set up one space for BBEdit (the favorite text editor of geeks everywhere) where I can edit my copy. Any applications I use to do any scripting, CSS, or HTML to build my pages open in a separate space. Photoshop opens in a third space so I can get my images ready to put up. Finally, I can create a space where different Web browsers will open to check the site. If I had to do all this on one screen, I would be moving, minimizing, opening, and closing windows 100 times an hour. To set applications to always open in a particular space, go to the Apple menu, select System Preferences, choose Exposé & Spaces, and click the Spaces tab. Directly below the Application Assignments section (the white box in the middle), click the plus sign (+) button, then navigate to the location of the first application you want to assign to a space. When you locate it, click Add. By default, the application is assigned to Space 1. To assign it to a different space, click the little up-and-down triangles at the far-right of the section and select one of the options. Applications you don't assign will simply open in whatever space you happen to be in at the time.

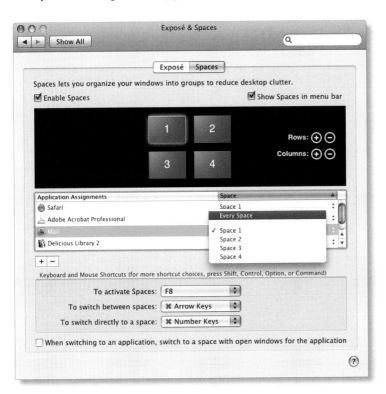

   SEE ALL YOUR SPACES AT ONCE

You can see miniaturized versions of all the spaces you have set up at one time (think of it as Exposé for Spaces) by pressing F8. This is very helpful when the number of spaces you're working on exceeds your ability to remember what's where, which is pretty much any time I have more than one space. To get out of this bird's-eye view, simply click anywhere on the screen.

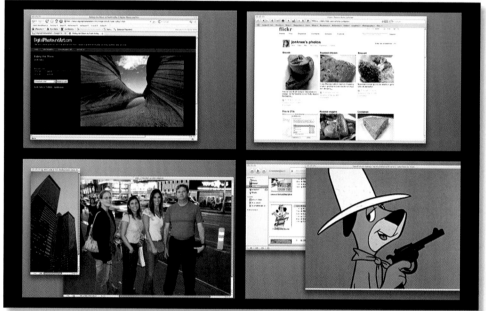

DAVE GALES AND SCOTT KELBY

   MOVING DOCUMENTS TO A NEW SPACE IS A DRAG

If you want to move something to a different space, just press F8 to see all your spaces at once, then click on the space that contains the window you want to move. Now simply move your cursor over the window, click-and-hold your mouse button, and drag the window to a different space. If you want to drag all the windows for one application, press-and-hold the Command key while you drag.

TRADING SPACES

If you want to move one of your spaces to a new position, simply press F8, position the cursor over the space you want to move, then click-and-hold the mouse button and drag the space to the new location. Just make sure when you click-and-hold the mouse button that you're not over one of the open windows in the space or you will move only that window, not the entire space.

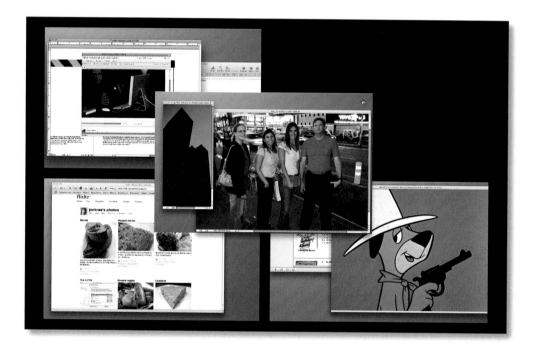

   MOVE EVERYTHING TO ONE SPACE

Spreading out documents in different spaces keeps things neat and organized. But sometimes you just want to stack everything up in one big pile. If you want to consolidate all the stuff in all your spaces into one space, press F8 to switch to Spaces' bird's-eye view, then press C. That's it. If you want to put everything back the way it was, just press C again.

Chapter 2

SHOW ME THE WAY

NAVIGATING YOUR NEW WORLD

The title of this chapter, "Show Me the Way," is an obvious tribute to musician Peter Frampton. I feel that I owe him this tribute

Show Me the Way
navigating your new world

because one day I received an email from a reader of one of my other books leading me to a website about Peter Frampton. On the site, Peter names his favorite movies, books, albums, etc., and among his favorite books he listed my book Photoshop Down & Dirty Tricks. *Of course, being a Frampton fan myself, I was really tickled, and learning this has changed my life in immeasurable ways. For example, if Peter Frampton (who is currently touring, by the way) is appearing in concert at any nearby venue, I can just drop by the box office, pay the admission price, and they'll give me a ticket to his upcoming performance. Not only that, but if I go to the local record store and try to buy any Peter Frampton CD (including his classic "Frampton Comes Alive" double-album set), they'll let me. No questions asked. All I have to present is my ID and credit card. How cool is that?*

CREATING ALIASES WITHOUT THE WORD ALIAS

Do you find it as annoying as I do that Leopard adds the word "alias" every time you create an alias? (I know, previous versions of the Mac OS did that, as well, and it annoyed me there, too.) Well, you can bypass the "adding the word alias" ugliness altogether by holding down the Option and Command keys and clicking-and-dragging the original file outside the Finder window it's currently in (I usually just drag mine to the desktop). This creates an alias without the word "alias" attached. *Note:* Don't worry, you'll still know it's an alias, because its icon will have a tiny arrow at the bottom left-hand corner.

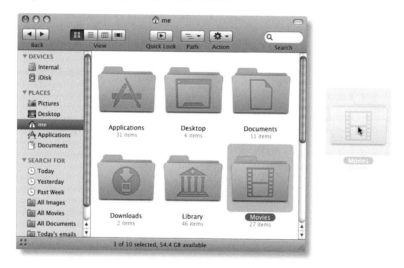

INSTANTLY FIND THE ORIGINAL FOR AN ALIAS

Since an alias is just a copy of the file's icon (not the actual file itself), you may need to find the original at times. To do that, just click on the alias, press Command-R, and the "real" file will appear onscreen in its Finder window. If you prefer, you can also Control-click on the alias and select Show Original from the contextual menu.

   USE LABELS TO FIND FILES FAST

If I'm working on a project (writing a book, for instance), I don't have enough extra brain cells to remember what needs to be done with every file in a folder. Some need corrections, others are done, etc. If you've attached a label to a file, you have an instant visual indication of what the file is, what project it's from, what needs to be done with it, or whatever else you need to track. To label a file or folder, just Control-click its icon, and choose a Label color. Of course, you'll have to remember what the colors stand for. If you have set red for files to delete and green for ones to back up, you don't want to mix them up.

   CREATE YOUR OWN LABEL NAMES

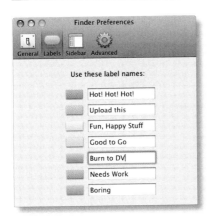

Don't like the names Apple created for the colors used in the Color Labels feature? Then just create your own by going under the Finder menu and choosing Preferences (or use the keyboard shortcut Command-, [comma]). When the dialog appears, click the Labels icon along the top, and you'll see a column of color swatches next to some text fields you can use to input custom names. This is great for designating a color for "Hot Projects" or "Back Up These Files," or perhaps a project name like "Cross Catalog" or "Vegas Blackjack Table Scam."

   MOVING ICON NAMES TO THE SIDE: IT'S UNNATURAL

The practice I am about to describe can only be labeled as "freakish." It's one of those things in life that falls under the category of "Just because you can, doesn't mean you should." Let me state for the record that I do not encourage you to dabble in this practice. Why? Because an icon's name is supposed to appear beneath the icon. It has been this way since the beginning of Mac-time, and moving the name to the right of the icon, rather than the time-honored tradition of positioning the name below it, is just plain sick. Nevertheless, here's how to do it: Click on the desktop and press Command-N to open a Finder window. If it's not already set to Icon view, press Command-1. Now open the View Options by pressing Command-J, go halfway down to Label Position and click on the Right radio button (shown here, circled in red). There, now the name of each icon will appear to its right (yeecch!). Since you've already crossed the line, you may as well go ahead and click the Use as Defaults button at the bottom of the dialog. However, "right is wrong!" Just so you know.

   ADDING WORDS TO THE END OF FILENAMES

Josh and Otis_5.psd   Josh at computer.psd

DAVE GALES

Josh first lesson_1.jpg   Josh first lesson.psd

If you want to add some text to the end of an existing file's name (for example, if you had a Photoshop file named "Hawaii Collage" and you wanted to add the words "Summer 2005" to the end), just click on the filename, press Return, then press the Right Arrow key to jump to the end of the existing name. Then all you have to do is type "Summer 2005" and press the Return key to lock in your new name. *Note:* To add characters at the beginning of the name, do the same routine—just press the Left Arrow key instead.

   HOW TO CHANGE A FILE'S ICON

Just as in previous versions of the Mac OS, if you don't like a file's icon you can change it—but it's easier than ever in Leopard. Go to the file whose icon you'd like to replace and press Command-I to open the Info window. Now go to the file that has the icon you want to use and drag its icon over the icon you want to replace (the one in the Info window). That's it! (Check out www.iconfactory.com and www.xicons.com. They both have fantastic selections of photo-quality Mac OS X icons ready to download.) *Note:* If you have Show Icon Preview turned on in the Desktop preferences, the icon will change in the Info window, but not on the file itself. Just press Command-J to open the Desktop preferences and turn off the Show Icon Preview checkbox.

● ● ● STEAL A FILE'S NAME, THEN WRITE RIGHT OVER IT

If you're saving a new file, you can
use the name of an existing file by
just clicking on it in the Save dialog
navigation window. Even if the
file is grayed out, you can still click
on it, and when you do, its name
appears as your new filename at
the top of the Save dialog. This is
a huge time saver. When you click
Save, it will ask if you want to
replace the existing file with the
new file you're saving. However, if
you're saving a different version of
a file and all you want to do is add
a version number (like "Brochure

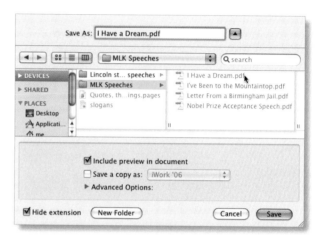

Inside Cover 2"), you'd just click on the existing file, named "Brochure Inside Cover" in the Save
dialog, and once the name appears as your new filename, just type "2." *Note:* If you are working on a file that has previously been saved, you'll need to press Command-Shift-S to open the
Save As dialog.

● ● ● CLONE FILENAMES TO SPEED THINGS UP

If you're naming a number of files with similar
names (such as "Bridal Shoot 1," "Bridal Shoot 2,"
"Bridal Shoot 3," etc.), you can save time by naming the first file, then highlighting the words
"Bridal Shoot" and pressing Command-C to copy
those words to the Clipboard. Then, when you
come to the next file you want to rename, click
once on its filename, press Return to highlight it,
press Command-V to paste in the words "Bridal
Shoot," then press the Right Arrow key, enter a
space, and enter the number for this file (like 4),
and so on. You can also copy-and-paste a name
from one folder to another, as long as these two
identically named folders don't wind up in the
same place. That's a big no-no, and you will be
severely disciplined if that should happen (or at
least a mean warning dialog will appear).

  OUTSMARTING THE ALPHABET

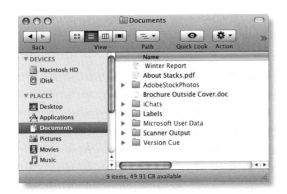

Want a particular file to appear at the top of your list when sorting in List view by Name? Just type a space in front of its name and it will jump to the top of the list (in the image shown here, after adding a space before "Winter Report," the document now appears at the top of the alphabetical list instead of the bottom).

  SET UP THE SIDEBAR THE WAY YOU WANT IT

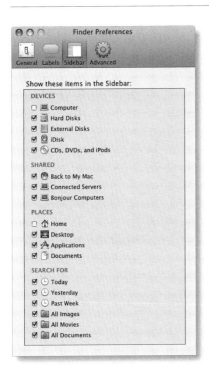

The sidebar that you see at the side (I probably didn't need to point that out) of every Finder window is the perfect place to put stuff you need to access frequently. The good news is Leopard tries to help you keep your sidebar organized by putting items in categories. The bad news is you are stuck with the categories Apple has determined you need. Luckily, you can at least decide what items appear in the sidebar, but Leopard will still decide which category you can put them into. From the Finder menu, select Preferences, then click the Sidebar icon (up top) to see a list of the default sidebar items. Turn off the checkboxes beside any items you don't want cluttering up your sidebar. If there's just one sidebar item you want to get rid of, it's easier to Control-click on it in the sidebar and select Remove From Sidebar from the contextual menu.

⬤ ⬤ ⬤ ADD YOUR OWN STUFF TO THE SIDEBAR

Once you've cleared some of the default items off the sidebar (see previous tip), it's time to add your own. You can put pretty much anything you want in the sidebar, but they're going to have to go in the Places section. Find the item you want to put in the sidebar and click-and-drag it into the Places section. That's it. If you ever want to remove the item, just drag it off and watch it go poof. *Note:* Adding or removing items from the sidebar doesn't affect the original item at all. You're not really moving the file, just putting (or removing) a "link" to it in the sidebar. The original file stays where it is.

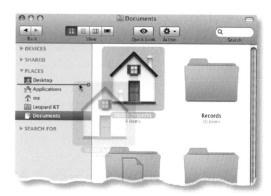

⬤ ⬤ ⬤ USE TOOLBAR AS "OVERFLOW PARKING" FOR FAVORITE FILES

Okay, you know the sidebar is for storing frequently used files and folders, but it can get full pretty fast. If yours gets "packed," try parking some of your most-used files right on the toolbar at the top of your Finder window. Here's how: Click-and-drag the file up to the toolbar. Hold it there for just a second, and you'll see a thin rectangle appear, letting you know to release the mouse button. When you do, the

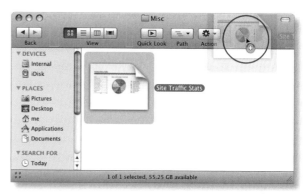

file will appear on the toolbar, where it's always just one click away. If you decide to remove it one day, just press-and-hold the Command key and drag it off the toolbar.

   ALWAYS TAKE THE SHORTCUT (MENU)

I'm riddled with ADD, and if I have to break my concentration to go up to the menu bar to hunt around for a menu item I need, it's highly likely I'll see something interesting on the way and take a 30-minute side trip to check it out. The fastest, easiest, and least likely way to get me off track in selecting menu items is to press-and-hold the Control key and click the mouse button. A contextual menu will open showing all the available menu items for whatever you're working on. You can Control-click on a folder, the desktop, a document, a word within a document, a webpage—heck, you can open a contextual menu from nearly everywhere. The options available will be different, depending on what you click on, but you won't have to go far to select them.

 GET A TWO-BUTTON MOUSE FOR CRYIN' OUT LOUD

The one thing that will make navigating your hard drive easy is a two-button mouse. If you use a two-button mouse (and honestly, I can't think of a single reason you shouldn't, unless you just love to Control-click several hundred times a day to use contextual menus), you can skip the whole Control-click thing by just clicking the right-hand button on your mouse. Can't get any easier than that.

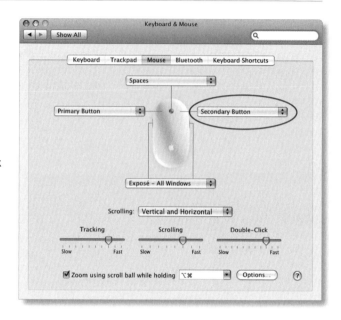

 HAVE A TRACKPAD? USE YOUR FINGERS TO CONTROL-CLICK

If you have one of Apple's newer laptops, you can experience the bliss of right-clicking by having two fingers on the trackpad when you click the trackpad's button. I love it! First, however, you need to activate this feature. Here's how: Go to the Apple menu, select System Preferences, and choose Keyboard & Mouse. Now click the Trackpad tab and turn on the checkbox next to For Secondary Clicks, Place Two Fingers on the Trackpad Then Click the Button. Now you can Control-click without using the Control key.

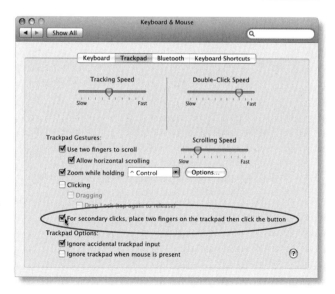

   CREATING YOUR OWN KEYBOARD SHORTCUTS

One thing that kicks butt in the productivity department is that you can create your own custom keyboard shortcuts. Here's how: Go to the Apple menu, select System Preferences, then choose Keyboard & Mouse. When the dialog opens, click the Keyboard Shortcuts tab, and then click the plus sign (+) button at the bottom of the list of existing shortcuts. A pop-up menu will open at the top of the dialog that lets you choose whether this shortcut works across all applications, or in just an individual app (or just the Finder if you like). In the Menu Title field, enter the *exact* name of the menu item the shortcut is for, then type the shortcut you want to use and click Add. It's that easy. *Note:* Make sure the application that you're making the shortcut for isn't open. Also, if you want to use a shortcut that's already in use, you can disable that item (assuming you don't use it much) and use its shortcut for a different command.

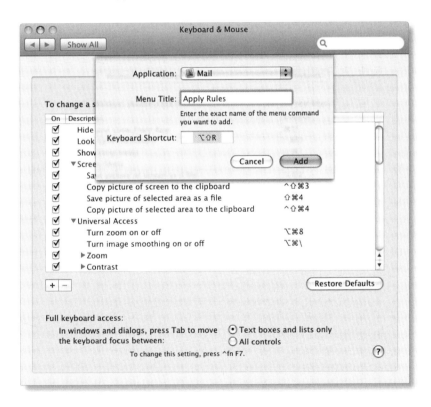

   MENU SPEED TIP

If you spend way too much time every day digging around in menus to get to the one you want, you'll love this tip. The next time you're in a menu, instead of mousing down to the command you want to use, just type the first letter of its name to select it, press Return and the first (alphabetically) item in the menu that begins with the letter you typed will be selected. If this isn't the menu item you want, just type the first two or three letters of the menu item you want and that should do it. For example, if you are in the Finder and want to connect to another Mac, click on the Go menu, then type "con" and Connect to Server will be selected. Speed menus, baby! By the way, the same thing works for selecting items in a folder.

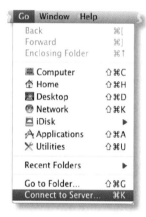

   BECOME THE ULTIMATE MENU MASTER

Want to really speed things up? How about jumping right to the Apple menu without even clicking the mouse? Just press Control-F2, press Return, and the Apple menu pops down (if you're using a laptop, press Function-Control-F2). Oh, but there's more! Now that you're in the Apple menu, press the Right Arrow key on your keyboard to move to the other menus (Finder, File, Edit, View, etc.) and the Left Arrow key to move back. Once you get to the menu you want, press the Down Arrow key to open the menu. Now you can use the Down Arrow key to

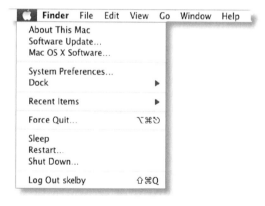

move to the menu item you want (or use the previous tip: type the first letter of the command you want). Now press Return to choose the command and you're done. The best part is that you did it all without ever touching the mouse.

   THE HIDDEN "GO TO ANY FOLDER" TRICK

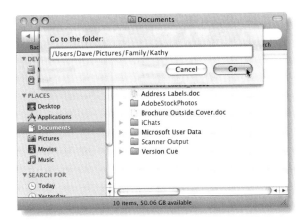

You can go straight to any folder on your hard drive by pressing Command-Shift-G while you're in any Finder window. When the dialog shown here opens, simply type in the path to the folder you want. For example, to get to a folder of pictures of my wife, I would type in "/Users/Dave/Pictures/Family/Kathy" and then press Return. So why would you want to go through all this just to open a folder that is only a few mouse clicks away? Beats me, but you can do it. Seriously, for the geeks out there, you can use this tip to access invisible folders. (If you don't know what invisible folders are, you really don't want to mess with them. They are invisible for a good reason—to keep you from messing up the really important things that are in them.) For instance, type "/usr/libexec" and get ready for a full evening of crazy fun.

   LOOK INSIDE MULTIPLE FOLDERS AUTOMATICALLY

Need to see what's inside more than one folder while in List view? Pressing Shift-Right Arrow will expand the current folder. But if you want to expand all the sub-folders and sub-sub-folders and sub-sub-sub-folders, press Option-Right Arrow.

SEE WHERE A FILE IS STORED

Since the Finder's job
is to store the things
you are working on
and help you find them
again, it gives you a few
different ways to locate
files. Here's one way: If
you have a file opened
on your desktop and
want to know where it
is stored on your drive,

Command-click its name at the top-center of its window and a list of folders appears, tracing
the path backwards from the file to the root level of your hard drive. Think of it as onboard
navigation for your files.

   FIND OUT WHERE AN APPLICATION LIVES WITH ONE CLICK

Okay, so you see an application's icon in the Dock, but
you have no earthly idea
where the app really resides
on your hard drive. It's there
somewhere, but you really
don't know where, and that
scares you (well, it scares me
anyway). To find where the
docked application really lives,
just Command-click its icon
in the Dock and the window
where it lives will immediately
appear onscreen.

    ADD A PATH BUTTON TO THE TOOLBAR

Another way to track down a file is to add a Path button to the toolbar. First, make sure you're in a Finder window (click the Finder icon at the far-left end of the Dock if you're not sure), then Command-Option-click the pill-shaped button in the top-right corner of the toolbar. In the top row of the set of buttons that opens, click the Path button and drag it to the toolbar. The next time you want to see the path to a file, all you have to do is click the Path button. This is probably stating the obvious, but that's never stopped me before: You can only customize the toolbar if the toolbar is visible. If you've hidden it, you'll have to unhide it before you can add the Path button.

   ALWAYS SEE A FILE'S PATH

If you're the type that always wants to know exactly where you are, this tip will make you feel safe and secure. One of the new features introduced in Leopard is the option to add a bar to the bottom of Finder windows that always shows a file's path. To turn on this feature, just go to the menu bar, select View, and choose Show Path Bar. That's it. If you look at the bottom of the window, you'll see the new bar already at work. One big advantage of using the path bar is that you can drag a file to any folder in the path. You have instant access to any location on the path without having to navigate your way back upstream.

   TOGGLE THROUGH OPEN APPLICATIONS

If you are using an application and want to switch to another one, just press Command-Tab. A bar of icons for every application that is currently open will appear. Each time you press Tab (make sure you keep the Command key pressed), the next icon in the line will highlight. When you get to the one you want, just release the Command key. The cool thing is you don't have to be in a Finder window for this to work. You can be in any window in any application. Sweet!

   TOGGLE THROUGH OPEN WINDOWS

When you're using an application, it's easy to end up with several windows open. If you press Command-` (the key right below the Escape key. In school it was called the "grave" accent. In programming it's commonly called the "Backtick." There's your punctuation trivia for the day), you can toggle between all the open windows for the active application. This is really handy if you are making changes to a document and have the old and new versions both open and want to be able to switch back and forth between them without taking your hands off the keyboard to use the mouse.

   STOP THE SCROLLING BLUES

If you don't like sliding the scroll bar up and down in your documents, you can turn on a feature called Jump to Here, which lets you jump to any position in the scroll bar by just clicking on it (rather than using the scroll handles themselves). To turn this on, go to the Apple menu, choose System Preferences, and click on the Appearance icon. When the Appearance dialog appears, for the setting called Click in the Scroll Bar To, choose Jump to Here.

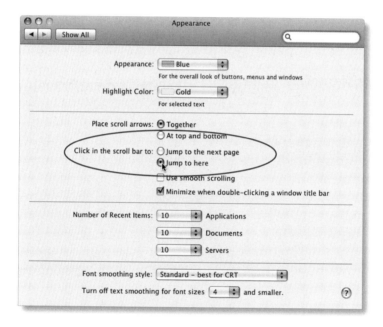

   ANOTHER ANTI-SCROLL BAR TIP

Speaking of hating to use the scroll bars, you can always use the Page Up/Page Down keys on your keyboard to move up and down. Hey, think of it this way—your hands are already resting on the keyboard—now you don't have to grab the mouse at all. (*Note:* If you have a laptop, press-and-hold the Function (fn) key and then press the Up Arrow key for Page Up and the Down Arrow key for Page Down.) Also, you can jump to the top of any document (except Word documents—surprise…) by pressing the Home key on your keyboard (fn-Left Arrow on laptops) or to the end of the document by using the End key (fn-Right Arrow on laptops).

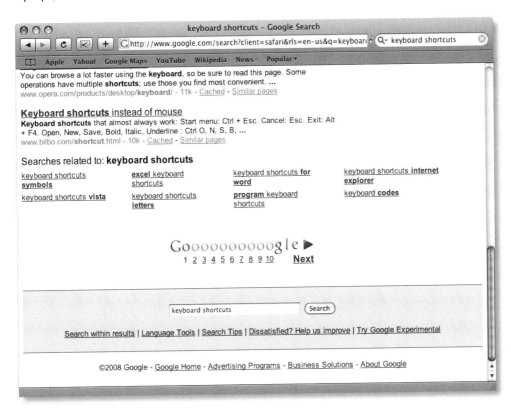

Chapter 3

FOR THOSE ABOUT TO DOCK!

Docking Miracles Made Easy

You have to hand it to Apple: When it comes to application launching and switching, they have created the Venus de

For Those About to Dock!

docking miracles made easy

Milo of application launchers and switchers with Mac OS X's Dock. Okay, that just sounds weird. How about "the crème de la crème" of launchers and application switchers? Nah, it just doesn't sound sexy enough to describe all the really cool things the Dock lets you do. Okay, how about this: "When it comes to doing it, the Dock totally rocks!" Nah, that sounds too "Eminem." Instead, perhaps we should look at the word "Dock" itself. It's clearly a derivative of the popular Latin phrase "One, two, three o-clock, four o-clock, Dock," which, if memory serves me correctly, is inscribed on the torch held high by Lady Liberty in New York Harbor (and Lady Liberty was presented to the United States by French Prime Minister Bill Haley, around five, six, seven o'clock).

   STACK THE DOCK

With Leopard, Apple has added a new feature called "stacks" that lets you keep groups of files or applications together in the Dock and access them with one click. Think of stacks as piles of papers and file folders that you set on your desk while you're working on a project like your taxes, for instance. Instead of going to your filing cabinet a hundred times to pull out the stuff you need, you sort your receipts into various categories and stack them nearby so they're handy when you need them. Stacks do the same thing with the files on your Mac. Apple did extensive research (I heard they taped some file folders on the wall and threw darts at them, but I've not been able to confirm it) and determined that the two folders you need most often are your Downloads and Documents folders. Just to the right of the Dock's divider line, you'll see these two default stacks. Click on one of them to see its contents, then click on the item you want to use. If it's a document, it will open. If it's a folder, a window will open and display the folder's contents.

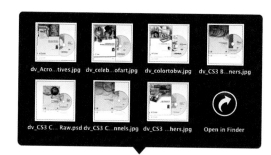

   DIFFERENT WAYS TO VIEW OPEN STACKS

By default, the option to select how you want the contents of your stacks displayed is set to Automatic. That means if there are nine or fewer items in the stack, it will open in Fan view. The only thing I don't like about Fan view is it's so cool, I can waste a lot of time opening and closing stacks just to see them fan. If there are 10 or more items in a stack, it will open in a grid with everything lined up neatly in rows and columns. It's okay, but not worth wasting any time over.

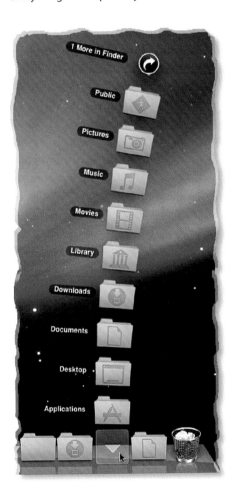

   SET YOUR PREFERRED VIEW FOR STACKS

If you have a definite preference for viewing the content of a stack, you can set a new default. Here's how: Control-click on any stack in the Dock and, when the contextual menu opens, go to the View Content As section and choose one of the available options. Fan is, as you know, the coolest. But it's really not practical when you have a lot of items in a stack. Grid is still pretty cool and it scales well, so the number of items isn't an issue. The option of last resort is List. Viewing stacks with List is just like viewing folders in the Dock in earlier versions of Mac OS X. So if you like living in the past, feel free to view the content of your stacks as a List. If you want to take a walk on the wild side, pick something else. *Note:* I must begrudgingly confess that List has a feature I am surprised the others don't—the ability to open files inside of folders directly. In the other views, if the file you want is inside a folder, your only option is to open the folder from the stack, then open the file.

   OPEN AN ITEM IN A STACK QUICKLY

When you click on a stack, you can navigate to the item you want by pressing the Arrow keys on your keyboard. The Left and Right Arrow keys move your selection left and right. The Up and Down Arrow keys move…well, I guess that's pretty obvious. If you don't feel like pressing the Arrow keys to select a file, click on the stack, start typing the file's name until it's highlighted, then press Return. Doesn't get much quicker than that.

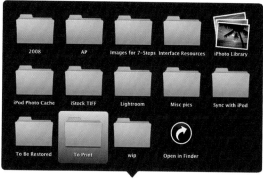

   PUT A PRETTY FACE ON A STACK

One thing I don't like about stacks is how the icons in the Dock change when you add items, depending on what item is first in the sort order. It gets very cluttered-looking and confusing to see different document and application icons instead of folders. Until Apple gives us the ability to give our stacks static icons (like every other folder), there are a couple of work-arounds. You can download a set of stack overlays which people have developed (search online for "Leopard, stacks, overlay" and you'll find a bunch) that will give your stacks a consistent look. A second thing you can do is create a new folder (Command-Shift-N), change its icon to whatever you want it to be, then give it a name that begins with a space to force it to be first in the sort order for the items in the stack. A third option, Apple's, is to Control-click on a stack and select Folder from the Display As section in the contextual menu. So now you have a stack disguised as a folder. The icon won't change when you add items to the stack—that's good. But you can't tell a folder in the Dock from a stack—that's bad. So take your pick. Personally, I go for option two. It's not particularly elegant, but it works for now.

   MAKE YOUR OWN STACKS

You can create your own stack in about three seconds. Pick the folder you want to use—pictures, movies, text files, folders, applications—it doesn't matter. Once you've picked the folder, drag it to the Dock. That's it. Done. Finished. No mas. Hasta la vista.

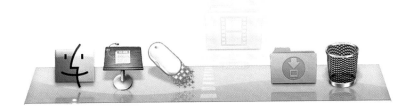

   ## MOVING ITEMS TO AND FROM STACKS

Moving stuff to and from stacks is as easy as eating an entire box of Girl Scout cookies in 15 minutes (not that I've ever done that or anything, but I have a "friend" who does it several times each year). To remove a file from a stack, click the stack, then click-and-drag the file you want to move. As soon as you start to drag it, the stack will close and you can drag the file to its new location. Adding files to a stack is even easier. Click-and-drag the item you want to move, and drop it on top of the stack.

   ## STACK IDEA: MAKE A SHORT STACK

A lot of people drag their Applications folder to the Dock, which really saves time. But I have dozens of applications, so even if I have my Applications folder in the Dock, I'm going to waste time looking for what I need. The fact is, I have a handful of applications I use every day, 20 or so that I use every week, another 20 I might open once a month, and about 100 that I downloaded because they were going to make me so much more productive, but now I don't even remember what they do. So what I do is create aliases of just the applications I use frequently and drop them into a new folder. Then I put that in the Dock where they are always one click away.

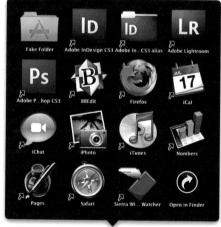

MOVE A FILE TO ANY FOLDER WITH STACKS

The tip on the previous page showed how to move a file to a stack, but because stacks are spring-loaded you can take things a step further and move a file to any folder on your hard drive. Click the file you want to move and hover over a stack (it doesn't matter which one) until it springs open and you see the contents of the stack in a Finder window. Since you're in a Finder window, you have access to any of the folders in the sidebar. So keep your mouse button pressed and drag the file over one of the sidebar folders (Documents, for instance) and hover there until it opens. Now just keep dragging-and-hovering over folders until you get to the one where you want to keep the file, then release the mouse button.

   OPEN AN ITEM IN A STACK WITH ANOTHER APPLICATION

When you double-click a document to open it, it will open using the default application for that particular file type. But if you're tired of the same-old-same-old, you can open a file in one of your stacks with a different application. Click the stack to open it, then click the file you want to open and drag it onto the icon for the application you want to use to open it. Say, for example, you have a photo someone sent to you and you want to crop out part of the background. You have set iPhoto as the default application to open photos, but Preview can handle a simple crop, and it will be a lot quicker since it opens in about one second. So instead of double-clicking the photo to launch iPhoto, click-and-drag it onto the Preview icon in the Applications folder or Dock. Preview will launch (if it's not already open), and you can do your crop, but iPhoto will still be the default application for image files.

   HIDE THE DOCK AUTOMATICALLY

The Dock is one of the seven wonders of the computing world, but it does take up some screen real estate, especially for laptop users. If you find yourself cussing a lot because the Dock is always in your way, you can turn on a feature that will keep the Dock hidden until you need it. Control-click on the Dock divider line and choose Turn Hiding On from the contextual menu. Now, the Dock will go into hiding but will kind of "pop up" so you can access the Dock when you move the cursor to the edge of the screen where the Dock had been. When you move your cursor away, it goes back into hiding. If you think you might use this function often, you'll probably want to memorize the Turn Hiding On/Off shortcut, which is Command-Option-D.

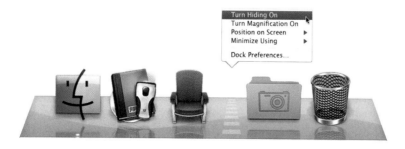

    INSTANT DOCK RESIZE

If you want to make the Dock larger or smaller, there's a slider in the Dock preference pane, but that's way too much trouble. Instead, put your cursor over the Dock divider line that separates your application icons (on the left side of the Dock) from your folders and Trash icon (on the right side). When you are over the divider line, the cursor will change to a horizontal bar with two arrows: one facing up and one facing down. When it does that, just click-and-drag your cursor upward to make the Dock bigger, or downward to shrink it.

    THE ONE-CLICK TRICK TO MOVING THE DOCK

Okay, so you're working in a program that takes up every vertical inch of the screen. You can set the Dock to hide automatically, and when you go to adjust something near the bottom, the Dock keeps popping up. Oh sure, you could move the Dock to where it's anchored on the left or right side of the screen, but that just feels weird. But what if you could move it temporarily to the left or right and then get it back to the bottom when you close Final Cut Pro (or whatever) with just one click? Here's how: Press-and-hold the Shift key, click directly on the Dock's divider line (on the far-right side of the Dock), and drag the Dock to the left or right side of your screen. Bam! It moves over to the side. Then, once you quit your application, just Shift-click on that divider line and slam it back to the bottom (okay, drag it back to the bottom). A draggable Dock—is that cool or what?!

   FOR THOSE WHO DON'T WANT TO HIDE: MAGNIFY

If the Dock seems to be in your way a lot, but you don't like the whole "hiding the Dock" thing, try using magnification. Control-click on the Dock divider line and select Dock Preferences. When the dialog opens, set the normal size of the Dock by using the Size slider. Next, make sure the Magnification checkbox is turned

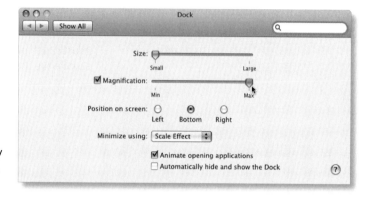

on and use the Magnification slider to set the size you want the Dock icons to be when you roll the cursor over them. Close the dialog and roll the cursor over the Dock to try it out. Cool, huh?

   THE CURE FOR BIG DOCK ENVY

I like a tiny Dock that takes up the least possible space on my screen. But there are times I look at other peoples' big Docks and have a twinge of big Dock envy. I know, I could turn on magnification, but I find it incredibly annoying to have it trigger every time I go to the bottom of my screen (which, I've discovered, is hundreds of times each day). After years of envy and feelings of inadequacy, I discovered that even if you have magnification turned off, you can turn it on temporarily by pressing Control-Shift as you drag your cursor over the Dock. Now I can enjoy the benefits of a big Dock whenever I want and never have to feel inadequate again.

   FORCE QUIT AN APPLICATION FROM THE DOCK

Occasionally, you're running an application in Mac OS X and for some reason it just sits there and refuses to do anything while the dreaded little beach ball spins. You press Command-Q to quit, but the beach ball will just keep spinning and taunting you. It's a power struggle. Option-Control-click on its icon in the Dock, select Force Quit from the contextual menu, and boom! That'll teach 'em. Now you can relaunch the application and odds are it's learned its lesson and will behave itself. Unfortunately, it will have the last laugh because you'll lose any unsaved changes you made before you force quit. But, don't worry about force quitting. It's not as big a deal as it might seem (or as it was in some previous operating systems), and you're not going to mess anything up.

   ACCIDENTALLY LAUNCH A PROGRAM? UN-LAUNCH IT

Because it takes only one click to launch a program from the Dock, you're just one click away from launching the wrong application (sadly, I do this all the time—and it's always one of those applications that takes five minutes to open). If you do launch a program you wish you hadn't, immediately Control-Option-click its Dock icon and choose Force Quit from the contextual menu. The application will realize it's not wanted and will give up and quit without arguing with you.

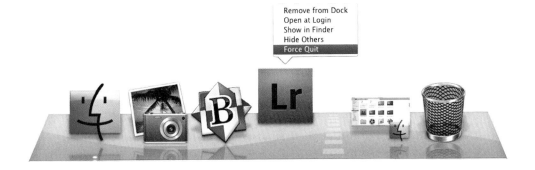

KEEPING AN APPLICATION IN THE DOCK

If you're running an application and you say to yourself, "You know, I use this app a lot," you can keep its icon in the Dock, so next time it's just one click away. The next time you're using the application, Control-click its icon in the Dock and choose Keep In Dock from the contextual menu. Of course, there is another way. A cooler way. Just click on the application's Dock icon and drag it to a new position in the Dock. It's really not faster, but it makes you look (and feel) less menu-dependent.

KEEP YOUR DOCK IN SYNC

If you have multiple Macs, you can use MobileMe's sync capabilities to keep the Dock the same on all your machines. Go to the Apple menu, select System Preferences, choose MobileMe, and then click the Sync tab. Be sure the Synchronize with MobileMe checkbox is selected, use the pop-up menu to set the sync options, and turn on the checkbox next to Dock Items in the list of items you can sync. Now just do the same for any other Macs that share your MobileMe account, and you'll never have to look at an unfamiliar Dock again.

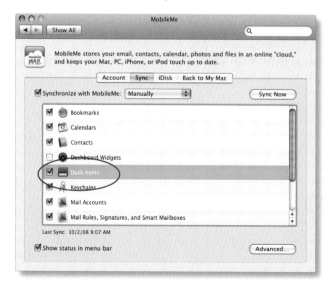

   UNCLUTTER YOUR DOCK

If you have a few apps running and you like to keep things uncluttered and organized by minimizing document windows to the Dock, it doesn't take long before your Dock gets pretty crowded. If that's the case, here's a tip that might help you bring some welcome space and order back to your Dock. When you're switching from one application to the next, press-and-hold the Option key before you click the new application's icon in the Dock. This helps unclutter the Dock by hiding all of the icons for minimized windows from the application you just left. When you switch back to that application later, its minimized windows reappear in the Dock.

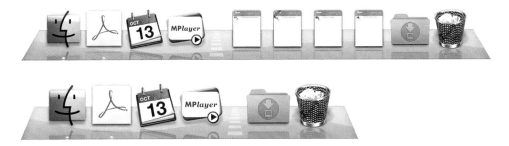

   OPEN DOCUMENTS BY DRAGGING THEM TO THE DOCK

If you find a document on your drive and you're not really sure what kind of file it is (TXT, JPEG, DOC, AI, PSD, NEF, LSMFT, or whatever), just drag it over the applications in the Dock. If one of them thinks it might be able to open it for you, the icon will highlight, basically telling you to "let 'er rip!" If you don't get any takers in the Dock, you can open your Applications folder and do the same thing. Odds are pretty good that you've got something that will open it for you.

LEOPARD

FORCING A SPECIFIC APPLICATION TO OPEN A DOCUMENT

Sometimes docked apps don't want to open your document, even though they may be able to, so you have to coax (okay, force) them to give it a try. For example, let's say sometime in the last century you created a document in WordPerfect for Mac. If you drag the document to Pages' icon in the Dock, chances are it won't highlight (which would normally be the indication it can open that document). If that happens, press Command-Option, then drag the WordPerfect document's icon to the Pages icon in the Dock, and Leopard will force it to try to open it, whether it wants to or not. By the way, if you ever get nostalgic about the good old days of computing, you can download WordPerfect for Mac for free from the Corel website. While you're there, get a copy of WordPerfect for DOS for a PC-using friend—you don't have to mention it was free.

MAKE DOCK ICONS STOP MOVING

In a previous tip, I showed how you can open a file by dragging it onto an icon in the Dock. But if you don't aim exactly right, Leopard thinks you're trying to add the document to the Dock itself, so it kindly slides the icons out of the way to make room for your document. That's incredibly polite (for an operating system anyway), but it can also be incredibly annoying if that's not what you're trying to do. If this happens to you, just press-and-hold the Command key as you drag your document and all the Dock icons will stay put. I guarantee you'll have a much higher success rate if you don't have to hit a moving target.

  BE CAREFUL WHEN DRAGGING ITEMS OFF THE DOCK

Dragging things into the Dock is easy, and there's really nothing you can do to mess things up. But dragging items from the Dock… well, there you can cause yourself to have a very, very bad day if you're not careful. Here's why: The icons in the Dock are just pretty graphics that look like the real thing, but aren't. When you drag an icon from the Dock and watch it go "poof," it's no big deal. You know how there are a lot of things in life that can be really cool if you use them correctly, but really uncool if you don't? Well, the Command key is the same way. Probably 350 of the tips in this book involve using the Command key. In 349 of those instances, it helps you do things faster, smarter, and better. Here's the 350th: Imagine you want to clear out your Dock. Knowing how cool the Command key is, you press-and-hold it while you drag icons from the Dock to the desktop. "That's strange," you say to yourself, "none of the icons went 'poof' when I dragged them onto the desktop. I think it made copies of all of them because there are still icons in the Dock plus all these on the desktop." You're tired and decide you'll figure it out tomorrow, so you go ahead and trash the copies of the icons from the desktop. The next day you click on an image to launch Photoshop and nothing happens. You click on the alias of an iMovie project you've been working on for six months and it says it can't find the original. You get a really bad feeling when you realize that everything you took out of the Dock is no longer on your hard drive. Here's what you need to learn from this mini-autobiography: When you press-and-hold the Command key and drag an icon out of the Dock, you're moving the real file. If you don't believe me, try it. (It's okay if you don't believe me. I understand. I've just told you that the Command key you love and trust is capable of unspeakable evil.) Drag the Mail icon to the desktop, then open the Applications folder and see if you can find it. Don't turn your back on the Command key—it does so many good things—but watch your back or it can burn you big time.

Chapter 4

Spotlight on Sam & Dave

Spotlight Search Tips

If there was ever a product that richly deserved its own chapter, it's Leopard's amazing Spotlight search feature. That's because

Spotlight on Sam & Dave

spotlight search tips

we spend a ton of our time searching for things on our Macs. Why? Because we don't know where anything is. Ever. Take my car keys, for example. You might as well take them, because I generally have no idea where they are. For some reason I can clearly remember undocumented keyboard shortcuts from Mac OS 7.1, but I have no idea where I laid my car keys last night. You know what I need? I need Spotlight outside my Mac, in my regular life. I would just type in "car keys" and it would say "in the kitchen, just to the left of the bowl of fruit" or, more likely, "they're still in the ignition." So, how does the name of this chapter, "Spotlight on Sam & Dave," fit in? Well, that's the hook from the classic oldie "Sweet Soul Music" by an artist named Arthur Conley. In the song, he "spotlights" other singers, like James Brown and Otis Redding.

   YOU CAN'T USE IT IF YOU CAN'T FIND IT

One of the most important features of any operating system is the ability to search the contents of your storage devices and find the files you need. Hard drives are getting bigger all the time, which is good because we keep filling them up. But bigger drives mean there are more places for your files to hide. Some operating systems use a little dog to distract you while it finds the file you need. Leopard doesn't have a dog, but it does have a search engine, Spotlight, that kicks butt. Spotlight was introduced in Tiger, but has undergone a major upgrade in Leopard. Every time you do a search you're using Spotlight, but it has a couple of different "doors," depending on where you are and what type of information you want to retrieve. I'm telling you, Spotlight rocks with a funky beat and is going to be your new best friend.

   SPOTLIGHT MENU: IT'S FAST, EASY, AND ALWAYS THERE

The Spotlight menu is used for quick searches when you pretty much know what you're looking for and just want to find it without sifting through thousands of files. Let's say I need a copy of a hotel bill from a recent trip to Portland to submit for reimbursement. I press Command-Spacebar and the Spotlight menu opens in the top-right corner of my screen. I begin to type in "Portland" to start searching. As soon as I type "P," possible matches start appearing. As I continue typing, the list of hits gets smaller. By the time I've finished typing "Portland," I am down to 39 hits—still too many. I know I stayed

in a Marriott, so I add that to my query. Now I'm down to only four hits, including the one I need. It took me about five seconds to find the one file I need out of the 599,420 files currently on my drive. How amazing is that?

   OPEN YOUR TOP HIT FAST

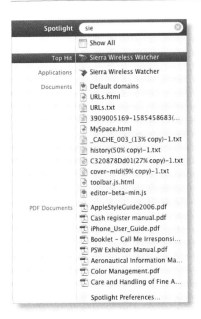

If you do a Spotlight menu search and the file you're searching for is the one that shows up as the Top Hit in the results list, just press Return and it will open right up. If the application the file needs isn't already running, Leopard will launch the application, then open the file for you. Now that's service!

   GET SMARTER WITH JUST ONE CLICK

If you want to get ahead, you need to use your prosencephalon

The title for this tip sounds like something you would hear on an infomercial, but it happens to be true. The next time you're reading a document (it can be an email, a text document, a webpage, etc.), and run across a word or topic you want to know more about, just Control-click it and select Look Up in Dictionary from the contextual menu. By default, Dictionary will search for your word in the *New Oxford American Dictionary*, the *Oxford American Writer's Thesaurus*, the Apple Dictionary, and Wikipedia, then it will display any results it finds.

   DANIEL WEBSTER WOULD BE JEALOUS

I've heard of people who read dictionaries for fun. Seriously. Why go out on a date when you can spend the evening with Merriam-Webster? For the rest of us, Leopard has at least four ways (there could be more that I haven't stumbled on yet) to look up definitions for words. Here's the quickest way: Press Command-Spacebar and type the word you want to look up in the search field. If you have entered a word Spotlight "knows," a new results category (Definition) will be visible along with the first few words of the definition. If you want to see the entire definition, roll your cursor over the Definition line, pause for a second, and it will appear in a yellow box. If you want to launch Dictionary so you can get even more detail, just click the Definition line.

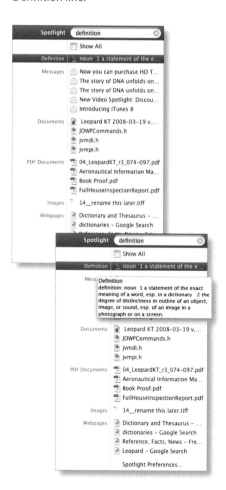

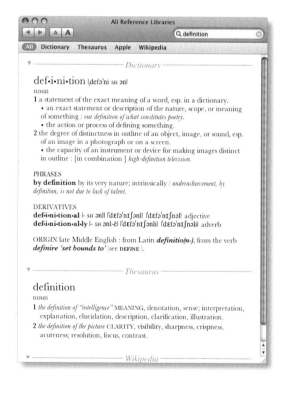

   BREAK THE TOP 20 BARRIER

The Spotlight menu only shows the top 20 results from your search, but if the file you're looking for didn't make the list, or if you just want to be sure you have every copy of a file, click
Show All at the top of the results list. This will open the Spotlight window and show you the
complete list of results for your search.

   PUT SOME LIMITS ON SPOTLIGHT

Spotlight is able to perform lightning-fast searches by creating and constantly updating an index of the files on your drive. It is annoyingly thorough (kind of like an IRS auditor. Just kidding. Really, you guys do a great job. Some of my favorite people, actually) and will index every file on your drive so it will know where it is if you ever ask for it. That's not all bad, because you don't really want a search engine that skips a lot of files. Since Spotlight is eager to please, if it has indexed a folder on your drive, it's going to look in it when it's searching. But if you're looking for an article you wrote last year entitled "The Negative Effects of Using Vista on a Person's Happiness and Sense of Well-Being," is it really necessary for Spotlight to search your Photoshop Presets folder, rummage through the Curves folder, and find the "Color Negative" curves preset? Save some processor power by setting some areas of your drive "off limits" when Spotlight is doing its indexing and searching. Here's how: Go to the Apple menu, choose System Preferences, and click on the Spotlight icon. Now click the Privacy tab and use the plus sign (+) button near the bottom to add folders or disks you want Spotlight to skip. You can also drag-and-drop folders and volumes into the window, if you prefer.

     SEE WHAT YOU WANNA SEE

While I might not need Spotlight to keep track of every file on my drive (see previous tip), I do want it to keep track of things like email messages and iCal events. But if I'm looking for a picture I took of my daughter Megan, for example, I don't want to have to scroll through a list of hundreds of emails and iCal entries that are linked to her or contain her name just to find the picture. Conveniently, you can limit the file types Spotlight will display in search results. Select System Preferences from the Apple menu, click on the Spotlight icon, and then turn off the checkboxes for any items on the list of categories you don't want to see when you perform a search. Since Spotlight has still indexed my Mail messages and iCal events, I can search them from within those applications. It just keeps things a little neater to not see them every time I do a search with Spotlight.

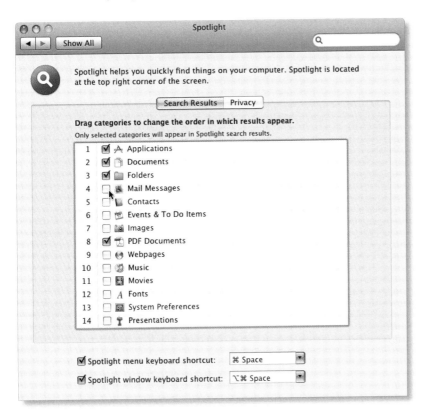

   CHANGE THE ORDER OF THE RESULTS

Not only can you limit the types of results Spotlight will show you, but you can also customize the order in which they are displayed. Let's say you're a creative type and find that most of the time you search for music, movies, and photos. By default Spotlight will display text files, Address Book contacts, and others at the top of the results list and put your items near the bottom. If you want to see the files you are most likely to want displayed first, go to the Apple menu, select System Preferences, then click on the Spotlight icon. The file categories are listed in the order they will appear in your search results. To change the order, just click-and-drag them up or down the list. From now on, the most important files will be right at the top of the list where they belong.

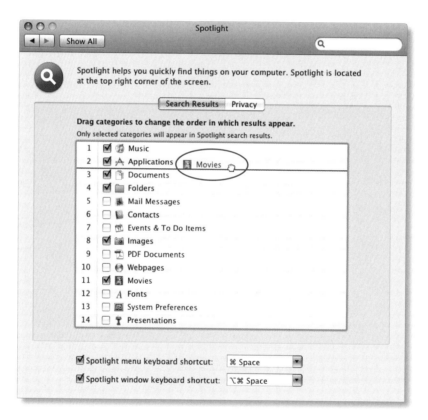

   USE QUICK LOOK TO BE SURE YOU HAVE THE RIGHT FILE

Does this ever happen to you? You do a search, get the list of results, say, "Oh, yeah, that's the one," click to open it, wait for the right application to launch, wait for the 300-MB Photoshop file to open, look at it and realize it's not the file you want? No? Never happens to you? Okay, well in case you have a friend who has had this frustrating experience, here's the solution: Instead of opening one of the files Spotlight found, click Show All to see the results in the Spotlight window. Now click (don't double-click) on one of the results, press the Spacebar, and enjoy the beautiful preview Quick Look serves up for you. If you want to check out several files, just Command-click on them before you press the Spacebar, and Quick Look will open a slide show of all the files you selected.

   SPOTLIGHT WINDOW

So far in this chapter, we've looked at the Spotlight menu, which is great when you want to search your entire drive and get back lots of results. But there's another search option in Leopard, Spotlight window, for those times you want to focus your searches on certain kinds of files, date ranges, etc. Using the Spotlight menu is like sending a man to Home Depot to buy one bag of wimpy screws to hang a picture. He'll wander up and down every aisle in the store looking at all the new power tools, nail guns, and pressure washers—you know, manly stuff. Two hours and three hundred dollars later, he comes back home with a fifty-cent bag of screws, along with a few extra things. Using the Spotlight window, in contrast, is like emptying all the money and credit cards from your husband's pockets (leaving $0.54 to cover the screws and tax, of course) before he heads out to buy the screws. To use the Spotlight window, press Command-Option-Spacebar. When the window opens, you'll see that every file on your drive is listed. All you have to do now is scroll down the list until you see the one you want—just kidding. The power of the Spotlight window is the ability to filter your search results by using the criteria and location bars. The next few tips will show you some nifty stuff you can do with the Spotlight window.

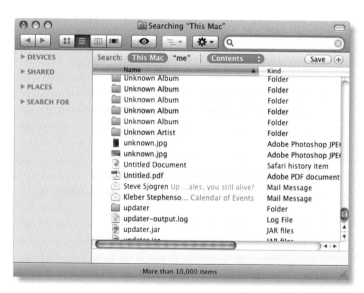

    REFINE YOUR SEARCHES IN SPOTLIGHT WINDOW

When you're putting in your contacts in the morning and drop one, you don't search the whole house to find it—you're reasonably certain it's in the immediate area. When you're searching your Mac, most of the time you have some idea of what you're looking for and where it is. You know it's a photo, for instance, or a file that you created last December. If you refine a search using the information you already know, you'll end up with a shorter list of results to look through. One of the ironies of searching is that, in many instances, the best search is the one that gives the fewest results. I'm searching because I want to be able to go right to the file I need, not so I can have the fun of sifting through 1,218 results to locate it. Here's how you start narrowing your searches: Open a Spotlight window (press Command-Option-Spacebar) and click the plus sign (+) button at the far-right end of the search bar, right next to the Save button. A second bar will open with some buttons you can use to add various types of filters. Each time you click the plus sign button and define another search filter, you'll see the list of results get smaller until (hopefully) you'll see the file you're looking for.

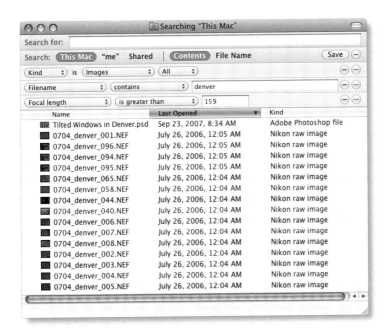

ADD ITEMS TO THE SEARCH CRITERIA POP-UP MENUS

When you are searching in the Spotlight window and use the pop-up menus to add additional search criteria, there are a limited number of choices on the menu. But if you scroll down to Other, there are 148 additional criteria (trust me, I counted—twice!) you can use. If some of these are ones you routinely use in searches, you can add them to the menu by simply turning on their checkboxes in the In Menu column. From now on, you can select them directly from the pop-up menu and save yourself a long scroll.

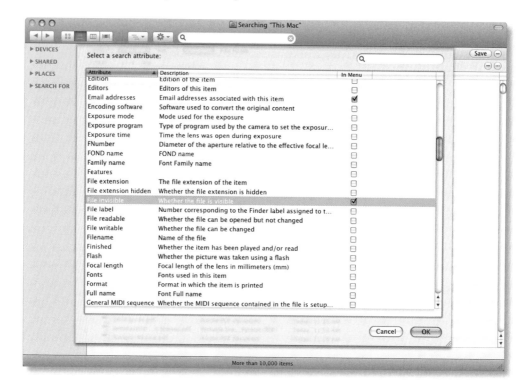

     SAVING SPOTLIGHT SEARCHES AS SMART FOLDERS

If you initiate a search from the Spotlight window or the search box that's in the top-right corner of every Finder window, you get a bonus—you can save your search to use again. For example, press Command-Option-Spacebar to open a Spotlight window, then click the plus sign (+) button at the far-right end of the criteria bar (next to the Save button). Now click on Any, scroll to the bottom of the list to Other, and type "address" (no quotes) into the text field that appears. As soon as you start to type, you'll see the contacts from your Address Book displayed in the results widow. Click the Save button in the top-right corner of the window, type in a name for the search (something like "Contacts" perhaps?), press Return, and you'll see a new folder appear in the sidebar. But this is no ordinary folder, my friend. No, this is a Smart Folder. Why is it smart? Because the next time you need to find a contact, all you have to do is click on the folder and it will run the same search again and show you the results, which will include any contacts you have added since the last time you searched. That's smart.

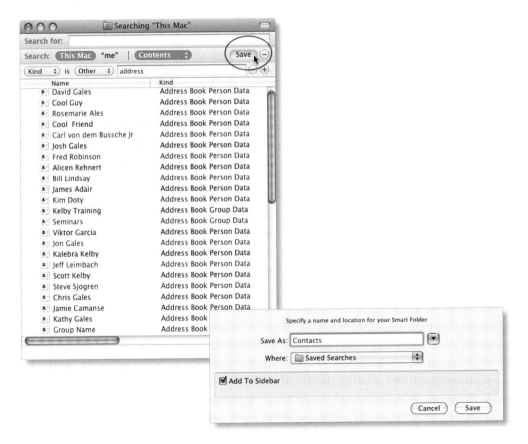

   POWER SEARCHING IS, UHHHH, POWERFUL

This tip takes you into territory rarely visited by normal humans. If you do this, you must never let anyone know or they will fear you. Imagine you have music files in all different formats scattered all over your drive which you want to consolidate. Easy. Press Command-Spacebar and type "kind:music" (without the quotes) into the Spotlight search box and you will instantly see a list of every music file on your Mac. Wow! Try this one: type "kind:mail" (again, no quotes) into the search box and be amazed at the number of emails you have stashed away (you'll need to click Show All to see the whole list). The magic behind power searching is the ability to pair an operator (kind) with a keyword (music). Tiger (the previous version of Mac OS X) had a few operators available, but Leopard has…well, no one knows for sure how many operators are available for searches in Leopard.

   SOMETIMES LESS CAN BE MORE

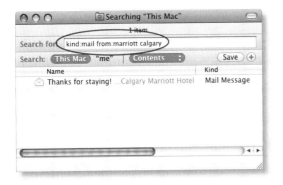

If you didn't read the previous tip, now would be a good time, or this one won't make much sense. Done? Good. So now you know how to take an operator, pair it with a keyword, and do a search. But if you tried some searches using the examples I gave, you probably had too many results to be useful. Here's how you can eliminate some of the junk by adding additional operators and keywords to your search. On my machine, "kind:mail" returns 2,374 results. (Yikes! And that doesn't include the ones I have archived on the server.) But if I search for "kind:mail marriott" (don't forget the space between the keywords—oh, and no quotes), I get 127 results. Adding one keyword eliminated 2,247 results I didn't need! But the remaining results include emails I sent to and received from Viktor Garcia, the thick-skinned young lad who books the travel (and takes serious abuse over middle seats) for the Photoshop Seminar Tour. I read all of Viktor's emails, but I'm looking for one particular email received from the Marriott in Calgary (it's a satisfaction survey that I can complete and possibly score some free Rewards points). So I make a small change and type in "kind:mail from:marriott calgary" and am now down to one, that's right, one result. It's amazing what a couple of words and a colon can do. To recap, you can narrow a search by adding keywords—add as many as you need—just be sure to leave a space between them. You can also narrow searches by using a second "operator:keyword" query. If this seems a bit confusing, it's because it is. But if you experiment, you'll get the hang of it and you'll love it. It is, in my experience, the absolute fastest search method.

   I SEARCH, THEREFORE I FIND

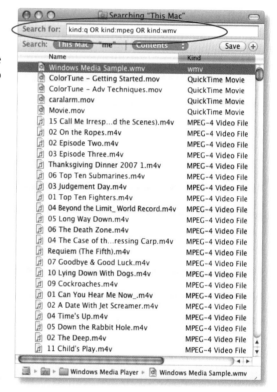

In college, I had to write a 10-page paper on René Descartes' brilliant observation, "Cogito Ergo Sum" ("I think, therefore I am"). To be honest, at the time I didn't see the value of the assignment. But now, too many years later, it has paid off: I came up with a lame play on Descartes' words for the title of this tip. And what a tip it is! Spotlight now has the capability of doing AND, OR, and NOT searches (Boolean searches, for the nerdly inclined). Let's say you want to find all the WMV (Windows Media) files on your drive so you can convert them to another file format. Simple: enter "kind:movie wmv" and you'll have your list. But what if you want to find all the WMV, MPEG, and QuickTime files? In previous versions of Mac OS X, it would have been impossible. But thanks to Boolean search capability, here's what you would type in: "kind:quicktime OR kind:mpeg OR kind:wmv". If your brain works like mine (a terrifying thought, isn't it?), wouldn't you think that if you wanted to find all the QuickTime, MPEG, and WMV files you would use AND instead of OR

in your search? But if you use AND, you're asking for files that are all three formats at once. You can have multiple personalities, but don't even think about having multiple file formats. One more quick search type—finding all files except ones you don't like (you don't have anything personal against them, you just don't need them right now): enter "kind:movie NOT mpeg" and you'll get a list of every movie except those kinds of files. *Note:* I wasn't yelling when I did the searches here. You need to use all capital letters whenever you use Boolean search terms.

A LITTLE HELP WITH MORE COMPLICATED SEARCHES

Spotlight's ability to do some rather complex searches is great, but getting the terms, colon, spaces, and file types right can be tough. (For example, kind:jpg gives you zip, but kind:jpeg works. Or kind:il gives you all your Adobe Illustrator files, but kind:ai finds nothing—even though the suffix for Illustrator files is AI. Things like that drive me crazy.) When you get to the point that you're ready to give up and go watch a chick flick on Oxygen for a couple of hours, use a different strategy. Start by pressing Command-Option-Spacebar to open a Spotlight window. Now that's what I'm talkin' about—I'll bet you've got over 10,000 results already. Now that you've put the TV remote down, click the plus sign (+) button at the far-right end of the location bar. Now go to the plus sign button that's on the bar you just added, but instead of clicking it, Option-click it. You'll notice the plus sign changes to an ellipses (…) and two additional search bars are added. What you're looking at is a way to do Boolean searches by clicking menus and pressing buttons instead of typing in file types, colons, and the other stuff. It's a bit clunky (the official technical term, I believe), but it can make things a lot easier sometimes. Here's the trick: To stay in the same search level, click the plus sign button to add your criteria. To nest criteria, Option-click the plus sign button. The example you see here is a search I've saved to have instant access to my travel itineraries for this year. I want to find any PDF created this year whose name contains at least one of the following words: "hotel," "flight," or "boarding." The best way to learn is to play with it.

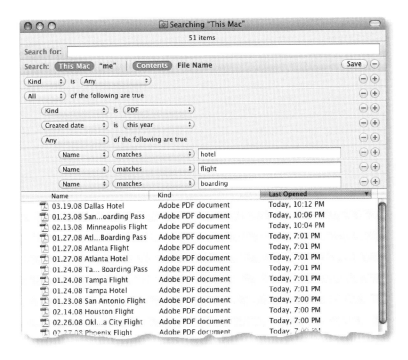

DON'T KNOW THE EXACT FILENAME? NO PROBLEM

What are the odds that I'm going to remember the exact filename for something I saved last month? About the same as remembering the name of a file I saved five minutes ago—nada. Fortunately, Spotlight's not picky and will take whatever information you can give it and start searching. If you know you created the file during a certain time period, enter the dates in the search box like this: "date:1/1/08-1/17/08" (no quotes, in case you haven't caught on to that yet). You sent an email to some friends about how you might have to put on jeans instead of shorts because it's supposed to dip below 50° in Tampa tonight, and you want to be sure to send it to your buddy in Chicago who just got buried by a blizzard. You know the subject line included "Brrrrrr," so type "kind:message subject:brrrrrr" and see what you get. You get the idea. Start typing and see if you get close enough for Spotlight to figure out what you're looking for.

SOMETIMES IT'S WHAT'S INSIDE THAT COUNTS

Not only does Spotlight search filenames, it can also search the content of files. Last year I was in Denver for a Photoshop seminar, and our team stayed at the absolute coolest hotel any of us had ever stayed in (with the possible exception of the Jefferson in Richmond, VA). Six months later, we were scheduled to go back to Denver and naturally wanted to stay at the same hotel. The problem was, we couldn't remember the name. But I knew I had received an email with the itinerary for the earlier trip that would have included the hotel information, and assumed I would recognize the name when I saw it. I simply pressed Command-Option-Spacebar and typed "denver" into the Search For field. Since Spotlight displays the subject lines of emails in the search results window, all I had to do was glance down the list until—bada boom, bada bing!—there it was. The Curtis—that's the one, baby.

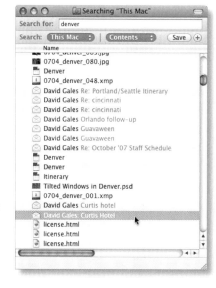

   AVOIDING JUNK SEARCH RESULTS

There is one caveat to the previous tip. If the word you are looking for is contained within another word, you'll get a bunch of "junk" hits. For example, search for "he" (I can't think of an instance when you would want to search for "he," other than when you need an example for a Spotlight search tip, but you never know) and if you leave off the quotes, Spotlight will find things like she, the, help, where—you get the idea. So if you know the exact word or phrase you are looking for, put it in quotes and Spotlight will eliminate the junk for you. The same thing applies to multi-word searches. If you know the name of the file you're looking for is 2005 Bucs Roster, you would search for "2005 Bucs Roster" with quotes around it.

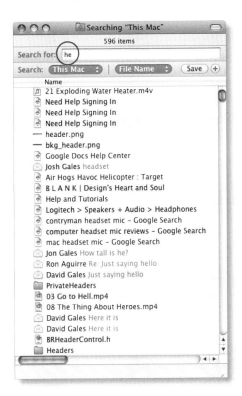 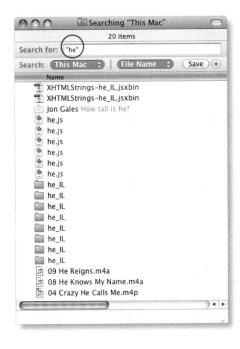

⬤ ⬤ ⬤ SEARCH INSIDE YOUR PHOTOSHOP DOCUMENTS

Here's another example of searching inside a document. I've got to warn you—this one's a mind blower. If you've got a layered Photoshop document (saved in PSD format), Spotlight will even search your Type layers to help you find the file that has the word you're looking for (as long as you're using Type layers—not rasterized layers, in which case they're not Type layers anymore). For example, here I did a search for the words "north rim," which resulted in Spotlight finding the layered PSD file I wanted.

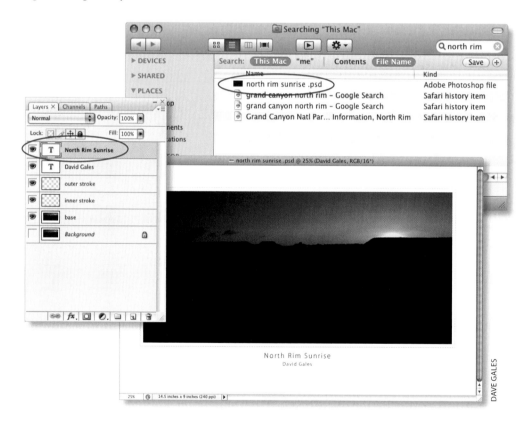

   SPOTLIGHT MENU VERSUS SPOTLIGHT WINDOW

Since the Spotlight menu is so convenient (it's right there in the menu bar, no matter which program you're using) and you can just press Command-Spacebar to activate it, why not always use it instead of the Spotlight window? Well, the Spotlight window has some big advantages. First, you see all your results for a search. The Spotlight menu only shows the first 20. Second, the Spotlight window gives you the option to view the results in List, Icon, or Cover Flow view, which means you can use Quick Look to preview the results. Third, you can drag files to new locations or delete them directly from the search results window in the Spotlight window. Finally, your ability to refine searches using additional search criteria and the ability to save searches make the Spotlight window much more powerful than the Spotlight menu. The bottom line is Spotlight is awesome, whether you use the Spotlight menu (Command-Spacebar) or the Spotlight window (Command-Option-Spacebar). But for serious searching, the Spotlight window gets the nod.

   SEARCHING THE SYSTEM PREFERENCES

Can't remember where a particular option is found within the System Preferences? (For example, for some reason I can never remember where to set the date format for my Mac. No, it's not in Date & Time.) No sweat, because Spotlight also lives right within the System Preferences dialog (in the upper right-hand corner). Just open the System Preferences dialog from the Apple menu, and type the name of the preference setting you're looking for (in my case, I'd type "format" [without the quotes]), and then Spotlight puts a little "spotlight" around the System Preferences that have a control for Format. If there's more than one, it will highlight several icons, but to help you even further, a pop-up search menu will appear with the names of all the "Format" stuff. Click the one you want in the list (in my case, Date Formats), and it immediately takes you to that preference. That ain't bad, folks.

   OPENING? SAVING? SPOTLIGHT WILL HELP

Okay, it's time to save a file, so you choose Save As (press Command-Shift-S) and the Save As dialog appears. You want to save your document in a particular folder, but you can't remember exactly where that folder is. No sweat, because Spotlight lives in the Save (and Open) dialog, as well—it's everywhere! Just type the name of the folder you're looking for in the Spotlight search field near the upper-right corner of the Save As dialog. When you see the folder you're looking for, press Return. *Note:* If you don't see the search field in the Save As dialog, click the blue triangle to the right of the field where you typed in the filename and the dialog will expand.

Chapter 5

YOU'VE GOT MAIL

TIPS FOR USING MAIL

All right, you're probably thinking, "Hey,

that's not a song or a movie, that's the

AOL greeting when you have mail in your inbox,

You've Got Mail

tips for using mail

right?" Well, it actually was a movie based on AOL's email greeting, and it had Tom Hanks and Meg Ryan. It actually was a pretty decent movie, but it was clearly not the Sleepless in Seattle, Part 2 *they hoped it would be. The problem was that it wasn't shot in Seattle, and that's what* Sleepless in Seattle *was really about. It wasn't about Tom and Meg, it was about Microsoft (as all things ultimately are). The whole love story was just a subterfuge for what was really going on—which was a thinly veiled marketing campaign by Microsoft designed to draw potential Microsoft employees to the Seattle area. See, it's all so simple when you break it down. Anyway, what does all this have to do with Apple's Mail application? Well, I was hoping we wouldn't get to that. Hey, how about that Tom Hanks, though, he's some actor. Did you see him in* Apollo 13?

   Address Book: CUSTOMIZE YOUR CONTACT CARD INFORMATION

Don't let your contacts know this, but they're not all equally important. That means you don't need to keep the same information for everyone. If you have a friend who lets you borrow his Ferrari whenever you want, you'll want to have every scrap of information you can get your hands on so you can always get in touch with him. Things like phone numbers (don't forget the satellite phone you got him for his birthday), email addresses, IM info, and numbers for places he likes to hang out at. Your other friend—the one with the 1990 Chevy Venture minivan—the address for the spam account he checks once a month will be good enough. One of the things I like about Address Book is the ability to customize the information fields on a contact card. To

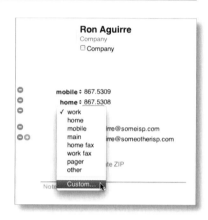

customize a person's card, launch Address Book, then click the name of the contact whose card you want to customize. Now, click the Edit button below their information card and if there's a field you don't need, click the red button to the left of the field's name and it's gone. If you need an extra copy of any field, click the green button (you can't add an extra field until you enter something in the existing one, however). If you click the button to the right of a field's name (it has two triangles pointing up and down), a list of field names will open. Choose the one you want, or choose Custom and enter the name you want to use.

   Address Book: ADD A BIRTHDAY FIELD

People love it when you remember their birthday, so it's very important to write them down. Where (you might ask) should you write them down? Right with their contact info in Address Book. Open Address Book and click on the contact's name. Next, go under the Card menu, under Add Field, and choose Birthday. This puts their card in Edit mode and adds a new field that's already highlighted and ready for you to enter a date. When you're done, click the Edit button under the card. That's it, you've got their birthday entered. Now comes the hard part—remembering it. Sorry, I don't have a tip to help with that.

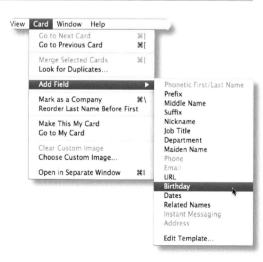

   Address Book: CUSTOMIZE THE CONTACT CARD TEMPLATE

The last couple of tips showed how to customize individual contact cards. But you can also customize the Address Card template so that every time a new card is created, it will have the fields you want. Here's how: Go under the Address Book menu, choose Preferences, and then click the Template icon on the toolbar. A blank contact card will open, showing the default fields. Now it's pretty much like customizing an individual card: Click red buttons to delete fields, click green to add them within the same category, and use the triangle buttons just after the field names to edit the labels. To add fields such as family members' names, job titles, etc., click the Add Field pop-up menu near the top of the window. If you want to make any changes to the way phone numbers are formatted, click the Phone icon on the toolbar and use the pop-up menu to pick one from the list of existing formats or create your own. That's it. The next time you create a new contact card, it will have all the right fields.

Address Book: MAKING YOUR OWN vCARD

I know, I know, you want to be all trendy and hip, so here's how to make your own vCard (Virtual Business Card). (*Note:* The first step in being trendy and hip is not to use the 1970s word "hip.") Here's how: First, set up your own personal card the way you want it, then go to the Card menu and choose Make This My Card. This will change the icon for your personal contact to a silhouette of a person rather than a square photo icon, letting you know which card is "your card."

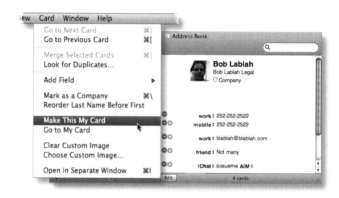

Address Book: HIDING YOUR PRIVATES

If you're sending someone your vCard, depending on who they are, you might want to limit how much info you give them. For example, if this contact is a business contact, you might not want them to have your private email address, or your home phone number (if you still have a land line phone), or your credit card number. Well, luckily, you can decide which fields are saved as your vCard, and which are kept private, by going to the Address Book menu, to Preferences, and then clicking the vCard icon. When the vCard pane opens, turn on the Enable Private Me Card checkbox. Now, go back to your vCard in the Address Book, click the Edit button, and a series of blue checkboxes will appear. The info in any checked fields will be included in your vCard, so uncheck any fields you want kept private. It's as easy as that.

    Address Book: SHARE YOUR vCARD WITH FRIENDS

One of the favorite pastimes of trendy people like you and me is to swap vCards. How many times have you been at an "A-list" party and had people come up to you and say, "Dude, let's swap vCards"? On the outside chance you've never participated in this social bonding ritual, here's how: First, if you have so many contacts that it's difficult to find your own card, click any-where in the Name column and start typing your name until you see it in the list. If you want to email your card to somebody, drag your name to the Dock, and then drop it onto the Mail icon. Mail will open a New Message window with your vCard already attached. All you have to do now is put in an email address, add a subject line and a message to let the recipient know just how lucky they are to be getting your information, and click Send.

Address Book: SENDING NOTES WITH YOUR vCARD

For some freaky reason, when you send someone your vCard, by default it sends them every single field except the Note field. Why? I have no earthly idea, but it doesn't have to be that way. To send your Note field along with your vCard, go to the Address Book menu, select Preferences, and click on the vCard icon at the top. In the vCard panel, turn on the checkbox for Export Notes in vCards, and from then on, your Notes will be sent along as well.

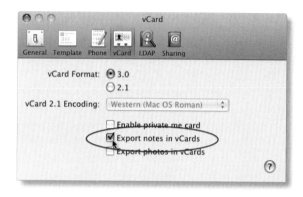

Address Book: IMPORTING vCARDS THE EASY WAY

vCards are getting so popular that they now have an "industry standard" format. Luckily, Address Book not only supports them but also makes it easy for you to import vCards. If you've received a vCard via email, double-click its icon, then click Add when the message shown here opens. If that's too easy, you can also drag it from the email and drop it into any open Address Book window or onto Address Book's icon in the Dock.

   Address Book: SEND SOMEONE'S vCARD TO SOMEONE ELSE

If you want to send a copy of someone's vCard to a friend, just click on the card you want to send, drag it to the Dock, and drop it onto the Mail icon. Another way would be to drag the card to the desktop, then open Mail and attach the vCard to an email. Take your pick. Sending multiple cards works the same way. Shift-click the first and last cards (or Command-click if they're not contiguous) and drag them all at once. Here's the thing: When you look at the email message that's created, it will look like only one card is attached. Trust me on this one, they're all there.

   Address Book: RUN A QUICK SEARCH ON YOUR CONTACT

If you're looking at a contact in your Address Book and you want to quickly find an email or a file they sent you, just Control–click on their name, and then choose Spotlight: "Kleber Stephenson." (Of course, you'll see the name of your contact instead of Kleber.) Spotlight will run a quick search for all instances of that name on your computer (not just within Address Book) and display the results for you. Here's a tip within a tip: If you want to limit the search to just emails, type "kind:mail" before or after the name of the contact in the search box.

Address Book: GET RID OF DUPLICATES

If you think you have multiple cards for the same person in your Address Book (it happens more than you'd think—at least to me), you don't have to track them down manually. Just go to the Card menu and choose Look for Duplicates. Address Book will do its search (it looks for exact duplicates and cards with duplicate names, but different information) and report on what it found, then ask if you want to cancel or merge. Here's the problem: It never tells you which cards it wants to merge. What's the deal? So it's decision time. If you get to this point and get cold feet—it's okay. No one's going to think you're a wimp if you hit Cancel. But how do you get rid of the duplicates? You read the next tip, that's how.

Address Book: MERGE MULTIPLE RECORDS

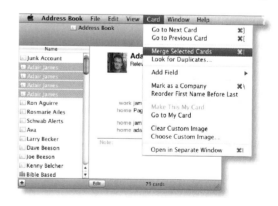

If you read the last tip, you know Address Book makes it easy to determine that you have duplicate contacts—it just keeps their identities secret for some reason. Here's a workaround that's less than elegant, but will at least allow you to know which cards you're merging. Basically, you're going to have to find the duplicates yourself (a potentially tedious operation), then have Address Book merge them. To make finding the duplicate names a little easier, go under the Address Book menu, and choose Preferences. Click the General icon and then select the option to Show the First Name Following the Last Name. This will make the duplicates easier to spot. Now you're going to have to scan down the list of contacts in the Name column until you spot the dupes. When you find them, Shift-click their names to select them. Then go under the Card menu, select Merge Selected Cards, and the two shall become one (like the way I switched writing styles there? "The two shall become one." Hey, if nothing else, I'm versatile).

    Address Book: CREATE SMART GROUPS

Let's say you're the coach of your kid's soccer team, and you have all the parents' numbers in your Address Book in case you have to call them and cancel a game because of rain or extreme apathy. Of course, you could create a group of just the parents' names, and then drag their addresses into this group one by one. Or you can create a Smart Group that will not only add the names for you when you create it, but also every time you add another kid to the team, the parent's contact info will automatically jump right into that group. Here's how it's done: Press-and-hold the Option key and click the little plus sign (+) in the bottom-left corner of the Address Book window (this is the shortcut for creating a Smart Group). A dialog will open with a couple of pop-up menus and a text entry field you can use to pick the contacts that will be added to your new Smart Group. In the example here, every Address Card that contains the word "soccer" in the Note field will be included. Now, whenever you add a player to the team, so long as the word "soccer" appears somewhere in the Note field, the card will be included in the group.

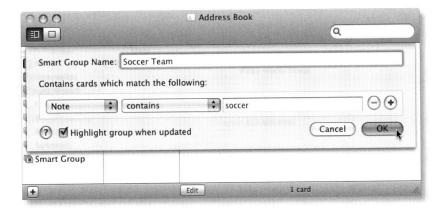

Address Book: SMART GROUP IDEAS

Here are some ideas for Smart Groups:

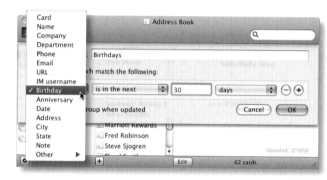

- Create one for your co-workers by setting the first pop-up menu to Company, then entering the name of your company in the text entry field. As new people are added to your company, they'll automatically be added to your Co-workers group. If someone gets laid off, when you update their card, they'll move out of the group and into your Federal Witness Protection Program Smart Group. (Kidding. I hope.)

- If you enter birthdays for friends and co-workers in your Address Book, why not create a Smart Group of all the people who are having a birthday in the next 30 days? "Brilliant," you say, "but how do I do it?" Here's how: Click the first pop-up menu and select Birthday. The second pop-up menu will change to "is in the next," and now just type "30" in the text entry field and click OK. What's particularly cool is that you only have to do this once—it will automatically update every day.

Address Book: SEE WHICH GROUPS A CONTACT IS IN

If you have a contact who appears in more than one group, you can instantly see which ones. Here's how: Click the name of the person you suspect is hanging out in multiple groups, then press-and-hold the Option key. When you do this, every group this person is in will be highlighted. Now it's up to you to decide if they stay or go. If you want my opinion, that Corey kid is

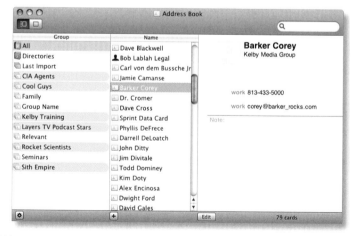

my kinda people and should be in any group he wants to be in. I'm not too sure of that Sith thing, though. I guess everybody has a dark side.

   Address Book: SYNC YOUR BOOK WITH MOBILEME

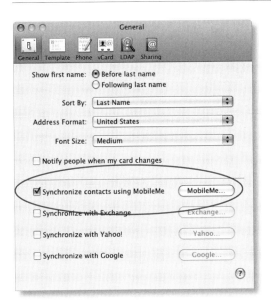

You can have access to your contacts' information from any computer by keeping the Address Book on your Mac in sync with the one on your MobileMe account. To set it up, go to the Address Book menu and choose Preferences. When the preference pane opens, click the General icon and turn on the Synchronize Contacts Using MobileMe checkbox. *Note:* If you have Yahoo!, Google, or Exchange contact lists, you can also sync them with Address Book by simply selecting them in the General preferences pane.

   Address Book: SUPER-SIZED PHONE NUMBERS

Okay, the phone numbers in the contact window are pretty small, but don't sweat it; you can make the numbers so large that someone standing a good 15 to 20 feet from your monitor could make them out. Open one of your contact's cards and click-and-hold on the name of the field for the number you want to read (Work, Home, Mobile, etc.), and then choose Large Type from the pop-up menu. The menu item should really read "Huge, Gigantic, Billboard-like Type" because it plasters a huge number across your entire screen. (Try it on a 30" display—it's stunning.) To make the huge numbers go away, just click anywhere and they disappear, making the original numbers appear even smaller than they did before.

 Address Book: SHARE YOUR ADDRESS BOOK WITH OTHERS

Let's say you want to share your Address Book with a co-worker. For example, I share my Address Book with my Executive Assistant, the wonderful and highly amazing Kathy Siler. We work on a lot of projects together, so when she makes a contact we both need, rather than emailing it to me, she just adds it directly to my Address Book herself. Here's how: First, go to the Address Book menu, choose Preferences, and then click the Sharing icon. When the Sharing panel opens, turn on the checkbox for Share Your Address Book and wait for a few

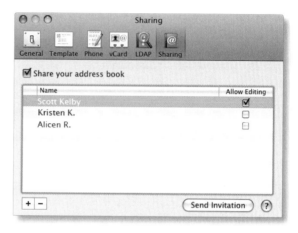

seconds while Leopard does some secret stuff to get everything set up. Now click the Add (+) button in the bottom-left corner of the panel, and select the person's name that you want to share your Address Book with. (This would probably be a good place to mention that if the person you've selected doesn't have a MobileMe account, none of this will work.) If you want this person to be able to edit your Address Book (rather than just read the information), turn on the Allow Editing checkbox. Now all you have to do is click Send Invitation to let them know the good news that they've been chosen to join a very elite group, and give them directions on how to access your Address Book. So as long as they're connected to the Internet, they'll be able to access your Address Book (from their Group column) and make entries and changes directly. How cool is that? Very.

   Address Book: PRINT A MINI-ADDRESS BOOK

If you've ever wanted a nice, small printout of all the contacts in your Address Book (maybe you want to keep it tucked away in your wallet), it's easy. Just go to the Address Book, click on the word All in the left column (or Command-click on specific names if you don't want to include everyone), and choose Print from the File menu (or press Command-P) to open the Print dialog. When it opens, click the Style pop-up menu, choose Pocket Address Book, and then click Print. That's it! You now have your own printed mini-address book. *Note:* If you don't see the Style menu in the Print dialog, click the button to the right of the Printer pop-up menu (it has a triangle pointing upward) and the full dialog will open.

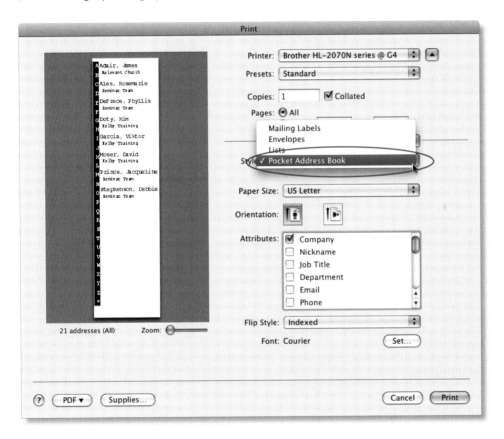

   Address Book: PRINT A CONTACT LIST

Another helpful list to have around is a contact list you can use for quick reference. To put one together, follow the steps in the previous tip, except when you get to the Print dialog, select Lists from the Style pop-up menu. Before you actually print, go down to the Attributes section and turn on the checkboxes for the items you want to include in your list. When you have everything set up the way you want, just click the Print button.

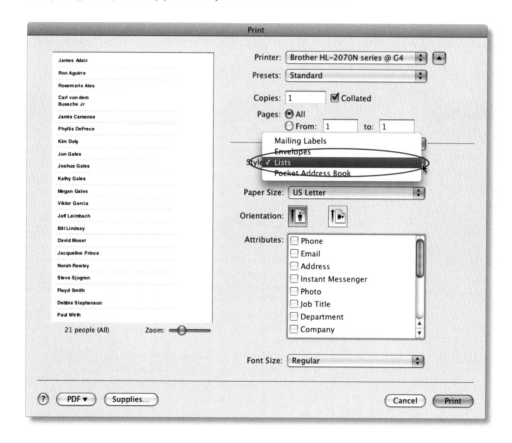

   Address Book: THE WORLD'S EASIEST BACKUP PLAN

If you're not using a MoblieMe account to sync your Address Book (and if that all sounds very foreign, then you're not), you'll definitely want to make a backup copy of your contacts just in case anything unspeakable happens to your Mac (it being dropped, stolen, confiscated by the FBI, or just taking a really nasty hard disk crash). And since backing up is so incredibly simple, there's no excuse not to. Just go to the File menu, choose Export, then choose Address Book Archive. This exports a copy of your entire Address Book, which you should then put on a removable drive, burn to a CD, email to a close family member, etc. Now, the unimaginable becomes manageable (that doesn't make much sense, but it would make a great tag line for a company: "We make the unimaginable manageable").

   Mail: CUSTOMIZE MAIL'S TOOLBAR

You can customize Mail's toolbar just like you can customize Finder windows' toolbars. Since most people will only take advantage of a few tools, why clutter the toolbar with tools you won't ever use, right? Just as with Finder windows, if you Command-click on the white pill-shaped button in the upper right-hand corner of the title bar, you'll step through the various toolbar icon/text configurations. To add or remove items from the toolbar, press Command-Option while you click the same button, and the all-important Customize Toolbar sheet will appear. Now you can drag items on or off the toolbar until it's set up the way you like it. *Note:* Besides being able to customize Mail's toolbar, you can also customize the toolbar in the New Message window, and to do that you only have to make one little move—first click the New Message button to create a new message, then go to the View menu and choose Customize Toolbar.

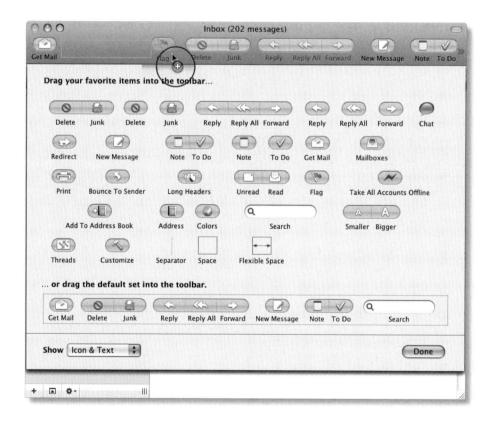

Mail: ADD MORE FIELDS TO THE NEW MESSAGE WINDOW

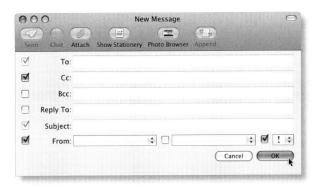

There are some handy fields you can add to the template for new email messages. To add them, click the New Message button on the toolbar, then click the Customize button to the left of the subject line in the new window. Choose Customize at the bottom of the menu to open a window showing the fields available. Simply turn on the checkboxes for the ones you want to show, then click OK. For me, the handiest fields are the two at the bottom that allow me to choose which of my accounts I want to send a message from and which server I want to use.

Mail: DON'T CHECK YOUR SPELLING UNTIL YOU'RE DONE

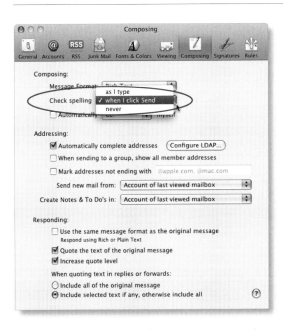

If you need a little help with your spelling (as I do—just ask the platoon of editors who check my spelling), by default Mail checks your spelling as you go (underlining misspelled words in red). But if you find that underlining obtrusive, you can change it so it just checks the spelling once—when you click Send. To do that, go to the Mail menu and choose Preferences. Click the Composing icon and, from the Check Spelling pop-up menu, choose When I Click Send. Now you can misspel to yor harts contant and enjoy the bliss that comes with ignorance, until you click Send and see all the words underlined in red. When you Control-click on one of the misspelled words, a pop-up spell-checking menu will open and display some of its best guesses of what you were trying to type. Click the one you want and no one will ever know you were never the spelling bee champion in the third grade.

   Mail: SEND FANCY EMAILS BY USING STATIONERY

Mail now comes with a bunch of templates you can use to send emails that, frankly, will make ordinary emails look pathetic. They are all professionally designed with coordinated fonts and colors. Think of it as having a designer write your emails for you. If the template you want to use includes a spot for a photo, you can use the Photo Browser that's right on the toolbar to find the one you want. To use stationery, just create a new message, click the Show Stationery button in the toolbar, and browse the various categories. When you find the one you want, just click it and type in your message. If you want to hide the thumbnail previews at the top, click Hide Stationery in the toolbar. You can preview your message in the other templates just by clicking on the templates. When everything is set, click Send.

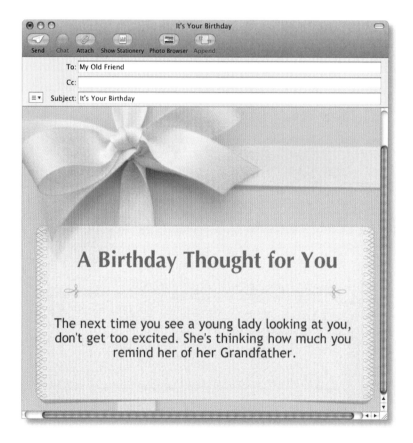

  Mail: UNCOVERING THE PRIORITY POP-UP MENU

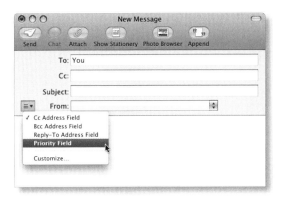

Just to make sure the recipients of your emails clearly understand how important those emails are, you can assign a priority to the messages you send. Here's how you do it: First, click on the New Message button on the toolbar (or press Command-N) to create a new message. Next, click the Customize button to the left of the Subject field, and choose Priority Field. From now on, when you create a new email you can click the Priority button (it's on the far-right side, below the Subject field) and set a priority that your recipients will be able to see.

  Mail: ATTACH A PHOTO TO AN EMAIL

Mail makes it painless to attach a photo or graphic to a new message. When you open a New Message window (click the New Message button on the toolbar) you'll see a Photo Browser button in the top right-hand corner. When you click on it, the contents of your iPhoto folder are displayed. Now all you have to do is navigate to the picture you want to attach and drag it into the message viewer window. How easy is that?

DAVE GALES

Mail: RESIZING PHOTOS FOR EMAILING

Picture this (I know you'll never believe me, but I didn't use that pun intentionally): Grandma and Grandpa Beeson are sitting in Indiana with their dial-up account, and they get an email from you with a picture of the grandkids. It was really nice of you to send it, but it would have been even nicer if it wasn't a 34 MB layered Photoshop file! It's going to take a couple of weeks to download, for crying out loud. Not everyone has the luxury of fiber optic like you do, and they get a little freaked out when they see a big attachment. Do the folks a favor and resize photos before you send them. After you attach a photo to your email message (either by clicking the Attach button in the New Message toolbar or just dragging the image into the New Message window), take a look in the bottom-right corner and you'll see the Image Size pop-up menu. When you click the menu and choose a new size, the image is automatically scaled down in the viewer window, and its new size is shown just below the scaled down image. Trust me on this one—friends with slow internet connections are going to like you a lot more if you send them a 248 KB picture instead of a 34.1 MB one.

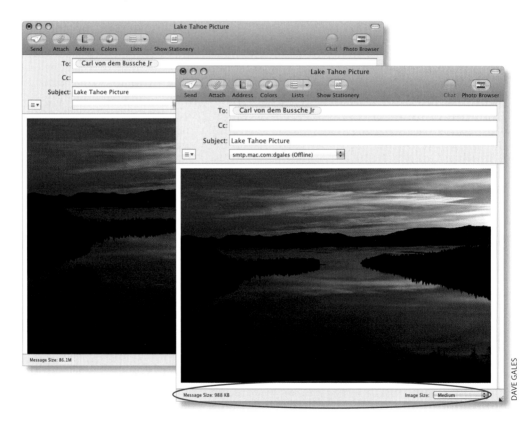

   Mail: HOW TO LOSE FRIENDS AND TICK OFF PEOPLE

I love it when acquaintances do their part to perpetuate an urban myth by forwarding something they received to 300 people, including me. How do I know there are 299 other lucky people getting the same email? Because the person who sent it kindly included email addresses for all 299 of them in the Cc field. So now 299 potential joke-sending, myth-perpetuating, chain-letter-loving, sob-story-believing people (not to mention all those clever little bots and spiders crawling around harvesting email addresses to sell to spammers) have the address I tried so hard to keep spam-free. If you must send annoying emails to people, at least enable the Bcc field (it stands for blind carbon copy. What's a carbon copy? Ask your grandparents— they'll know) so everyone's address will be hidden from everyone else. (You do this by going under the View menu and selecting Bcc Address Field.) Or you can create a group—call it "People I think will enjoy getting useless email"—in Address Book. Then click on Mail, select Preferences, and click the Composing icon. In the Addressing section, turn off the checkbox for When Sending to a Group, Show All Member Addresses option. Oh, and please don't send me a copy.

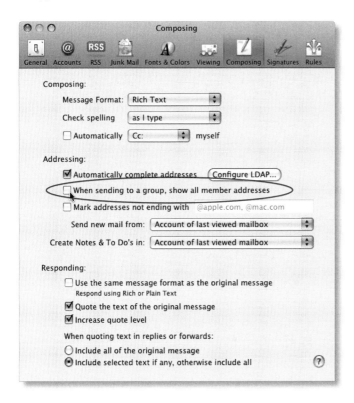

Mail: FORWARD AN EMAIL AS AN ATTACHMENT

When you start forwarding emails, it doesn't take too many hops before you think about calling your cousin at the CIA to see if she can make sense out of it. You've got multiple headers, five levels of indentation, and little notes included with each forward that you think might be part of the first forward, or possibly the second forward of the first forward of the original. See what I mean? Mail now has an option to send email as an attachment to a message instead of having the entire message included as quoted text. To make your friends very happy, go to your Inbox and select the message or messages you want to forward, then go to the Message menu and select Forward as Attachment. It's easier for you (the Forwarder) and for the Forwardee.

Mail: SEEING MULTIPLE MAILBOXES IN ONE WINDOW

If you have multiple mailboxes, clicking on the Inbox will display the contents of all of them in one window. But if you want to see only the contents of certain mailboxes, Command-click on each of their names (they're nested under the Inbox) and their contents will be temporarily merged and displayed in one window. (Or you could merge, say, your Inbox and Sent box, as I did here.) The mailboxes themselves (and the mail in them) don't change at all and will be displayed individually again as soon as you click on any one of them.

   Mail: CONTROLLING YOUR SEARCH OPTIONS

If you're searching for a particular piece of mail (aren't we all?), you can tell Mail where to search and what to search for. As soon as you start typing in Mail's search field, some search options will appear right under Mail's toolbar. You can expand your search by clicking the All Mailboxes and Entire Message buttons. If you want to narrow your search to only the From, To, or Subject field, just click the corresponding button in the search options bar.

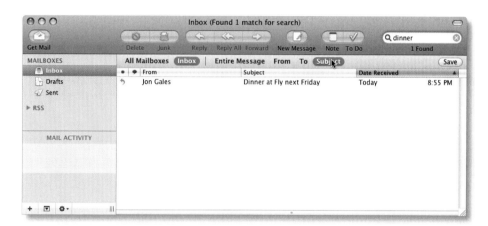

   Mail: DOCTOR! DOCTOR! GIVE ME THE NEWS!

If you're having a hard time making a connection to the Internet to get your email, the Mail Connection Doctor might be able to help. Go to the Window menu and choose Connection Doctor. The MD (Mac Doctor) will use some powerful medicine to try and cure your Internet aches and pains (yes, that was a lame attempt at humor. I'm not proud of it, but I did it, and I'm man enough to own up to it).

   Mail: FIND OUT WHAT MAIL IS DOING RIGHT NOW

Okay, so you're downloading your email, and the little status circle beside your email account keeps spinning and spinning. You're wondering if a huge email attachment is being downloaded. You're wondering if it's doing anything at all. The sad truth is that you don't know what Mail is doing. You don't know, I don't know.

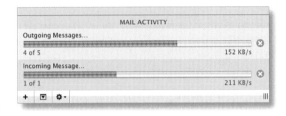

I'm not sure Apple even knows. It's a mystery wrapped in a riddle. Okay, Apple does know, and actually you can, too, by pressing Command-0 (that's zero, not the letter O). This brings up the Activity window, which shows you exactly what (if anything) Mail is doing. So if, for example, it's downloading a huge email attachment, you'll be able to tell. Now you can breathe a sigh of relief. It doesn't make the download go faster, but it does have a surprisingly calming effect simply knowing what's going on. If you just want a bare-bones, cut-and-dried, down-and-dirty look at what's happening, click the little triangle in the bottom-left corner of the main Mail window (between the plus sign and the gear icon) and you'll get what you're looking for.

   Mail: MAKING AN ARCHIVE OF YOUR MAILBOXES

If you have a mailbox that's accumulating a bunch of emails, you may want to create an archive to clean out the older items. To do that, Control-click on the mailbox you want to archive and choose Archive Mailbox from the contextual menu. Now all you have to do is pick a location to save your archive and click the Choose button. Your original mailbox stays right where it was and, in fact, all the messages are still in it because Mail doesn't delete the messages when it creates the archive. If you want to clear it out, just press Command-A to select all the messages, then press Delete. Just one more thing about creating an archive: it's a good idea to save your archive to an external drive (a USB thumb drive will usually do it) so in the unlikely event that you have a hard drive go bad or another person decides they need your laptop more than you do, you'll still have your email.

   Mail: CREATING SMART MAILBOXES FROM SEARCHES

Smart Mailboxes sort through your email and collect messages that match certain criteria into a mailbox so you can easily read them without ever having to search for them again. Here's how you create one: Let's say, for example, you want to create a Smart Mailbox for all incoming emails from a particular person. Enter the person's name in the search field in Mail's toolbar and choose From in the bar below the toolbar. When the results appear, you'll see that a Save button has been added to the far-right end of the criteria bar. Click it, and a Smart Mailbox dialog will appear with all the information pretty much filled out already—so just enter a name for the mailbox and click OK. Now you'll have a new Smart Mailbox that contains all the email you've received from the person, and (this is the really cool part) from now on, any new email from this person will automatically appear in that Smart Mailbox. Oh, and if this person goes nuts and switches to a Windows machine, you can delete their Smart Mailbox and it won't delete their emails—so when they come to their senses and come back to Mac, you'll still have their messages.

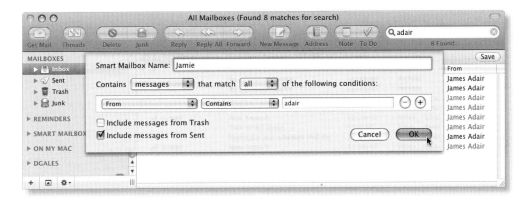

Mail: CREATE AN EVEN SMARTER MAILBOX

Let's take the previous tip a couple notches up the coolness scale. Instead of doing your search from within Mail, press Command-Option-Spacebar to open Spotlight and type the following into the search field: "kind:mail from:someperson" (leave off the quotes). Make sure there is no space within the search terms but there is a space between them. And unless the person you are searching for happens to be named "someperson," put their name and email address after "from:". As you type, you should see any emails they have sent you show up in the search results window. Now go back up to the search bar and click the Save button, then type in a name for the new Smart Mailbox. Below the save options is the key to making a cool thing (a Smart Mailbox) even cooler—a Smart Mailbox in the sidebar! Make sure the Add To Sidebar checkbox is turned on, then click the Save button. Now any time you want to see an email from this person, all you have to do is click the Smart Folder that is now in the sidebar of every Finder window. And to make it even more amazing, it is auto-magically updated whenever Mail is running.

KILLER TIPS

   Mail: SMART MAILBOX IDEA #1: ARCHIVE OLD MESSAGES

You can use Smart Mailboxes to automate some of the tasks you do all the time—or should do, anyhow. I've come to the realization that old emails never really go away, they just sit in my various mailboxes as a continual reminder of all the stuff I haven't taken care of yet. Well, here's how you can clear old mail out of your mailboxes to get it out of sight, but still keep it around just in case you ever decide to answer some of it. Click the plus sign (+) button in the lower-left corner of the Mail window and select New Smart Mailbox. Type in a name for this mailbox (feel free to use the one I used in the example, or use something a bit more normal, like "Archive," for instance). Now click the From pop-up menu and select Date Received. Click the next pop-up menu button and select Is Not In the Last from the list. Finally, enter a number in the text field and select a time period from the last pop-up menu. Click OK and all your email that is older than six months (or whatever time period you set) will now show up in the new Smart Mailbox. Now you have two options: To delete that old email, just click on the Smart Mailbox, press Command-A to select it all, then press the Delete key on your keyboard. The second option is to Control-click on the mailbox and choose Archive Mailbox. Pick a destination and a copy of the contents of the mailbox will be saved. Now you can burn it to a CD for safe-keeping if you want, and then go back to Mail, select all the messages in the mailbox, and click Delete. Now all that old stuff is gone, but not forgotten. You can always import it back into Mail if you ever need it. *Note:* If you want to archive mail more than a year old, don't configure your Smart Mailbox to look for messages where the Date Received is in (or not in) the last 1 year. Here's why: Mail doesn't use days to calculate the date, it just looks at the year. If today is January 2, 2009, and you tell mail to find all messages received in the last 1 year, it will find everything you got on January 1. So do the math for Mail. Set your selection to 365 days instead of one year.

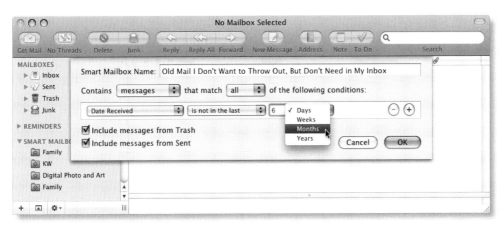

Mail: SMART MAILBOX IDEA #2: SAVE YOUR LIFE

Setting up this Smart Mailbox could save your life! With the amount of email most people get every day, it's easy to overlook one you really need to read—like one from your boss, for instance. Here's how you can avoid the pain of failing to respond to his or her "request" for immediate action on something. First, click on an email message from your boss, then create a new Smart Mailbox (as shown in the previous tips). By default, the first field will be set to From, the second field will be set to Contains, and the third field will have your boss's email address already filled in. You might want to add more criteria (like a second email address they might use) just to cover all your bases. When everything is set, just click OK. Mail will do its part, but you'll have to remember to check the new Smart Mailbox.

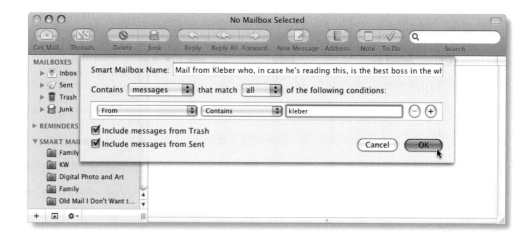

   Mail: SMART MAILBOX IDEA #3: NEW MAIL

A lot of users (myself included) have more than one email account. For example, I've got a public email address that's posted on several websites that is the recipient of floods of spam, then a private address I only give my friends, and another address I only use for shopping online. So, if you have multiple email accounts, you can make your life easier by creating a new Smart Mailbox for all your unread mail. That way, no matter which account the mail comes into, you'll be able to see all your new unread mail in just one nice, neat Smart Mailbox. Here's how: Click the plus sign (+) button in the bottom-left corner of the Mail window and choose New Smart Mailbox from the pop-up menu. When the Smart Mailbox dialog appears, from the first pop-up menu, choose Message Is Unread. That's it—that's the only choice you have to make. Now click OK and all your unread mail will be just one click away. As you read a message, it removes itself from the Smart Mailbox. This thing's not smart—it's brilliant!

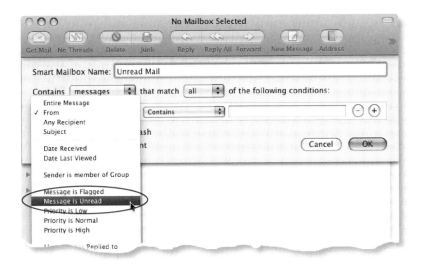

Mail: MAKE A NEW TO DO ITEM IN MAIL

In my lifetime I have used about every time-management system ever developed. I've had notebooks, cards, pads, PDAs, computer calendars—I've tried everything to remind me of what I need to do. Not being one to give up easily, I now have a new tool in my war against forgetting things—the new To Do feature in Mail. Part of the reason I'm optimistic is because it is so easy to create a new To Do. The obvious way is to click the To Do button in the toolbar. A less obvious (and very "power user-ish") way is to highlight some text in the body of an email you're reading, then click the To Do button. A goofy graphic that looks like a legal pad with your handwritten To Do item opens above the message window. If you're a real go-getter and have finished the task in the time it took the legal pad thing to open, you can go ahead and turn on the checkbox to mark it as done.

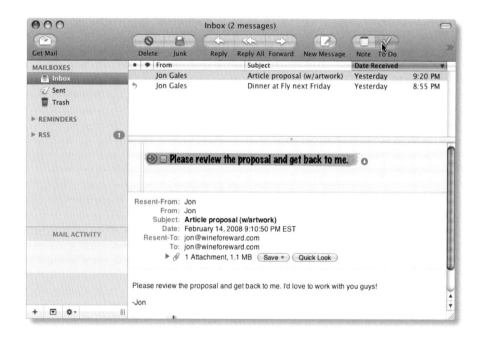

   Mail: GETTING RSS FEEDS IN MAIL

Keeping up with new content in websites that update frequently can be harder than keeping track of a politician's position on an issue. In the Safari chapter, there are some tips on using RSS (Really Simple Syndication) to have sites let you know when they've added new content. But you can also subscribe to RSS feeds in Mail so they'll be available any time you check your email. From the File menu, choose Add RSS Feeds. You can browse any feeds you have already set up in Safari and simply turn on the checkbox next to any of them you want to access from Mail, then click the Add button. If you want to subscribe to a new feed, choose Specify a Custom Feed URL, then type the URL in the box. If you look at the bottom of Mail's sidebar, you'll see all the RSS feeds you just selected.

  Mail: SEE YOUR RSS FEEDS IN YOUR INBOX

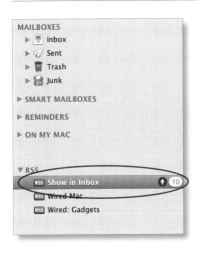

If going to the bottom of the sidebar to check your RSS feeds is too much trouble, you can click the title of the feed, then click the little arrow just to the right of its name, and it will now show up in your Inbox. If you ever decide to move it back to the spot it's supposed to be in, just select the feed's name (in the Inbox) and click the arrow again (this time it's pointing down), and you'll be in compliance with the rules again. There, that feels better.

Mail: GET A GOOGLE MAP OF AN ADDRESS IN AN EMAIL

This one just blows my mind. Say you get an email that contains an address for an event you are invited to attend. When you roll your cursor over the address, it will be boxed, and if you click the arrow in the lower-right corner of that box you will be presented with several options. Choose Show Map, and Safari (or whatever browser you've set as your default) will launch and go to Google Maps, and a detailed map of the address and its surrounding area appears. Wow! How's it do that? Data Detectors, that's how. Simple Data Detectors.

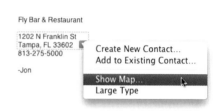

 Mail: GETTING EMAILED PHOTOS INTO iPHOTO FAST

If someone sends you some photos and you want to add them to your iPhoto library, you don't have to save them to your hard disk, and then import them into iPhoto manually—that takes too long. Instead try this: Go to your Inbox and click on the email (don't double-click to open it, just click once to select it), then look in the message preview window and press the Save button that's just to the right of the information about the attachment(s). Now choose Add to iPhoto from this menu, and iPhoto will open automatically and import all the attached photos. Amazing!

DAVE GALES

   Mail: ADD A PHONE NUMBER TO YOUR ADDRESS BOOK

Fly Bar & Restaurant

1202 N Franklin St
Tampa, FL 33602
813-275-5000

Create New Contact...
Add to Existing Contact...

-Jon
Large Type

Here is another Data Detector trick. Someone sends you an email that contains a phone number somewhere in its header, body, or signature. Roll your cursor over the number, click the down-facing arrow, and you get the option to either create a new contact or add this number to an existing one.

   Mail: CREATE AN iCAL EVENT FROM A DATE IN AN EMAIL

If you have an email that contains a date, name of a day of the week, or time, move your cursor over it, click the down-facing arrow, and a box will appear, giving you the option to create a new iCal event or show the date in iCal. If you take Mail up on the first offer, iCal opens, a new event is created, and the subject line of the email is automatically filled in as the title for your iCal event.

We're all getting together for dinner next Friday (02/22/08) at Fly. No need to RSVP, but it would be great if you could make it. If you don't make it that means we could spread terrible rumors about you. But seriously, no pressure. We'll be there around 9pm.

Create New iCal Event...
Show This Date in iCal

Fly Bar & Restaurant

1202 N Franklin St
Tampa, FL 33602
813-275-5000

-Jon

Chapter 6

TALKING HEADS

iCHAT TIPS

If you're not chatting, you need to be, because there should not be a single second of any waking moment that you're

Talking Heads
ichat tips

not communicating with somebody about something using an electronic gismo of some sort. As far as electronic gismos go, iChat is among the coolest. So much so, that I have an entire chapter of cool tips for using it. In fact, I use iChat every day, and wind up talking to people I would never normally wind up talking to. But since they can see I'm online and available, I can't just ignore them, so I wind up wasting valuable time talking about how hot it is in Florida. Sometimes it trashes my productivity for the entire day, but I keep reminding myself that chatting, video conferencing, and text messaging are necessary tools that would otherwise require me to (gasp!) pick up the telephone. Unthinkable!

   LET ME SEE WHAT MY BUDDY CAN DO

Unless your parents were hippies (in which case you're too young), you have probably experienced the childhood ritual of humiliating your peers by utterly crushing them in some pointless competition, then reminding them of it every chance you got. Ahhhh, so many wonderful childhood memories. At this point, you might be wondering what any of this has to do with tips on iChat. Here's the point: Just like when you were a kid and not everyone in your peer group exhibited the same level of physical abilities (there was always someone in the group you could beat in something), not all of your iChat buddies will share the chatting capabilities you may have. The difference is you don't have to beat them up anymore to find out what they can do. You can just Control-click their name in your buddy list (they have to be online), choose Show Profile, and then look in the Capabilities section to see what types of chats they can handle. Just remember that you're an adult now, so don't go around talking trash about them because they can't do something you can do.

  FORGET MY BUDDY—WHAT CAN I DO?

Obviously, iChat can do a lot of things, but depending on your setup, you might not be able to do them all. This is, in my opinion, an excellent reason to get a new Mac. If your spouse doesn't share my opinion, try this: "It's not really about me, it's about the children. Twenty years from now, when they can't find good jobs, will we wonder what might have been, if only we had provided them with the tools they needed to utilize the full capabilities of iChat?" (Heck, after hearing that, she might want to get each of you a new Mac!) Before you make the pitch, however, it might be a good idea to find out exactly what your current capabilities are. Go to Video on the menu bar, then select Connection Doctor. Now click the Show pop-up menu and select Capabilities. A dialog like the one shown here will give you the results. Here's the thing: There is an inverse relationship between your current Mac's level of compatibility with iChat and your chances of getting a new one. So, for your sake, I hope your report doesn't look anything like the one shown here. Results this good would be really bad for you—in an inverse relationship kind of way.

   YOUR BUDDY DOESN'T NEED A CAMERA TO VIDEO CHAT

Invite to Chat...
Send Instant Message...
Send Direct Message...
Send Email...
Send SMS...
Send File...
Open URL

Invite to One-Way Video Chat
Invite to Audio Chat
Share My Screen with Joshua Gales...
Ask to Share Joshua Gales's Screen...

If your buddy doesn't have a camera connected, but you do, you can still have a one-way video chat. That way, your buddy has the pleasure of seeing you on their end. The only downside is you don't get to see them, but that's what you get for having cheap friends. Here's how it works: Click on your buddy's name in the Buddy List, and then go to the Buddies menu and choose Invite to One-Way Video Chat. Again, they'll see and hear you, but not the other way around. Well, technically, if they have a microphone built into their Mac, then you'll be able to hear them, too, but with your buddy being so cheap, don't get your hopes up.

  USE YOUR OWN PHOTO OF A BUDDY

Info for Kathy Gales

Profile Alerts **Address Card**

Picture: ☐ Always use this picture
Select this option to ignore the
picture set by your buddy.

First Name: Kathy
Last Name: Gales
Nickname:
Email:
AIM:
Jabber:

Show in Address Book

If you don't like one of your Buddy's iChat photos, believe it or not, you can replace it with one of your own (of course, I mean a photo you have of them). Here's how to play the ol' photo swap-a-roo: Control-click on their name in the Buddy List, select Show Profile, then click the Address Card tab. Now drag-and-drop the photo you want to use for them right onto the Picture box, and turn on the Always Use This Picture checkbox (otherwise, the photo your buddy has set will reappear). That's it—from now on that photo will be displayed for them instead. By the way—unless you tell your buddy, they'll never know, because this change is only visible in your iChat, not theirs. Just be sure they never borrow your computer or you may have some splainin' to do.

   STAY ALIVE EVEN WHEN YOU'VE QUIT

Just because you've quit iChat AV doesn't mean your buddies can't send you an instant message. Well, actually, that's exactly what it means, if you don't make one little change to iChat AV's preferences. In the iChat menu, select Preferences, click General, and turn on the Show Status in Menu Bar checkbox. This will add a tiny menu icon to your menu bar that looks like a "talk bubble" that you can click and see (and change) your status as well as see which buddies are available. Unless your status is set to Offline, even when you quit iChat, you'll still be logged into AIM and Bonjour. That's why your buddies can still send you an IM. If you want to log out of everything when you quit iChat, go back to the General preferences and turn on the When I Quit iChat, Set My Status to Offline checkbox.

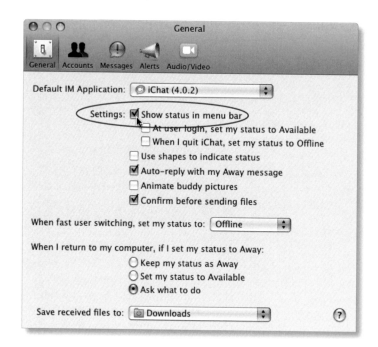

   SHARING YOUR MUSICAL TASTE WITH YOUR BUDDIES

If you listen to iTunes while you're chatting, you can give the people you're chatting with a glimpse into your musical genius. Go to your Buddy List and under your Status pop-up menu, choose Current iTunes Song. Now the song you're listening to will be displayed to the person you're chatting with, which basically tells them that they're not important enough to demand your full attention, and that you must do other things, like listen to music, to keep yourself occupied while mindlessly chatting with them. Okay, I'm not sure it means all that, but you get the drift. Okay, so what if they really like the song? They can click on it, and it will take them directly to that song in the iTunes Store, so they can buy it themselves, and then they'll be the one who looks cool. It's a vicious cycle.

MANAGING LOTS OF BUDDIES

If you're fairly popular with the iChat crowd (and my guess is you are, because only very cool people buy this book), you've probably got lots of buddies in your Buddy List, which means your life is filled with an awful lot of scrolling. But it doesn't have to be that way, because you can group related people together into groups (just like you do with groups of people in Address Book). So, if you have a number of people you chat with from your office, you can have a Work group with all their buddy names appearing within a collapsible group (which saves loads of space and scrolling, and just generally makes your Buddy List easier on the eyes). To create

a Buddy group, first go to the View menu, and choose Use Groups. Then click the plus sign (+) button in the bottom-left corner of the Buddy List window, choose Add Group, and give your new group a name. To add buddies to your new group, click the name in your Buddy List and drag it on top of the group name.

   ADD NEW BUDDIES TO GROUPS

If you are adding a new buddy to your Buddy List, you can save some time by adding them to one of your groups at the same time. First, click the plus sign (+) button in the bottom-left corner of the Buddy List window just like you did in the previous tip, except this time, select Add Buddy from the pop-up menu and enter their information in the appropriate text entry fields. Now click the Add to Group pop-up menu and select a group for your brand new buddy.

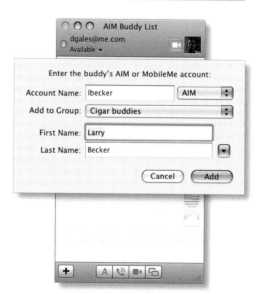

MOVING OLD BUDDIES AROUND

When I say "old buddies," I'm not talking about ones that are AARP members, just ones that are already in one of your groups but don't really belong there anymore. For instance, you have a buddy in your People Who Use Vista group (admittedly, a very small group) who comes to his senses and buys a Mac. All you have to do is click the People Who Use Vista group name in your Buddy List, click your buddy's name, and then drag it into your Recent Converts group. You can also put a buddy into more than one group by clicking his or her name in the current group, and pressing-and-holding the Option key while you drag the name into another group. So you could have someone who is in your Almost Eligible for AARP group also in your Everest Expedition and Bungee Jumping Buddies groups.

SAVING TRANSCRIPTS OF YOUR CHATS

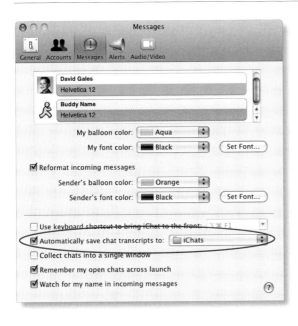

There are a dozen reasons why you might want a written log of your text chats: maybe someone gave you instructions, a recipe, or just typed a bunch of stuff that cracks you up. Well, luckily, you can ask iChat to keep a running log of your text chats. Go to the iChat menu, select Preferences, then click on the Messages icon, and turn on the Automatically Save Chat Transcripts To checkbox. By default, the transcripts are saved to a folder cleverly named "iChats," which is automatically created in your Documents folder. If you want them to be saved to a different location, just use the pop-up menu provided.

SPECIAL ALERTS FOR SPECIAL BUDDIES

Alerts are handy, but they can drive you nuts if you have a lot of buddies. When I'm working and hear the "Someone on your buddy list just became available" alert, there's no way I can ignore it and keep working—I have to check to see who it is. If you are as distractible as I am, you can take advantage of iChat's ability to create custom alerts for a particular buddy. All you need to do is Control-click the name in your Buddy List, select Show Profile, and then choose Alerts. Now just click the Event pop-up menu and select an event, then turn on the Play Sound checkbox and click the pop-up menu to pick the sound you want to hear whenever this buddy does the action you just selected.

ENJOY A THREE-WAY CHAT

Video chatting with someone is so cool. But it gets even cooler when you add more people to your chat. While you're chatting away with one buddy, all you have to do is click on the little video camera icon next to another buddy's name and invite them to join you. When they do, they don't just pop up in another chat window. Oh no, that would be much too ordinary. No, when they join, they look like they are seated at a shiny, black conference room table. You can have up to four people (including yourself) in a chat. I'd love to show you a screen capture of what that looks like, but I don't have that many friends.

RECORD AUDIO AND VIDEO CHATS

New with Leopard is the ability to record your audio or video chats so you can access them later. Start a chat with one or more of your buddies. Now click Video from the menu bar, and select Record Chat. To keep everything legal, ethical, and non-voyeuristic, iChat will send a notice to your buddies letting them know what you're up to, and asking their permission (as shown here). Assuming they agree, you'll see a blinking red light in the corner of your screen to let you know the recording is in process. When you want to stop, click the button or simply close the chat window. To access your chat recordings later, go to the iChats folder, which is in your Documents folder.

   AVOID UNWANTED CHATS

When you open iChat, you are basically inviting anyone who knows one of your various chat service names to stop by and say hello. That's cool if you're sitting around doing nothing, but if you're trying to get some work done, it can drive you crazy. Rather than just ignore all the chat invitations (which will lead to people texting your cell phone or emailing to ask why you're not answering their chat messages), you can set up some Privacy Levels in iChat's preferences. Here's how: Press Command-, (comma) to open iChat's preferences, click the Accounts icon, select an account other than Bonjour, and then click the Security tab and you'll see the list of Privacy Level options available. Once you select a level, anyone who is not allowed according to the criteria of the level, or people you specifically block (it's okay, we all have people we move from a Buddy List to a "Bug Me" List), will see your status as Offline.

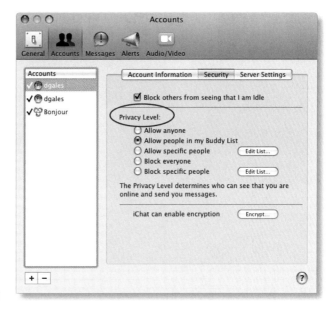

   AVOID UNWANTED CHATS BY USING STEALTH MODE

When I was a kid, I thought the coolest thing in the world would be to be able to turn invisible. You could be right in the middle of a room and see everybody, but they wouldn't know you were there—until whatever you did to become invisible wore off, then everyone would see you. Sometimes I just want to launch iChat to see if a particular person is on-line, but I don't want other people to know I'm online. Even if I set my status to Away when I log in, my name is going to pop up on everyone's Buddy Lists and they'll know I'm at my computer, and that's information I don't want to broadcast. iChat now has a status named (are you ready?) Invisible! All you have to do to be able to log on without anyone seeing you is click on your status in the Buddy List window, and select Invisible. How cool is that? You can finally live out your childhood fantasies of being invisible. Well, maybe not all of them, but it's a start.

   AVOIDING LATE-NIGHT AUDIO CHATS

If you're working late at night and your spouse and kids are in bed, you may not want one of your buddies calling you for an audio chat. If that's the case, select Video from the menu bar, then select Microphone Enabled to disable it. Nope, that's not a mistake—go to Video to disable your audio. Now, when your insomniac friend sees you in their Buddy List, the green Audio Chat icon will be hidden. So if they want to talk to you, they'll have to let their fingers do the talking and use text chat.

SEND A BUDDY A FILE—EVEN A GIGUNDO ONE

If you're in a text chat with someone and want to send them a file, just click the file's icon on your drive, drag it to your chat window, and drop it in the message area. If you're video chatting, click-and-drag the file on top of the video window and drop it in the top section. One huge benefit of sending files through iChat is, unlike email, there is no size limit to the files you transfer. If you forget that your buddy lives in the middle of nowhere with a dial-up connection and send a 903 MB file, it's no big deal. When you send it, your friend will have the option to either accept the file and go ahead and start the download, or reject it.

   WHAT COLOR BALLOONS WOULD YOU LIKE?

Don't like the default color of your dialog balloons? Go to the iChat menu and choose Preferences. When the Preferences window appears, click Messages, and then pick a new color from the My Balloon Color pop-up menu. While you're there, why not go crazy and pick a cool font and a funky font color for your chat? Just be sure to change the settings for incoming messages as well to maintain the sense of balance and harmony in your chat world.

   SHARE YOUR BUDDY'S SCREEN

One of the best new features in Leopard is Back to My Mac. The only problem with it is I can only access other Macs that are on my MobileMe account. So if my in-laws are having some sort of an issue with their Mac, I have to tell them something to try, then have them tell me what they're seeing. But as long as they have Leopard, I can access their screen and fix the problem directly, even though they aren't on my MobileMe account. All you have to do to share a screen using iChat is click on the buddy's name in your Buddy List, then click the Start Screen Sharing button from the bar at the bottom of the Buddy List. You can either share your screen (allow your buddy access to your Mac) or ask permission to share your buddy's screen. Assuming your buddy agrees to give you access, their screen appears on your computer and your screen will appear as a large thumbnail in the corner of your desktop. To switch between their screen and yours, just click the one you want to use. When you're all done, just close the chat window or click the red screen sharing indicator in your menu bar.

DRAG FILES BETWEEN SHARED SCREENS

Here's a really cool thing you can do while you're sharing screens with iChat. If you want a file that's on your buddy's computer, all you have to do is click-and-drag it from their computer onto your desktop. Works the same way in the other direction: find a file you want to put on their Mac and click-and-drag it onto the thumbnail of their screen while you are sharing it. Does it get any easier than that? I'm thinkin' it doesn't.

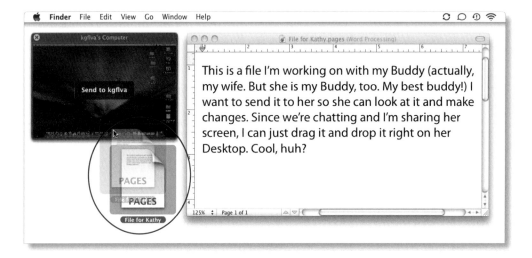

   IT'S LIKE SHOW AND TELL

Several times a day I'll find someone walking around the office and run up to them with my laptop and say, "Dude (we're old school at our office and still say dude), check this out!" I get funny looks from the janitor and UPS guy, but everyone else at least feigns excitement over my latest discovery or creation. Well, thanks to iChat Theater, I can do the same thing when I'm out of the office. When you're in a video chat with someone, click on a file you want to share (it can be basically anything: image, text document, song, movie, PDF, or anything else you can think of), drag it on top of the video chat window and drop it in the Share With iChat Theater box that pops up. On your Buddy's screen, your image will replace theirs in the small local video window, and the file you are sharing will take over the large video window.

Chapter 7

SURFIN' SAFARI

Tips for Using the Safari Web Browser

So how does Safari wind up getting its own separate chapter? Well, there are a number of reasons, none of them sound. First,

Surfin' Safari

tips for using the safari web browser

the Safari browser is one application that we use a lot. And by a lot I mean "a whole bunch." It is our access to the Web, and by Web I mean Internet, and by Internet I mean Information Super Highway, which is perhaps the corniest phrase ever conceived to describe the Internet, with the possible exception of Cyberspace. Politicians use these terms, because they don't actually use the Internet, but their staffers and interns do. Anyway, you (me, we, us, them, they) wind up using Safari a lot, but it got its own chapter because I had so many Safari tips that if I included those tips in another chapter it would be just too many tips. It would be "tip overload" (or, as the politicians refer to it, "Tipformation Super Overload"). By the way, it was Al Gore who invented the Safari browser. That's right, Al Gore. Not that Al Gore. The other Al Gore.

TABS, BABY! IT'S THE ONLY WAY TO SURF

For many people, tabbed browsing will forever change the way they work (or play) online. Here's how it works: Ordinarily, when you're on a website and click on a link, a new page opens, replacing the content of the original page. If you want to go back to a previous page, you either have to keep hitting the Back button or open the History and find the page you want. But if you use tabs, every time you Command-click a link, instead of replacing the current page, the link will open in a tab (they look like little file folder tabs) on the Tab Bar (located just below Safari's menu bar). By default, you won't see the new page until you click the tab. But if you Command-Shift-click on a link, a tab will be created and selected for you. You can change these default settings by going to the Safari menu, selecting Preferences, and then clicking on the Tabs icon. The beauty of tabs is you can Command-click to your heart's content and load up the Tab Bar. No matter how many pages you have opened, they are accessible with just one click on their tab. Like I said—it's the only way to surf.

     I WANT TO SEE YOU, BUT NOT RIGHT NOW

If you want to open a page in a tab, but want to keep looking at the page you're on, Command-click a link (instead of Command-Shift-click) and the link will open in a new tab, but it won't become the active tab until you click it. This is especially handy if there are several links on a page you want to check out, because you can click as many links as you want and line them up in the Tab Bar, instead of having your original page replaced every time you click a new link. It's like when you're at an awards ceremony and they ask you to hold your applause until all the recipients have been announced. Of course, if an involuntary clap slips out when your child's name is called, that's okay.

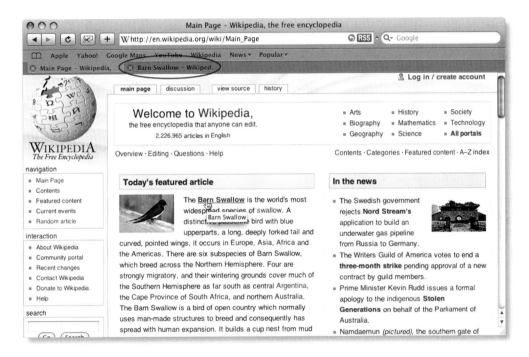

SOMETIMES YOU FEEL LIKE A TAB—SOMETIMES YOU DON'T

As much as I like tabs, there are times when I want to open a link in a new window (right off the top of my head, I can't think of an example of when I would want to do that, but I'm sure it could happen) instead of a tab. If such an occasion arises, Command-Option-click the link and it will open in a new window behind the current one. If you want to open the link in a window and have it visible, Command-Option-Shift-click the link. If you want to change these defaults, just press Command-, (comma) while you're in Safari, then click the Tabs icon. If you turn on (or off) any of the checkboxes, the descriptions of what the various commands do will be updated. Set it the way you want, and then close the preferences.

   MOVE A TABBED PAGE TO ITS OWN WINDOW

If you're browsing around the Web and have been opening pages in tabs, but then decide you want to see one of the pages in its own window rather than a tab, Control-click the tab and choose Move Tab to New Window.

   DRAG A TAB TO OPEN A NEW WINDOW

Here's another way to convert a tab to a separate window that is more fun than the way I just showed you. Click the tab you want to open in a new window and drag it down out of the Tab Bar without dragging it over another tab. As soon as it is off the Tab Bar it will turn into a thumbnail of itself. Now, just release the mouse button and it will open in its own window. So do you want to know what happens if you touch another tab while you're dragging it off the Tab Bar? Either your drive will immediately reformat and erase all your data, or the tab you're dragging will just swap places with the one you touch. As I recall, it's the second one, but go ahead and try it to be sure.

COMBINE ALL OPEN WINDOWS INTO ONE TABBED WINDOW

In case you've not picked up on it by now, I'm a tabbed browsing kinda guy. But there are times when I go into a clicking frenzy and click links with reckless abandon, only to discover that my desktop is littered with dozens (okay, six or seven, but it could be dozens) of browser windows. If that happens to you, go to Safari's Window menu, and select Merge All Windows. Safari cleans up your mess and leaves you with a beautiful window, all tabbed and ready to go.

   ADD AN OPEN WINDOW TO A TAB BAR

If you have a page open in its own window and want to add it to the Tab Bar of another open window, click on its favicon (the little icon just before its address) and drop it in an empty spot in the Tab Bar of the window you're moving it to. Make sure you don't drop it on top of an existing tab, or it will replace it.

   BOOKMARK A SET OF TABS

Rather than having several hundred separate bookmarks, I have them grouped into folders such as News, Crosswords, Blogs, Fun Stuff, etc. But there are certain sites (scottkelby.com, for instance) I go to every day so I can stay hip, cool, and on the cutting edge. Naturally, I have them all bookmarked, but they're not all in the same folder. It would be a pain to have to sift through several bookmark folders every morning to find the ones I want. So I created a "Read These Every Day" bookmark that opens all my regular sites with one click. Here's how: Open the sites you want to include in your set in separate tabs. When you have them all in the Tab Bar, go to Safari's Bookmarks menu, and select Add Bookmark For These [*the number of tabs you have*] Tabs. Give your new bookmark a descriptive name like "Sites I Read Every Day So I Can Stay Hip, Cool, and On the Cutting Edge." Another possibility might be something like "Daily Reads"—whatever works for you. Then save it to the Bookmarks Bar. Now your favorite sites are one click away.

OPEN ALL THE TABS IN A BOOKMARK FOLDER WITH ONE CLICK

If you have created some bookmark folders (see previous tip), you can click on the folder in the Bookmarks Bar and select an individual item you want to open. But if you Command-click the folder, all of the bookmarked pages inside will open—each in a separate tab. If you have a bookmark folder you routinely open like this, you can swap these shortcuts for that folder so just a simple click loads all the tabs and pressing Command-click lets you open individual tabs. You would think you would go to Safari's preferences to make this change. Nope. Go to the far-left end of the Bookmarks Bar and click the little book icon (technically, it's known as the Show All Bookmarks icon). Now go under Collections in the sidebar and click on Bookmarks Bar. Turn on the Auto-Click checkbox for any folder you want to open with one click. *Note:* If you click on a bookmark folder with three tabs in it, it's no big deal. If you click on one that has a couple of hundred items, you're going to wish you had the next tip memorized.

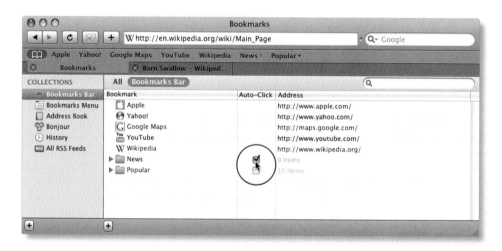

   HOW TO STOP MULTIPLE TABS FROM OPENING

Tabbed browsing has changed my life, but there's one thing about it that drives me nuts. I routinely Command-click on a link so it will open in a new tab. But at least once a day, I Command-click on one of the bookmark folders I have on my Bookmarks Bar—which tells Safari to open every bookmark in the folder in a separate tab. If there are over 50 links in the folder, Safari throws up a nice little warning that says, "Do you really want me to open 394 tabs for all these links?" But if there are only a couple of dozen links in the folder, Safari gets a smirk on its face, snickers under its breath, and starts opening tabs as fast as it can. If this ever happens to you, hit the Back button on Safari's toolbar and you will wipe that smirk off its face and bring the tab-opening to a grinding halt.

   JUMPING FROM TAB TO TAB

Tabbed browsing is about the coolest single thing in Safari, and jumping quickly from one tab to the next may well be second. To get from tab to tab in a flash, just press Command-Shift-Right Arrow to move right, and press…do I really need to mention how to move left? Didn't think so.

REARRANGE THE ORDER OF YOUR TABS

You can rearrange the order of the tabs on the Tab Bar by simply clicking-and-holding on the one you want to move and dragging it to its new location. The other tabs will step aside and make room for the new kid in the neighborhood.

 DELETE YOUR AUTOFILL INFORMATION

When you fill out a form on a website, as soon as you start typing, Safari looks in your Address Book and information it has stored from other forms you have filled out and tries to find a match. If it finds one, as soon as you enter a letter or two, it will fill in the rest of the field for you. Pretty sweet, unless you have

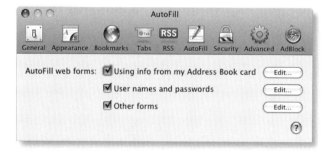

a mistake somewhere that AutoFill keeps pulling up. For example, I had a typo in my street address in my Address Book record. Every time I would start to enter my address in a form, AutoFill would take over and fill it in for me—typo and all. Fortunately, you can delete incorrect AutoFill information. Here's how: Go under the Safari menu, choose Preferences, click the AutoFill icon, then click the Edit button next to one of the items in the list. If you selected the Address Book option, your address card will open so you can make the necessary corrections. If you select either of the other two options, a list of the AutoFill information currently being used opens. You can't make corrections, but you can select it and press Remove.

   BOOKMARK AN EMAILED LINK WITHOUT OPENING IT

If someone sends you an email that contains a link, you can click the link and drag it into the Bookmarks Bar (or into a folder in the Bookmarks Bar) in Safari and you'll have it bookmarked without ever opening it. Since you don't have to open the link, you avoid the risk of getting distracted for the next hour because the page has tons of interesting links you feel compelled to check out. Not that it ever happens to me, but I've heard of such things.

DRAG BOOKMARKS AND TABS FROM FIREFOX INTO SAFARI

Firefox is another popular browser that's available for free. If you're browsing in Firefox and want to add a bookmark for the page you're viewing to your Safari bookmarks, just click the page's favicon in Firefox's address field, and drag it to a bookmark folder in Safari's Bookmarks Bar. If you have a tab in Firefox and want to have the same tab in Safari, just click the tab in Firefox and drag to an empty spot in Safari's Tab Bar. That's pretty darn cool.

   OPEN GOOGLE SEARCH RESULTS IN A SEPARATE WINDOW

By default, when you do a Web search using Safari's built-in Google search field, the results of your search replace what was in your browser window. That's okay, unless you're using that search to look up something relating to the page that you were on (which seems to happen, at least to me, more often than not). Here's a way around that: Once you enter your search term in the Google search field, instead of pressing Return, press Command-Return, and the Google results will open in their own separate window.

HIGHLIGHT THE ADDRESS BAR FAST

Want to enter a new address fast? Don't drag your cursor over the old address to highlight it—that's way too slow. Instead, just press Command-L and the URL address field will highlight (as shown here), ready for you to type the new address. For you former Windows users, you don't need to type in "www." before an address or ".com" after it—just the name of the site will be fine.

BROWSING IN STEALTH MODE

When you're on the Web, many sites secretly collect information about you and your browsing habits. That's not always bad—I like Amazon or the iTunes Store recommending things I might like based on my previous purchases. But if you prefer to remain anonymous (especially if you share a computer), you can enable Private Browsing. Go to the Safari menu and choose Private Browsing. Click OK when the annoying message pops up warning you that if you continue on this foolhardy course, none of the information you enter in forms, or addresses of sites you visit, will be saved. Exactly—if it kept track of those things, it wouldn't be Private Browsing, would it? So now that you are in stealth mode, you can go to Microsoft's or Dell's website without your Mac buddies finding out.

   HIDING YOUR TRACKS

Let's say that you've been visiting some sites (like PlasticSurgery.com, PreparationH.com, etc.) that you would rather not have the whole world know about. Just choosing Clear History from the History menu isn't enough. Heck, these days your average middle-school student could trace you back to those sites in about five minutes. If you really want to hide your tracks, go to the Safari menu and choose Reset Safari. This brings up a warning dialog that says, in essence, choosing this is the next best thing to a clean reinstall of your browser. It basically "cleans house," so don't click it unless you're on the run from the CIA (or a crafty middle-school student).

   REOPEN CLOSED WINDOWS

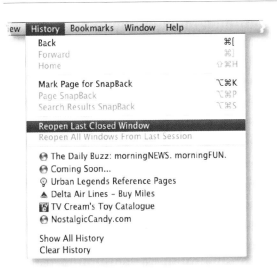

If you're checking out several sites and inadvertently close a window you didn't mean to, go up to the History menu, and choose Reopen Last Closed Window (as shown here). But what if you're working away and Safari decides to quit, like mine did about two minutes ago? You could go to your history and start opening the windows you need one at a time, or you can go to the History menu, and choose Reopen All Windows From Last Session. In less than a second, you'll be having a déjà vu moment as you look at your desktop and everything is just like it was before.

JUMP BACK FAST

If you're using tabbed browsing (and you should be), here's a great tip to keep you from un-necessarily reloading a page you've already been to. Let's say, for example, that you're visiting a site, and you click on a link that takes you to a different site. If you click the Back button, it reloads that page you were just at. Instead, try this—press-and-hold the Command key and click the Back button. This opens the original page in a separate tab, without reloading the whole thing from scratch. Need I say that you can do this with the Next button as well (as shown here)? Okay, I didn't think so.

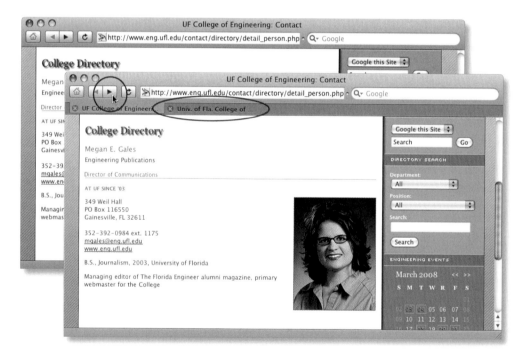

KILLER TIPS

IMPORTING BOOKMARKS FROM OTHER BROWSERS

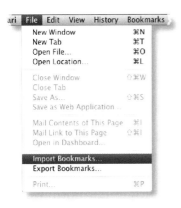

If you've been using another browser, it's easy to import the bookmarks (sometimes called Favorites) you've accumulated into Safari. If you've been using Firefox, for example, go ahead and open it, then go to the Bookmarks menu, and choose Organize Bookmarks. Now go to the File menu, select Export, and save the file. Switch to Safari, choose Import Bookmarks from the File menu and choose the file you just exported from Firefox. If you've been using Internet Explorer and you have some Favorites (as Microsoft called them) you want to salvage, go to your Home folder, open the Library folder, open the Preferences folder, and then open the Explorer folder. Inside, you should see a file named "Favorites. html." Drag this file to the desktop, then import it into Safari. Once you're done importing, you can drag the Favorites.html file and the file with the exported Firefox bookmarks to the Trash—you won't be needing them anymore.

SEARCH BOOKMARKS, HISTORY, AND GOOGLE SEARCH TERMS

It's amazing (and scary at the same time) how many footprints you leave when you go online. I'm just talking the ones on your computer, which is nothing compared to the stuff we leave behind on the sites we visit. If your memory is anything like mine, however, having Safari remember where you've been is a good thing. If you click on the Show All Bookmarks icon (it looks like a little open book) at the far-left end of the Bookmarks Bar and type a search term in the search field in the top-right corner of the Bookmarks window, your results will include bookmarks you created, pages you visited (whether they are bookmarked or not), and search terms you typed into the Google search box in Safari's toolbar.

A FASTER BOOKMARKS MENU

If you thought adding your favorite sites to Safari's Bookmarks Bar sped things up, wait till you hear this tip: Once your favorite sites are added, you can have even faster access to those sites than by just clicking on their bookmarks. Instead, press Command-1 to load the first site in the Bookmarks Bar. Press Command-2, Command-3, Command-4, and so on to instantly load the sites in order. *Note:* Sadly, this trick only works with individual sites added to your Bookmarks Bar—it doesn't work with folders.

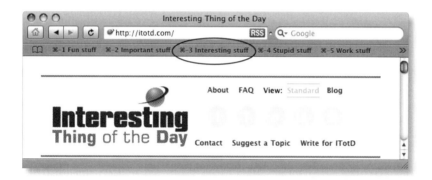

SHARING YOUR BOOKMARKS

It's easy to share your Safari bookmarks. Just go to Safari's File menu and choose Export Bookmarks. Enter a name in the dialog and click Save. This creates an HTML file with your bookmarks separated into their various categories and all the links live. Now, should you decide to use another browser (say it ain't so!), you can use this file to import your Safari bookmarks into your new browser (knowing all the while that you might feel a little bit guilty for turning your back on Safari like that). If you want to share your bookmarks with the world at large, you can upload the HTML file to a website, or email it to friends so they can get a glimpse into the in-ner workings of your mind. On second thought….

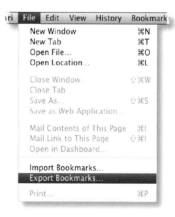

   BUILT-IN TIP FINDER

You can uncover a number of cool little tips from right within Safari itself by looking at the very bottom left-hand corner of the Safari window (if you don't see it there, choose Show Status Bar from the View menu). When you put your cursor over a link on a webpage, before you even click the link, it shows you what will happen when you do click it. For example, if you put your cursor over a link to my website, in the status bar it would say, "Go to http://www.scottkelby.com." Now, here's where it gets fun: Press-and-hold a modifier key (Command, Option, Shift, Control, etc.) and then take a look down there. As you hold down each key, the status bar changes to show you what will happen next. For example, if you hold down the Command key and move over the link, it would say something like, "Open http://www.scott-kelby.com in a new tab," so you now know that holding down the Command key and clicking a link does just that—it opens that site in a new tab. I won't spoil the rest for you, but try it yourself by moving over a link and pressing Control, Option, Command-Shift, Command-Option, Command-Shift-Option, etc., and a number of cool little tips will be revealed.

FASTEST WAY TO EMAIL A LINK TO A FRIEND

If you run across a cool website and want to email that site to a friend, the fastest way is to press Command-Shift-I. This opens your default email client and inserts the Web URL into the body of your email. Now all you have to do is type the recipient's email address, enter "Check this site out" in the Subject line, and click Send.

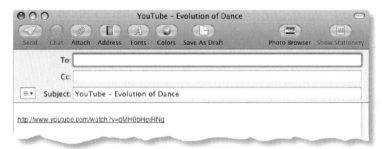

   USING GOOGLE'S SEARCH TERM MEMORY

When you're using the Google search field in Safari's toolbar, Safari keeps track of your last 10 searches, just in case you want to re-search using one of those same terms. To access one of your previous search terms, just click on the magnifying glass icon within the Google search field and a pop-up menu of recent terms will appear. If you want to erase Google's search memory, just select the Clear Recent Searches option at the bottom.

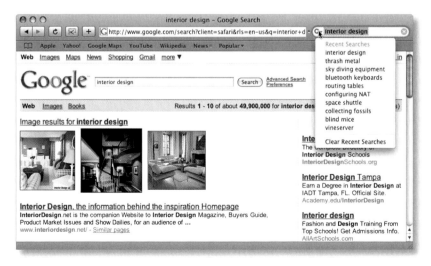

 HOW TO REMOVE SITES FROM YOUR HISTORY

If you choose Clear History from the History menu it wipes out the list of all the sites you've ever visited. If you want to remove only particular sites from your history but leave the rest, try this: Click the Show All Bookmarks icon at the far-left end of the Bookmarks Bar, then click on History in the Safari sidebar. Now simply click the history item you want to remove and press the Delete key. If you have a few items you want to remove and they happen to be together, keep pressing the Delete key. Each time you press it, the next item in the list will be deleted. If you have a lot of items, you can click the first one, then Shift-click the last one to select everything between the two. Now when you press Delete, they'll all be removed from your History folder.

SKIP THE LINK—SEND THE WHOLE PAGE!

If you run across a webpage you want to share with a friend, instead of just sending them a link to it, you can send them the contents of the page (complete with all the graphics, formatting, links, etc.). To send the page, just press Command-I. Mail will open a New Message window with the contents of the page already in the message area. Now all you have to do is fill in your friend's email address, add a subject, and type a message if you want. When you're done, just click Send. When your friend receives your email, they'll see the webpage in the message viewer (complete with live links), saving them the trouble of launching a browser, clicking on a link, and waiting for the page to load.

   FINDING YOUR DIGITAL BREADCRUMBS

Like any browser, Safari keeps track of where you've been, page by page. If you want to hop quickly back to a page where you've been recently, just click-and-hold on the Back button in Safari's toolbar. The sites you've visited in the current tab will appear in a pop-up menu. If you've hopped back, and want to jump ahead, click-and-hold on the Next button. (I didn't really have to tell you that Next button trick, did I?)

FIND A WORD ON A WEBPAGE

If you want to find a particular word on a page you're viewing, press Command-F and type the word in the search field that will open (this isn't the Spotlight search field, it's a special one that opens under the Tab Bar when you press Command-F). If the word is on the page, it will be highlighted in bright yellow. If it's on the page more than once, these additional occurrences will be highlighted in white. You can use the arrows located to the left of the search field to move to the next (or previous) occurrence of the word.

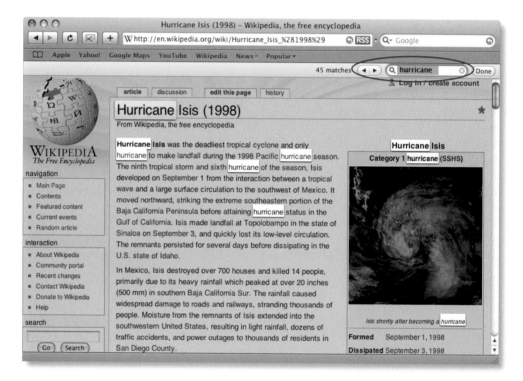

   MAKING ONLINE ARTICLES EASIER TO READ

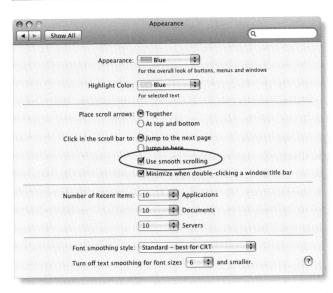

This is a great tip for people who read a lot of articles online, because when you're reading these articles and you come to the bottom of the page, using the scroll bar is a pain, and pressing Page Down usually moves too far. However, you can set up Safari to better accommodate reading articles using Smooth Scrolling. To turn it on, go to the Apple menu, select System Preferences, and click on the Appearance icon. Now turn on the Use Smooth Scrolling checkbox. From now on, when you hit the Page Down button, your article will move line by line, rather than page by page. You'll be amazed at the difference this makes.

   READING RSS FEEDS OUTSIDE OF SAFARI

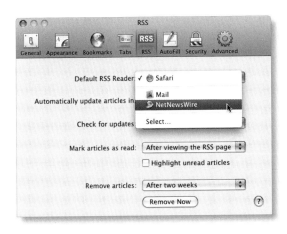

Safari has its own RSS reader that does a nice job of letting you read RSS feeds without leaving Safari. But if you prefer to use your favorite RSS reader, just make a quick trip to Safari's preferences (found under the Safari menu) and click on the RSS icon. When the RSS pane appears, from the Default RSS Reader pop-up menu at the top of the dialog, choose whichever program you prefer, and close the preferences. Now when you click on the RSS icon in Safari's address field, it will open that feed in your preferred reader.

LEOPARD

   CAPTURE THAT WEBPAGE

I'm sure this has probably happened to you: You find a website with some great information, so you bookmark it, but a few weeks later when you go back to that bookmark, the page you saved has been changed, and the info you need is long gone. Well, you can protect against that with Safari by saving that page as a Web Archive. When you save as a Web Archive, not only is the text on the page saved, but the entire page—just as you saw it (including the full layout, graphics, you name it)—is also saved right along with it, so when you open the archive, even years later, the page will look exactly as you remember it. To save a page as a Web Archive, just go to Safari's File menu and choose Save As. When the Save dialog appears, go to the bottom and select Web Archive from the Format pop-up menu and then click the Save button. To open a Web Archive later, just drag-and-drop the saved file directly onto Safari's icon in the Dock.

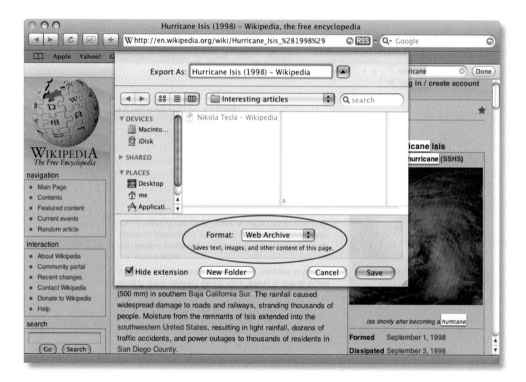

   MAKE A WEBPAGE WIDGET

If you can think of something useful to do with this feature of Leopard, have at it. I can't think of anything myself, but I use it to have fun. You can create a Dashboard widget from a portion of any webpage. Just Control-click on the page you want to use for your widget (you have to click on an empty space on the page, not on a photo or graphic or it won't work), then select Open in Dashboard from the contextual menu. Your screen will dim, except for a selection area that will never be the size or shape you want and is always in the wrong position. No problem. You can change its position by moving the mouse, and you can resize it by clicking the resize handles (the little circles) around the edges of the selection. When you have selected the area of the page you want to use as your widget, press Return (or click the Add button) and now you have a custom, one-of-a-kind, no-one-else-in-the-whole-world-has-one Dashboard widget. If you click the information icon in the bottom-right corner of the widget, you can add a frame to make it look professional. But here's the really cool thing—the widget is live, meaning it will update just like the original page every time you open Dashboard. Like I said, you might find a use for it. Me? I made a widget to check the weather where my wife's family lives so I can gloat—especially on days like today.

   STOP AND RESUME A DOWNLOAD

If you're downloading something and it's taking longer than you thought it would, you can pause the download and resume it later. Go to the Window menu, and choose Downloads. You will see a list of recent downloads as well as any files currently downloading. To pause a download, click the little icon with the X that's to the right of the file's title. I know you're afraid to click it because X is like the universal symbol for "get rid of this." Call me crazy, but it might have been nice if Apple had used an icon with the ubiquitous "pause" symbol like they do in every other application they make. Anyhow, when you click the pause button, it will change to an icon that makes sense—a nice round line with an arrow on the end that screams out, "Start moving." When you're ready to start downloading again, just open the Downloads window and click the "Start moving" button.

   KEEP YOUR KIDS FROM UNSAVORY SITES

If you're concerned about your children accessing sites that are inappropriate, you can help make sure that doesn't happen by turning on the Parental Controls. When you do this, your kids can only visit sites you have bookmarked in advance for them (they can't visit or book-mark sites on their own). To enable Parental Controls for Safari, go to the Apple menu, select System Preferences, then click on the Parental Controls icon. The controls that pertain to Safari are located in the Content section and are self-explanatory. Two things that I especially like: When the preference pane opens, near the bottom is an option to Manage Parental Con-trols from Another Computer (as shown here). Turn this checkbox on—it will make your life easier. The second thing I really like is the ability to keep logs of your children's activities. You can set this up by clicking on the Logs tab. I know some parents don't think it's right to "spy" on their children like this. Personally, I don't have a problem with it: my house, my computer, my child, and my responsibility to know what they're up to.

Chapter 8

Music
& Movies

Using iTunes, DVD Player,
Front Row, and More

At this moment I am being held captive by a gang of uniformed "attendants" who have put me inside a long aluminum tube,

Music & Movies

using itunes, dvd player, front row, & more

cut off my fresh air supply, wedged me into a cramped space, strapped me to my seat, and told me not to even think about trying to get up until they tell me to. Every time I manage to drift off to sleep, a speaker right above my head starts blaring. They give me a bite of food and a couple of ounces of water that's supposed to last me for the remaining five hours of my captivity. The only thing that's keeping me going is my iPod touch. I can plug in my ER 6i noise-blocking earphones and take my mind off my troubles with the help of Bublé, Norah, B.B., Shania, Faith, Stevie Ray, Van, and Satriani. Or I can watch Mike Rowe do another disgusting job and remind myself there are worse things than flying from Tampa to Los Angeles. It helps, too, knowing I'll be enjoying a Double Double with Cheese at In-N-Out Burger in a couple of hours.

iTunes: PLAYING A SONG

There are really four different ways to play a song within iTunes, so you should try them all to find out which one best suits your personal style. Here they are: (1) find the song you want to play and just double-click on it; (2) click on the song you want to play and press the Spacebar; (3) click on the song you want to hear, then click on the Play button in the upper left-hand corner of the iTunes window; or (4) click on the song you want to play and choose Play from the Controls menu (as shown here).

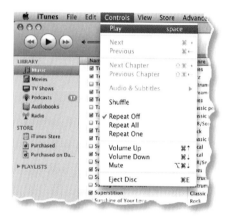

iTunes: SKIPPING A SONG

To the left of each song title is a check-box, and every checked song will play when you're listening to an entire play-list. If you want to skip a song, just turn off its checkbox. This also works when importing songs from an audio CD—checked songs are imported, unchecked songs are not.

  ◯ **iTunes: GRID VIEW IS BRAND NEW**

Back in the day when you went to a record store to buy albums, the covers they came in were more than just a way to protect the vinyl; they were pieces of art. Some of them (The Beatles' *Sgt. Pepper's Lonely Hearts Club Band* and *Abbey Road*, and Pink Floyd's *Dark Side of the Moon*, for example) became cultural icons. In iTunes 8, Album view has been replaced by the new Grid view, and it's pretty slick. If you click the middle View button in the toolbar, iTunes will display album cover art for all the music in your library (as well as TV shows, movies, and anything else in your library) all neatly lined up. You can use the buttons at the top of the iTunes window to group the albums in different ways, and you can adjust the slider at the top right to adjust the size of the covers.

   iTunes: ALBUM VIEW IS STILL AROUND

The Grid View button has replaced the Album View button in the toolbar, but you can still use Album view if you like. If you're in Grid view and double-click any album cover (or group art-work), Album view will open and display the contents of the album or group you're browsing. If you don't see the album's cover art in Album view, just click the little triangle at the top of the first column. If you're browsing your iTunes Library in List view, press Command-G to toggle between Album view and List view.

KILLER TIPS

   iTunes: USE BROWSING TO CREATE INSTANT PLAYLISTS

Let's say you want to hear nothing but country songs today, but you don't have a Country playlist. Or maybe you want to hear all your Aretha songs, but don't have a "Queen of Soul" playlist either. No worries. You can use the Browser feature to create a playlist with just a couple of clicks. First, go to your iTunes Library and select Music. Next, press Command-B to open the Browser window shown here. Now simply select a Genre, Artist, or Album, and all songs that fit the category you selected will be listed. Click on the songs (Shift–click or Command–click to select multiple items) you want to include in your new playlist then select New Playlist from Selection from the File menu. Finally, give it a name (unless you just really like "untitled playlist"), put in your earbuds, and start "Swayin' to the Music" (Johnny Rivers, 1977).

   iTunes: MAKE A TEMPORARY PLAYLIST

Here's a fast way for you to listen to all the songs by a particular artist or in a particular genre or album. Assuming you're in iTunes, click the Grid View button in the toolbar (the middle one), then use the buttons just above the album covers to select a group. Now just move your cursor so it's over the item you want to listen to and click the Play button that appears. So if I'm in the mood for some country music, all I have to do is switch to Grid view, select Genres, roll my cursor over Country and click the Play Genre button. Here's another cool thing: If you want to see what country albums you have, just move your cursor to the left or right while it's over the genre artwork, and you'll scan through all the albums for that genre.

    iTunes: CREATE A GENIUS PLAYLIST

Using the iTunes browser is an easy way to create new playlists, but the new Genius feature in iTunes 8 makes it even easier. Here's how you create a Genius playlist: click on any song in your iTunes Library, then click the Genius button in the bottom-right corner of the iTunes window. That's it! Genius will search your library and find songs that go great together and list them for you. If you want to save the list as a playlist, just press the Save Playlist button in the top-right corner of the window. If you're like me, chances are pretty good that you'll rediscover songs you forgot you had. It's kind of like buying them again…without having to actually buy them.

   iTunes: GENIUS SIDEBAR

Genius playlists are cool—they find songs you already have in your library. The Genius sidebar is dangerous—it tempts you with songs you don't have but, at least in my case, soon will. When you launch iTunes, you'll see the Genius sidebar on the right side of the window (if you don't see it, press Command-Shift-G), and it displays a list of songs the helpful folks at Apple think you should add to your library. They know that if you click the musical note by a song title to preview it, you'll also press the Buy button. So when I selected "1234" (that catchy song from one of the iPod commercials) to make the figure shown here, I ended up buying five songs. (In case you're wondering, none of them was from the Soccer Mom Chillout suggestions.) So here's the tip: If you are as impulsive as I am, don't open the Genius sidebar unless you're prepared to deal with the consequences. If it's already open, press Command-Shift-G to toggle it off.

   iTunes: **SHOW IN PLAYLIST**

If you're browsing your iTunes Library and run across a song you like, but you can't remember if you've added it to one of your playlists, all you have to do is Control–click on it. If you see a Show in Playlist option in the contextual menu, roll your cursor over it and you'll see the playlist(s) you've added the song to. If you only see an Add to Playlist option, that means the song is only in your iTunes Library.

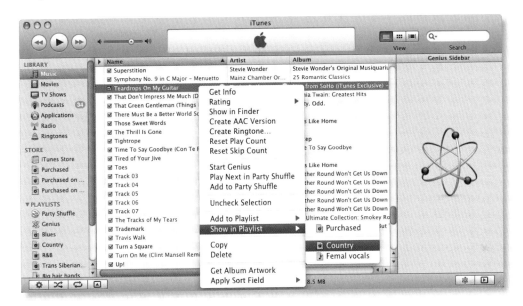

   iTunes: GET CONCERT TICKETS

If you are browsing one of your favorite artists or bands on the iTunes Store and are thinking, "I'd really like to see them in concert, but it's such a pain to track down upcoming venues and get tickets," then you're in luck. On the right side of the iTunes window you'll see several links, one of which is Concert Tickets. Click on it and you'll be taken to Ticketmaster where you'll see upcoming concert dates. Find one that works for you and you can purchase your ticket with a couple of clicks.

   iTunes: SET UP YOUR CDS TO IMPORT AUTOMATICALLY

If you've decided to import your entire collection of CDs into iTunes (and I wholeheartedly recommend that), then you're going to want to have as much automation as possible, so you don't go totally brain-dead during the process. Here's why: When you insert a CD, by default iTunes doesn't import the tracks. Instead, it just shows you what's on the CD, which is great if you only want to know what's on the CD. But it you're cataloging your entire collection, this is the last thing you want it to do. Imagine how much time it would save if you just inserted a CD and iTunes automatically imported all the songs, then spit the CD out, ready for you to insert the next disc. It can do just that—you just have to tell it to. Go to the iTunes preferences, click the General icon, then go down to the When You Insert a CD pop-up menu, choose Import CD and Eject, and then click OK. That's it—you just turned your computer into an automatic CD-importing machine, which enables you to pay your little brother to sit there and swap the ejected CDs for a few hours while you go to a concert. See, this is what life's all about.

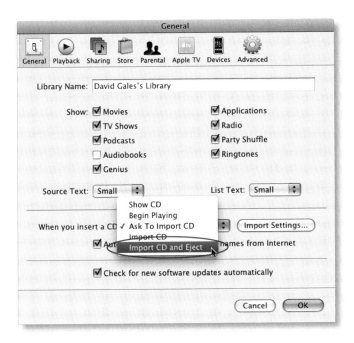

iTunes: GET CD TRACK NAMES AUTOMATICALLY

If you're importing songs from a CD and you have a continuous Internet connection, iTunes can automatically find the names (and other background info) for all the songs you're importing. Here's what actually happens: When you import songs, iTunes will go to the Web and search the massive Gracenote CDDB Internet Audio Database for the info on the CD you're importing. If it finds the information, iTunes will automatically download it into each song's info panel, naming the songs (artists, album names, etc.) as it goes (pretty cool, eh?). To set this up, go to the iTunes preferences, click General, and turn on the checkbox next to Automatically Retrieve CD Track Names from Internet. If you don't have a continuous Internet connection, just add all of your songs to your iTunes Music Library or playlists, connect to the Internet, then under the Advanced menu, choose Get CD Track Names (as shown here).

KILLER TIPS

   iTunes: CONSOLIDATING YOUR MUSIC IN ONE PLACE

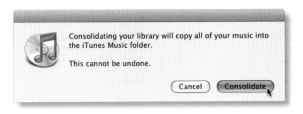

If you've already got music scattered all over your hard disk, it's not too late—you can have iTunes go to all those folders and copy all the songs listed in your Music Library into the iTunes Music folder on your hard disk in just two clicks. Go under the File menu, under Library, and choose Consolidate Library. Ignore the warning that Leopard is about to do what you just told it to do, and click Consolidate. I also recommend playing "Come Together" by The Beatles while iTunes does its thing.

   iTunes: COPY SONGS INTO YOUR iTUNES MUSIC FOLDER

If you have an MP3 song on your hard disk and you double-click on it, iTunes opens it and plays the song. It also creates an invisible shortcut (or alias) to the song from that folder on your hard disk. There's nothing wrong with this, but eventually you'll have folders scattered all over your hard disk with music in them. Well, you can make things much more organized than that (which makes backing up your music much easier) by having iTunes copy each song that it plays into the iTunes Music folder. That way, all of your music is in one place. To turn on this feature, go to the iTunes preferences and click the Advanced icon. In the Advanced section, turn on the checkbox for Copy Files to iTunes Music Folder When Adding to Library. Now you can click OK, with the peace of mind that can only come from bringing order and harmony to your music world.

   iTunes: ADDING YOUR OWN CUSTOM GENRES

Although iTunes comes with a list of popular genres, there are some it just doesn't include (like Salsa, Thrash, and New Wave), and you can probably come up with a dozen or so yourself. That's why iTunes lets you create your own custom genres (like Death Metal or Opera or Death Metal Opera). To create your own custom genre, Control-click any song, then choose Get Info from the contextual menu. When the Get Info dialog appears, click on the Info tab, and then just type the name you want for your new genre in the Genre field and click OK. If you want to create a genre that encompasses a number of different styles, just put a comma after each name (like "Metal, Jazz, Punk, Choral"). Assigning these multiple genres to a song will cause the song to appear in multiple categories when searching. For example, you might want the Brad Paisley song "Find Yourself" to have multiple genres, so it appears when you search for either Country or Soundtrack (it was part of the movie *Cars*). When browsing, it would appear in a new genre labeled "Country, Soundtrack."

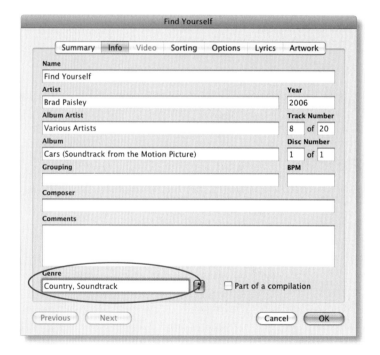

 iTunes: DELETING SONGS

If you've had enough of a song and you just want it out of iTunes (and out of your life), click on the song and press the Delete key on your keyboard. You can also delete a song by Control-clicking on a song and choosing Delete from the contextual menu. Either way, when the dialog appears, if you click Keep File, the song will be removed from your iTunes Library, but will still be in your music folder. So if absence makes your heart grow fonder toward the song at some point in the future, you can put it back in the Library. If you choose Move to Trash, one of two things will happen: If you selected the song from a playlist, iTunes will remove the song from just that playlist. If you selected the song from your Music Library, then iTunes removes the file altogether and puts it in the Trash. Don't freak out—you'll get a warning dialog, so you don't have to worry about hitting the wrong key and losing a beloved treasured favorite, like "My Sundown" by Jimmy Eat World.

iTunes: SELECT THE COLUMNS YOU WANT DISPLAYED

In the iTunes main Library window (where you see your songs), there are separate columns that display the song title, the artist, the album name, and a host of other information. Some of it you probably will care about (like the song name, artist, time, etc.), and some of it you probably won't need to see. Ever. Stuff like a song's Beats Per Minute (although this column is very helpful to DJs and people working out). Luckily, you can customize your columns and choose which ones are visible (and which ones are hidden), which makes for very clean, easy-to-read playlists, because they display just the info you care about seeing. Here's how to customize yours: Press Command-J on your keyboard to bring up the iTunes View Options dialog. Select which columns you'd like to be visible by turning on (or off) the checkboxes next to the column names. When you're done, click OK and only the columns you selected will appear in your main window.

View Options

🎵 Music

Show Columns

☐ Album	☐ Episode ID	☐ Show
☐ Album Artist	☐ Equalizer	☐ Size
☐ Album Rating	☑ Genre	☐ Skip Count
☑ Artist	☐ Grouping	☐ Sort Album
☐ Beats Per Minute	☐ Kind	☐ Sort Album Artist
☐ Bit Rate	☐ Last Played	☐ Sort Artist
☐ Category	☐ Last Skipped	☐ Sort Composer
☐ Comment	☐ Play Count	☐ Sort Name
☐ Composer	☑ Rating	☐ Sort Show
☐ Date Added	☐ Release Date	☑ Time
☐ Date Modified	☐ Ringtone	☐ Track Number
☐ Description	☐ Sample Rate	☐ Year
☐ Disc Number	☐ Season	

(Cancel)   (OK)

   iTunes: HIDING AND UNHIDING COLUMNS

If at any time you decide you want a hidden column to be visible or vice versa, just Control-click directly on any of the column headers and check (make visible) or uncheck (hide) the column name from the contextual menu.

   iTunes: VIEWING MORE INFO ABOUT YOUR SONGS

While a song is playing, the iTunes status display (that rectangular panel at the top center of the iTunes window) shows you the name of the current song, the artist, how much of the song has already played (the elapsed time)—in minutes and seconds, as well as in a progress bar—and how much time is left until the song has finished playing (the remaining time). But more information is just a mouse click away. If you'd like the name of the album the song came from, click directly on the artist's name (the artist's name and the album's name scroll continuously under the static song name). Want the total time of the song? Click on the remaining time (on the right side of the progress bar).

iTunes: EDITING YOUR SONG'S INFO

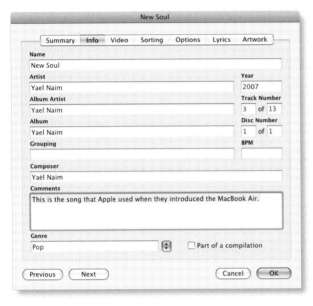

If you want to make some minor change to a song's information, select the song in your iTunes Music Library (or a playlist) then click on the field you want to change and wait a second until it highlights, then enter the updated info (as shown below). If you want to make changes to several fields, just Control-click on the song, and choose Get Info from the contextual menu. When the dialog appears, click the Info tab and you'll see the fields you can edit or use to store additional information about the song (as shown to the left). When you're done, just click OK and get back to enjoying some tunes.

   iTunes: EDITING MULTIPLE SONGS AT ONE TIME

If you have multiple songs that need some information updated, you can do it all at once. Just select the ones you want to modify, then press Command-I. Ignore the warning that opens and turn on the checkboxes next to the categories you want to update. The only thing left is to enter the new information and click OK. Just remember, the updated information will replace the existing info for every song you've selected. So it would be a bad idea, for instance, to select all the songs in your iTunes Library and then update the Artist information. Unless, of course, you happen to have a couple thousand songs by the same artist, in which case it would be a very good idea.

   iTunes: FINDING DUPLICATES

Because you'll wind up having hundreds, maybe thousands, of songs in iTunes, and lots of different playlists, you'll be amazed at how easy it is to have more than one copy of a song (maybe with a slightly different name, or just in different playlists, or different versions of the same song). Luckily, there's a quick way to get rid of duplicates—just go under the File menu and choose Show Duplicates. This will bring up a list of all your duplicate songs. Then, if you have two (or more) copies, you can quickly click on the one(s) you want to delete and press the Delete key on your keyboard.

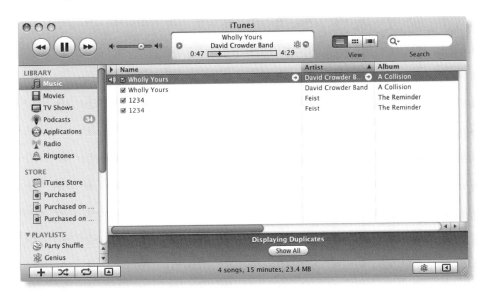

iTunes: LISTENING TO INTERNET RADIO STATIONS

If you've got an Internet connection, there's another side to iTunes that they don't talk about at parties, and that's iTunes Radio. Well, it's not exactly FM radio, but instead it's a list of hundreds of streaming Internet radio stations, broadcasting everything from reggae to talk shows, from metal to classical (and everything in between). All you have to do is click on Radio in your iTunes Library and start browsing around. When you find some stations you like, drag them into one of your playlists in the Source list on the left (or make one just for Radio). The next time you want to listen to some tunes, just go to the playlist and click on the station you want to hear. That's pretty darn cool if you ask me.

   iTunes: BURNING A CD OF A PLAYLIST

Burning a CD is a breeze, but there are a couple of things you should know before you do it, just so it's even breezier (if that's even a word). First, you can only burn playlists (not your Music Library), so click on a playlist in the Source list that you want to burn (also, don't insert a blank CD yet—wait until it asks you to). So now that you've selected a playlist, take a quick look down at the bottom center of the iTunes window to make sure you don't have more than 1.2 hours of music in your playlist (that's pretty much the maximum amount of time you can fit onto an audio CD these days). If you have too many songs, delete some until you have less than 1.2 hours. Then click the Burn Disc button (in the bottom right-hand corner of the iTunes window). The top-center status display will prompt you to Please Insert a Blank Disc (that's your cue). Once you insert a blank CD, iTunes will begin burning the songs in your playlist onto your blank CD. Now's your chance to abort burning the CD, if you so desire, by clicking the X in the status display, although the formerly blank CD will no longer be usable. Assuming all goes well, iTunes will spit your new music CD out of your optical drive.

   iTunes: SET PARENTAL LIMITS ON iTunes

The iTunes Store makes it so easy to buy things—sometimes too easy. If you have children, you can set limits on what they can see and purchase with iTunes. To set up the Parental Controls, log into your child's account (using their login information), go to the iTunes menu, select Preferences, and then click the Parental tab. Now just select the items you want to disable or restrict. Any of the items you disable won't even show up in your child's iTunes Source list. One very important thing you need to do before you close the preferences and log out is to click the lock in the lower-left corner. If you don't, your child will be able to undo everything you just did. Once it's locked, however, it will take an administrator's password to be able to make changes.

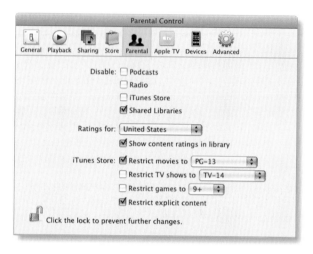

   iTunes: GET FREEBIES FROM THE iTUNES STORE

It's not often you hear about Apple giving away something for free, but on the front page of the iTunes Store there is a section called "Free On iTunes." I say it's on the front page, but unless you routinely scroll all the way to the bottom of webpages, you'll miss it. So go down to the iTunes "Bargain Basement," and click the See All arrow at the top right of the feature box and you'll see everything currently available. The nice thing is it's not just a bunch of junk—you can find some good stuff. It's also updated frequently, so make sure you check it whenever you stop by the store.

    iTunes: LET'S GET VISUAL

Remember all the psychedelic posters and album covers from the '70s? Of course you don't. But if you press Command-T, which turns on the Visualizer, you will get a glimpse of what life was like when your parents were in their twenties. When you turn on the Visualizer, it reacts to the music iTunes is playing, displaying constantly changing colors and shapes on your screen. To get the total Visualizer experience, press Command-F to go full screen, then sit back and stare at the screen for hours on end. When you find yourself saying things like, "Far out, man," and "Groovy" (a couple of sayings from the '70s), it's time to press the Escape key and go back to the regular iTunes screen. *Note:* If you want the Visualizer to always be displayed in full screen mode, go to iTunes' preferences by pressing Command-, (comma). Now press the Advanced button and select the Display Visualizer Full Screen option.

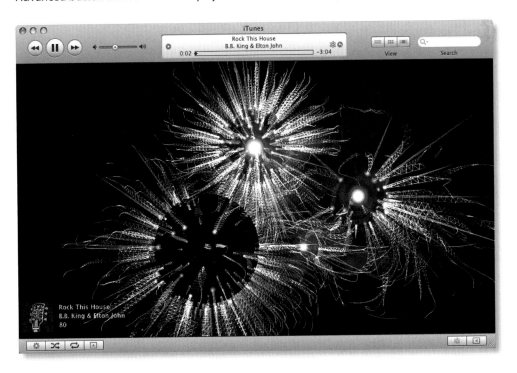

Front Row: **YOUR ONE-STOP MEDIA PLACE**

Everything you can do with Front Row, you can do with other applications. Listen to music or Internet radio: iTunes. View a slide show: iPhoto. Watch a DVD: DVD Player. Watch a TV show, movie, or podcast: iTunes. But Front Row lets you do them all. Even better, you can do it with a beautiful, elegant interface. Hook a spare Mac into your entertainment system (I like to think of it as the poor man's Apple TV) and you can enjoy big screen, big sound

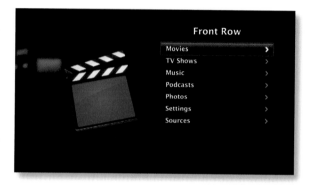

entertainment and control it with one remote that's smaller than two Hershey's Miniature candy bars, has six buttons, and doesn't require an engineering degree to operate. Front Row is a perfect example of what Apple does better than anyone else—making complex things easy and fun, then wrapping them in beautifully designed, user-friendly hardware and software.

 Front Row: **LAUNCH FRONT ROW WITH ONE CLICK**

If you are working away and are struck with a sudden urge to watch *Babette's Feast* (one of Scott's all-time favorites), press Command-Escape and Front Row will launch. Hey—that didn't even take a click!

KILLER TIPS

     Front Row: CHANGE THE SETTINGS FOR A SLIDE SHOW

Either slide shows aren't very intuitive in Front Row or I'm just stupid. But since I'm writing the book, I'll assume the first option. It looks easy enough: You launch Front Row, scroll down the options to Photos, start looking through the events from your iPhoto Library, press Return, and there's your slide show. But you never got to select which photos you wanted, what song you wanted to play, or the option to turn off the Ken Burns effect. Going back to the menu and selecting Settings is worthless. You can't get a menu bar like every other application. It's crazy. I'm ashamed to admit it, but I had to violate one of the fundamental rules of being a Mac user—I had to read the documentation. Here's the scoop: Before you play a slide show in Front Row, you put it together in iPhoto. Just open an event, select the photos you want to use, and click the Slideshow icon (if you can't find it, choose View, then Show in Toolbar, and select Slideshow). The window shown here will open (but yours won't have photos of the guy in the cool hat) where you can select the music you want, get rid of Ken Burns, set the duration of the slides, etc. Now when you go back to Front Row, and you select Photos, you will see your slide show listed as one of your options. Hopefully this will keep you from having to stoop to reading the manual, too.

DAVE GALES

   SOME NOT-SO-OBVIOUS WAYS TO WATCH MOVIES

In Leopard, there are at least seven ways to watch videos that I know of. The obvious ones are iTunes, QuickTime, DVD Player, and Front Row. But there are three that are less obvious.

- **Quick Look** If you want to watch a video and can't wait the ten seconds it will take to launch an application, click on the video in Finder, and press the Spacebar. That's right: Quick Look does videos.
- **Column View** If you're browsing a folder of movie files in Finder, while you're using Column view and select a video, a small video player will open in the Preview column (if you don't see the player, click the triangle in front of "Preview"). Just put your cursor on top of the player, click the Play button, and your video will start playing.
- **Get Info** Click on a video file, press Command-I, put your cursor on top of the player in the Preview section at the bottom of the Info window, and click the Play button.

But here's something else: Any of these options lets you scrub (move really fast) through a movie by putting your cursor on the preview and scrolling forward and backward using a scroll wheel on a mouse (or two fingers on the trackpad if you're using a laptop). You can get to any spot in your movie in just a few seconds. *Note:* Unfortunately, these three techniques won't work on movies you have purchased from the iTunes Store because of the copy protection.

   QuickTime: KEEP YOUR RESIZED VIDEO LOOKING CRISP

Images (moving or otherwise) are made of pixels, and look best at their original size. If you resize them to even sizes (like 30%, 80%, 150%, 200%, etc.), they still look pretty crisp and smooth. However, if you resize them to odd sizes (like 67.7%, 82%, or 129%), they tend to look a little jaggy (you Photoshop users know what I mean). Well, in QuickTime 7 you can just grab the corner of the Quick-Time Player window and drag it to any size you'd like. So, is there a trick to making the window snap to sizes that make your movies look their best when resized (like 50%, 25%, or 200%)? Yup. Just Option-click on a corner of the window, and start dragging. As you drag, it will snap to those ideal sizes.

   DVD Player: CONTROLLER MAXIMUS (THE HIDDEN CONTROLS)

If you're wondering whether DVD Player is missing some DVD functionality, you're only half right. It does have the ability to access DVD controls, such as slow motion, subtitling, camera angles, language, etc., but for the sake of space considerations, they're tucked away. To bring these buttons into view, double-click the little vertical gray lines on the right center of the Controller, and the Controller will expand to show two additional rows of buttons. If that's too much work, press Command-] (Right Bracket key) to show/hide the options.

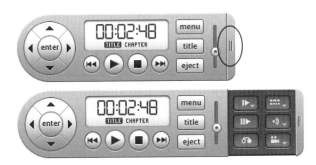

DVD Player: CONTROL CENTRAL

If you're watching a movie in Full Screen mode and need do something (like turn off the subtitles if you're watching a foreign film, so you can act like you can understand what they're saying), move the cursor to the bottom of the screen and the Controller Bar will appear and give you access to all the features and options you need to control the movie.

   DVD Player: GET BACK TO THE MENU FAST

There are a couple of ways to get back to the main DVD menu while you're watching a movie. If you're watching in Full Screen mode, you can either move the cursor to the bottom of the screen and click Menu in the Controller Bar, or you can press Command-D. If you're not in Full Screen mode, use the Command-D shortcut and it will instantly take you to the DVD's main menu.

   DVD Player: ENABLE PARENTAL CONTROL

If you have children you want to keep from viewing certain DVDs without your approval, you can enable parental controls by going under DVD Player's Features menu, choosing Enable Parental Control, then entering your administrator password. Now when a DVD is inserted, you have two choices: Play Once or Always Allow. If you select Always Allow, the next time the same DVD is inserted you won't need to enter your password. If you change your mind later and want to restrict a movie, just go back to the Features menu, and choose Deauthorize Media.

   DVD Player: PLAY MOVIE IN A FLOATING WINDOW

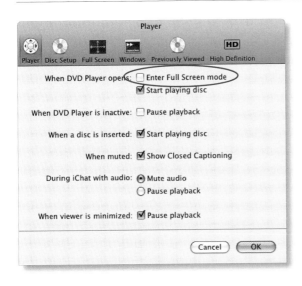

If you ever use DVD Player to watch training DVDs, you probably want to be able to jump back and forth between the DVD and the application you're learning, so you can watch a technique, pause the DVD, and then try it yourself. If that's the case, you can configure your DVD Player so it doesn't go "full screen" but instead displays the video in a floating window. To set up this mode as the default, go to the DVD Player menu, choose Preferences, click the Player icon, and where it says When DVD Player Opens, turn off the checkbox for Enter Full Screen Mode (it's on by default). The next time you insert a DVD, it will appear in a floating window.

⚫ ⚫ ⚫ DVD Player: SET YOUR OWN STARTING SPOT

When I want to watch a DVD, I don't want to have to sit through all the stuff they make you watch before they let you watch what you want to watch (I just used "watch" four times in one sentence, didn't I? Ouch!). Here's how to start playing your DVDs where you want to. The first time you play the DVD, when you get to the spot where you want to start in the future, press Command-= (equal sign) to set a bookmark. Enter a name for the bookmark, then turn on the Make Default Bookmark checkbox. Now you need to tell DVD Player to ignore the wishes of the studio, and always start playing this DVD at the bookmark you just set. To do that, go to the DVD Player menu, select Preferences, and click the Previously Viewed icon. In the Start Playing Discs From section, select Default Bookmark. Now whenever you insert this disc, it will automatically start playing right where you want it to,

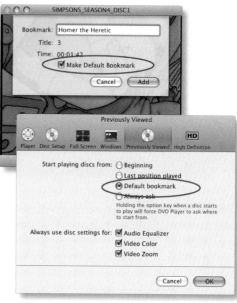

which means you can avoid seeing all the stuff they make you see before they let you see what you want to see.

⚫ ⚫ ⚫ DVD Player: TIME SLIDER MAKES MOVIES GO FAST

Sometimes it's the simple things that make a big difference—the time slider in DVD Player is one of them. When you're watching a movie in Full Screen mode, if you move the cursor to the bottom of the window, the Controller Bar will appear. Along the bottom of the Controller Bar is a time slider you can drag left or right to skim through the movie, or simply click anywhere along the bar to go directly to that spot. So when your friend loans you their favorite DVD and you really don't share the love for it, you can skim right through it. When they ask how you liked it, just say it was one of those movies that seems to go really fast. Then change the subject really fast before they start asking you about your favorite part (which was, of course, the end). *Note:* If you're not in Full Screen mode, the time slider is always visible whenever you move the cursor over the bottom of the player window.

   DVD Player: BOOKMARKING YOUR FAVORITE SPOTS

There are times you like to go straight to a particular spot in a DVD without having to fast forward and rewind a few times until you find what you're looking for. That's what bookmarks do. When you're watching a movie, every time you get to a spot you want to be able to go right to in the future, press Command-= (equal sign) to create a bookmark. Enter a more memorable name than Bookmark 1, then press OK. The next time you want to see Ned throw Homer out the window, press Command-B to show the Bookmarks window (shown here) and click the one you want to watch. If you forget the keyboard shortcut, you can also choose Go in the menu bar, select Bookmarks, and choose the bookmark you want.

Chapter 9

The Everyday Mac

Helpful Apps that Make Your Life Easier

I know what you're thinking: "Come on, Stickies is going to make my life easier? Winning the lottery would make my life easier.

The Everyday Mac

helpful apps that make your life easier

Spending six months a year in a cabin in the mountains, and the other six in a seaside villa, would make my life easier. But a sticky note?" But what if you were sitting on a plane a few years ago, watching a DVD on your eight-pound laptop and listening to a CD on your three-pound music player, and you suddenly had a brilliant idea for an amazing gadget that would fit in the palm of your hand and would play movies and music? You wouldn't have anything to write with, but who could forget such a great idea? Sure enough, you remember it. The only problem is it's two years later and you're watching Steve Jobs introduce this thing called an iPod. Bet you'll use Stickies next time.

   Time Machine: NO MORE EXCUSES FOR NOT BACKING UP

Time Machine does something we all know we should do, but don't do—no, not get a colonoscopy—back up our hard drives. You hear the horror stories of people who lost years of work when they had a drive fail (my son has a friend who spent $2,300 to recover the data from a drive that failed with no warning) and you make up your mind that you're going to start backing up. But then you discover that even with a good backup application, backing up is a pain. But Time Machine has changed that. It is possibly the feature that generated the most buzz and hype in the months before Leopard was released, and it has lived up to its own PR. Plus, it has a cool name and the user interface is like nothing you've ever seen on a Mac (is it a problem that it violates virtually every rule that Apple has prescribed for interface designers? Nah. You make the rules—you can break the rules). The first time you use Time Machine, you need to do some setup. It's absolutely imperative that you set things up properly, so read the following directions very carefully. Step One: Plug in an external drive (USB or FireWire). Step Two: Click on Use as Backup Disk. Step Three: Welcome yourself to the elite group of people who back up their computers.

   Time Machine: SET SOME PREFERENCES

I know what you're thinking: "Here it comes: I have to configure the preferences. So much for 'easy.'" Alright, I'm busted. I wasn't being entirely truthful when I implied Time Machine makes backing up easy. I should have said it makes backing up way crazy over-the-top stupid easy. Time Machine will work without any configuration at all, but there are some preferences you can set to fine-tune it to fit your situation. Here's how: From the Apple menu, select System Preferences and then click on the Time Machine icon. You've already told Time Machine what disk to use for your backups, but if you want to change drives, click Change Disk and pick a new one. If you click the Options button, you can tell Time Machine what *not* to back up. If you have a big backup drive, you can skip this. But if you need to conserve drive space, you can have Time Machine skip things like applications and all the system files that you probably already have on CDs or DVDs and could reinstall if necessary. The next preference you need to configure…wait, there are no more. Two preferences? Like I said, way crazy over-the-top stupid easy.

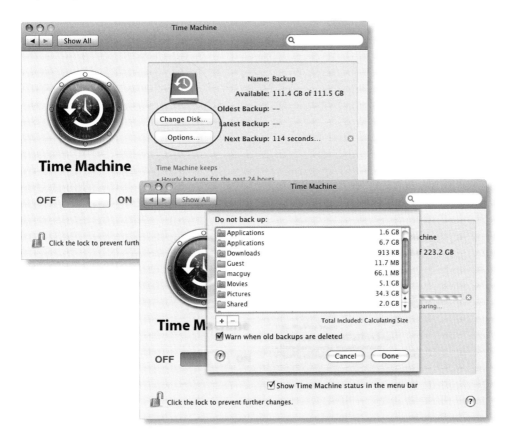

   Time Machine: RESTORING FROM YOUR BACKUP

You know that feeling you get when you realize you've just made a huge mistake? I'm not talking about wearing a black belt with brown pants here (a major fashion faux pas, to be sure), I'm talking a bigger mistake. Like deleting the folder containing all the files for a book you are writing about Leopard, along with some other things like the entire Adobe Creative Suite. Thankfully, Time Machine does as good a job restoring as it does backing up. If it didn't, you wouldn't be reading this book right now. If you ever come down with a case of extreme stupidity like I did, go to the Applications folder and open Time Machine. After you've played around with the interface for a few minutes, zooming back and forth saying things like, "All ahead full, Mr. Sulu," or "Mr. Scott, I need those shields up now!" use the Timeline along the right side of the screen to go back to a point in time where you still had the files you need. Now just select the files you need and click Restore, and in a few minutes you'll feel like a genius for having the foresight to have a backup.

   BACK TO MY MAC

This is one of the new features in Leopard that would be reason alone to upgrade. Back to My Mac gives you the ability to share any Mac on the same MoblieMe account from anywhere in the world. When you fire up your Mac, any other computer you have registered with your MobileMe account will show up in the Shared section of the sidebar, and can be accessed with one click. I can almost hear the geeks among you pointing out the fact that being able to connect to other Macs remotely is nothing new. That's true. What is new is the ease with which you can do it. I don't want to bore you with a long technical explanation of how Back to My Mac works (even if I knew enough to give you a long technical explanation, I wouldn't do it), so here's the bottom line. To connect remotely to other Macs, you have to know their Internet address. That's difficult because most Internet providers change your IP address periodically and you'll never know until you're out of town and try to connect remotely. The reason Back to My Mac works so easily is because it uses your MobileMe account to keep track of your home IP address. If it changes, MobileMe knows instantly (spooky, huh? I wonder if Steve Jobs sits at a computer all day typing in new IP addresses) and reconfigures the settings to let you connect. You'll never again be dead in the water because you forgot to pull a file off your computer at home or the office. *Note:* I've got to be honest with you, unless you are using Apple's Airport Extreme, it can be a bit tricky getting your network router configured to make this work. Airport Extreme comes preconfigured with the correct settings and works out of the box. Other routers will require you to do some port forwarding.

Fonts: FINDING WHERE THE © AND ™ SYMBOLS LIVE

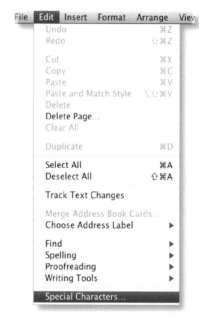

There are literally hundreds of special characters (stuff like ©, ™, £, ¢, ‰, ƒ, etc.) hidden somewhere in the dark corners of your Mac that you can use in any document. You can see all the characters available by using the Character palette, which you can access several ways: (1) from within most of the applications that come with your Mac, just go to the Edit menu and choose Special Characters (as shown here); (2) click the Action menu at the bottom of the Font panel and choose Characters; and (3) add Character palette access to your menu bar, so you can access it when you're working in other applications (like Word or Adobe InDesign). You do this by going to the System Preferences on the Apple menu, clicking on the International icon, and then clicking the Input Menu tab. Turn on the checkbox for Character Palette and it will now appear at the right side of the menu bar (its icon is a small flag). When you want to open the Character palette, just click the little flag and choose Show Character Palette.

   Fonts: USING THE SPECIAL CHARACTERS ONCE YOU FIND THEM

No matter how you open the Character palette (see previous tip), here's how you use it: choose All Characters from the View menu, then click the By Category tab. The left column shows a list of special character categories and the right column shows the individual characters in each category. To get one of these characters into your text document, just click the character and click the Insert button in the bottom right-hand corner of the dialog. If you find yourself using the same special characters over and over (like © and ™, for example), you can add these to your Favorites list, and access them from the Favorites tab in the Character palette. To see which fonts contain certain characters (they don't all share the same special characters), expand the Character palette by clicking the down-facing arrow next to Font Variation on the bottom-left side of the palette. This opens a section where you can choose different fonts. You can also ask that this list show only fonts that support the character you have highlighted.

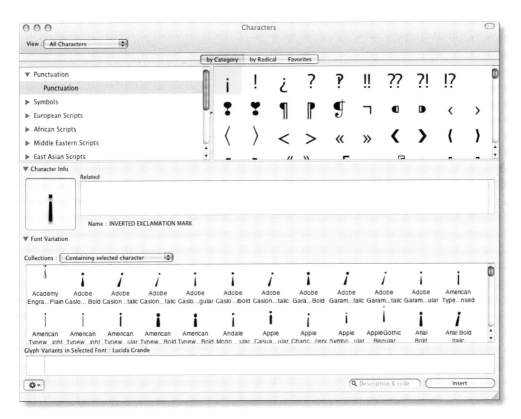

   Font Panel: SEEING YOUR FONTS BEFORE YOU USE THEM

Apple has heard your plaintive cries, and finally they've included a preview of your fonts so you can actually see what they look like before you decide which one to use. You access this new wonder of modern science in any application that uses Mac OS X's built-in Font panel (which is pretty much any application). Press Command-T to open the Font panel. When it appears, click on the Action button at the bottom left of the panel and choose Show Preview. A font preview will open at the top of the Font panel and display a live preview when you click on different fonts, styles, and sizes. So what you see is what you'll get!

   Font Panel: **GET A LEAN & MEAN FONT PANEL WITH ONE CLICK**

The Font panel is amazing, but it's also huge! If you want to use it, but don't want it to take up half your screen, click the green button in the top-left corner of the Font panel, and it will snap to a very convenient size. If you click the resize button in the bottom-right corner of the "mini panel" and drag it to the left, you can make it even smaller. But even at it's smallest size, you still have access to the main features of the full-sized panel by using the pop-up menus. If you need one of the other features, just click the green button again and it will switch back to the full-size version. Even if you don't use the Font panel, it's worth trying it once just to see this amazing technology at work.

   Font Book: **CHECKING FOR BAD FONTS**

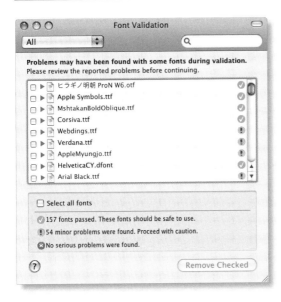

If there's one thing that can bring a document (or your system) to its knees, it's using a corrupt font (meaning a font that accepts bribes—sorry, that was lame). Here's how to search for rampant font corruption: Go to your Applications folder and launch Font Book. You can either click directly on any font that you might think is suspect, or Command-click on them, then go to Font Book's File menu and choose Validate Fonts. When the Font Validation window opens, you'll see which fonts are legit and which are suspect. If you want to know details about any of the fonts, just click the right-facing triangle next to them. When you're ready to eliminate the problem fonts (if you know what I mean), turn on the checkbox next to their names, then click the Remove Checked button in the lower-right corner of the dialog.

Font Book: RESOLVING DUPLICATE FONTS

If there's one thing that messes with an application's (or a system's) head, it's font conflicts (duplicate copies of the same fonts installed on your hard drive). Thankfully, Font Book kicks this problem in the butt. If Font Book detects a duplicate font, it puts a little bullet point in front of the font's name. Then it's up to you to choose which version you really want to keep open (you shouldn't have both open). Click on the version you want, then go to Font Book's Edit menu and choose Resolve Duplicates, and it will automatically turn off the duplicate, leaving you free and clear to enjoy a single-font family life.

Font Book: KEEP A SHORT LIST OF FONTS

Back when fonts used to cost big bucks (I'm talking hundreds of bucks each), there were always people who were eager to let you know they now had 20 fonts on their computer. But now that there are thousands of fonts available for free, those of us who were font-deprived back in the day now have drives full of them. But be honest, just between you and me, how many of those fonts do you use regularly? Unless you're a PC user doing a Power-Point presentation, I would guess you use maybe four or five fonts to do 90% of what you do. I have 259 fonts on my Mac. This book

uses one font—Myriad. If I had written this tip in the first chapter, I would have wasted a lot less time scrolling through lists of fonts looking for Myriad. I might have even made my deadline! But thanks to Font Book's Auto Activation feature (which is enabled by default), I can turn off all the fonts I rarely use and let Font Book activate them for me if I open a document that asks for one of them. All you have to do is click All Fonts at the top of the Collection column, then start selecting fonts you want to deactivate in the Font column. When you're done selecting, click the button that's just below the list (circled here in red). Now when you're working in an application and need to select a font, you'll have a nice short list to look through.

   Font Book: CREATING YOUR OWN CUSTOM PREVIEW TEXT

By default, the Font Book preview text shows "ABCDEFGHIJKLMNO…," and although seeing your fonts previewed like this can be helpful, it pales in comparison to seeing the font previewed using your own text from the project you're working on. Here's how to make that happen: Go to the font you want, then press Command-3 (the shortcut for Custom Preview). Now you can type in your own text over the highlighted copy in the preview window. Even cooler: You can copy-and-paste text right from your project straight into the preview window. Nice!

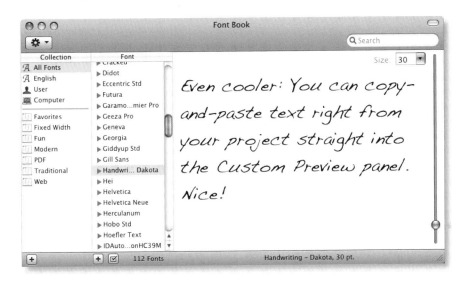

   Font Book: FONT FIELD SIZING TIP

If you want to see your font in various sizes, you could use the slider on the far-right side of the preview window, but it moves so quickly and so freely (it's not stopping at the common sizes used in page-layout applications) that you probably find yourself using the Size pop-up menu more. If you do, here's a tip on how to speed things up a bit: To choose your size quickly, just click in the Size field, then use the Up/Down Arrow keys on your keyboard to jump quickly to the size you want. Here's where it might throw you—unlike the slider, the font doesn't change size as you select sizes in the list, so what you have to do is highlight the size you want and press Return, or click on the desired size in the menu, and your font will resize to your chosen value.

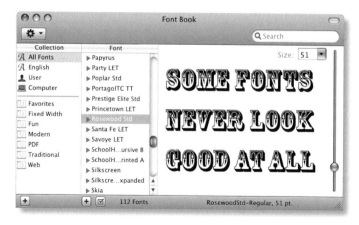

   Font Book: COMPARING FONTS SIDE BY SIDE

If you're trying to make a decision on which font to choose, and it's down to just a few choices, here's a great way to do some side-by-side comparisons. In the Font column, double-click on the first font you want to compare. This brings up a preview of the font in its own separate floating window. Then double-click on the next font, and its preview appears in another floating window, so you can position them side-by-side and see which you like better. You can open as many different font preview windows as you need to help you find just the right font. Also, once the floating preview window is open, you can choose different font weights and variations from the pop-up menu at the top of the window.

   Font Book: FIND ALL FONTS WITH THE STYLE YOU NEED

If you've ever been working on a project, and you know you need a bold font for the headline, but you're not exactly sure which bold font you should use, this tip is for you. Just type Bold into the search field in the top-right corner of the Font Book window. This instantly gives you a list of every font that has a bold variant, and once you click in the Font column, you can use the Up/Down Arrow keys on your keyboard to get a quick look at how each bold font looks.

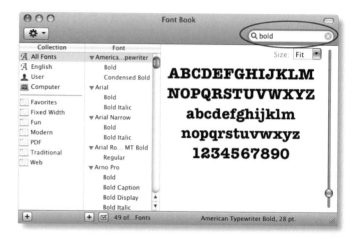

Of course, this isn't just for bold fonts, you could search for all italic fonts, or script fonts, or bold and italic…you get the idea.

   Font Book: EXPORT FONTS WITH A FILE

If you are collaborating on a project with someone or are sending some files to someone so they can do some work on them, you need to be sure they have all the fonts they need. It used to be a pain to collect a group of fonts because you had to hunt all over your drive to find where they were buried, then copy them to one location. But with Font Book, all you need to do is select the fonts you want to export (in Font Book, not by digging through your drive), go to the File menu, then choose Export Fonts.

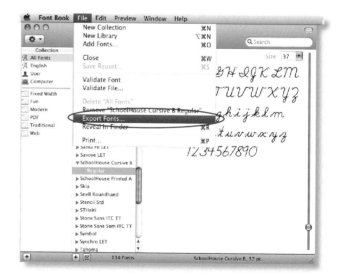

   iCal: CUSTOMIZING YOUR iCAL INVITE MESSAGE

If you're inviting people to a meeting using iChat, it sends them a pretty straightforward, business-sounding email invitation. However, if you'd prefer iCal's invitation to read something like "If you have any hopes of keeping your job, you'd better be at the 4:00 p.m. meeting today," you can do it pretty easily.

STEP ONE: Go into your Applications folder and Control-click the iCal application's icon. Choose Show Package Contents from the contextual menu that appears. This brings up a folder named Contents. Look inside that folder and you'll find another folder named Resources. Look inside this folder for a folder named English.lproj, then look inside that folder for a file named iTIP.string. Open this iTIP.strings in TextEdit.

STEP TWO: As you look through this file, you'll see a line that reads "/* Mail body when sending an invitation to an event (IP 56) */." Directly below this line, you'll see the default text that iCal uses when inviting someone to a meeting. This is the text you'll edit. However, iCal customizes part of this invitation with the recipient's name, the time you want your meeting, etc., so don't erase any characters that look like this: "%@". Leave those in place and work around them. For example, the default invitation reads "%@ has invited you to the iCal event: %@, scheduled for %@ at %@ (%@)." You could change that to "%@ is warning you to get your lazy butt into gear for my meeting about: %@, and if you have any hope of keeping your miserable job, you'd better be there at %@ in the %@." Now you can close the file, save changes, restart iCal, and scare the hell out of your employees.

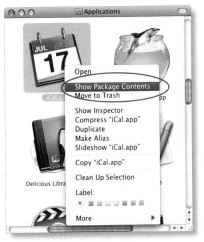 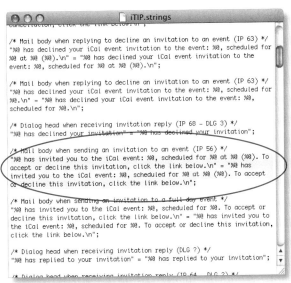

   iCal: BREAK THE ONE LINE PER EVENT RULE IN iCAL

When you're entering a new event in your calendar, you've probably already noticed that pressing the Return key to add a line break in the Info panel doesn't work—instead it just thinks you've finished typing and closes the field (that's because by default iCal doesn't allow multiple lines—go figure). But there's a little-known keyboard short-cut that lets you create a line break. Instead of pressing just Return, press Option-Return, and you get that so well-deserved line break. Seems like they could trust us with more than one line of information to begin with. So try to be responsible with this newfound power and maybe they'll reward us in the next version.

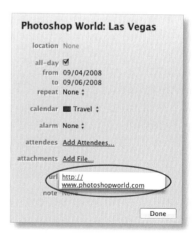

   iCal: ADDING A LIVE WEB LINK TO AN EVENT

If you're adding an event to your calendar, you can include a link with information about the event (map, registration info, hotel, etc.) so it's handy when you need it. When you create the event (or edit it later) just click None next to URL (near the bottom of the event window) and type in the Web address. To make it a live link, you have to have the full address (http://www.something.com). If you want the link to appear in the title of the event, instead of typing it in the URL field, type it in the Event Title field. One slight change is needed, however. You need to bracket the address, so it will look like this: <http://www.something.com>. This would be a perfect place to use the secret "multiple line" shortcut, by the way. You could put the name of the event on the first line and a link to it on the second line. How about that—a practical use for a tip!

   iCal: SETTING YOUR ALARM TO PLAY A SONG

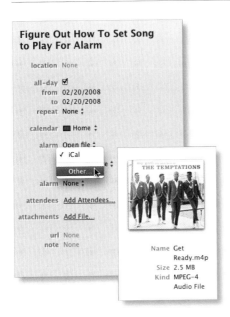

Why just have an annoying alert sound, such as your iCal alarm, when you can have it play your favorite song as your alarm? It's easy. All you have to do is double-click on the event you want to set an alarm for, click Edit, click on the current alarm setting next to the word Alarm (by default it's None), and then select Open File. You might assume that this would be a perfect time to open a window so you could choose the file you want to open—you know, to be consistent with how it works in every other application. But evidently, someone thought it would be fun to play the "Guess How To Figure Out How to Open the File You Said You Wanted to Open When You Clicked the Open File Option" game. If you look at the Alarm option in your Event window now, you'll notice that you now have three options from which to choose: Open File, iCal, and 15 Minutes Before (as an added bonus, there is also a second alarm available now). Of the three options, you can rule out the 15 Minutes Before option because that's obviously got nothing to do with opening a file. That leaves Open File and iCal. Hmmm. I'm going to take a wild guess and say that Open File would be the option to choose if I want to open a file. Oh man, those zany iCal developer kids really got me on this one. Boy, do I feel like an idiot! Isn't it obvious? To choose the music file for my alarm, I choose the iCal option. Wait a second, I clicked on it and I still don't see any way to navigate to my music folder and pick a song. I'm down to my last shot, so I click Other and whadda you know—I can go to my iTunes music folder, select the song I want to use, and then click the Select button. The next time this alarm goes off, I'll have The Temptations telling me to "Get Ready." Man, it doesn't get much easier than that!

   iCal: KEEPING RELATED CALENDARS TOGETHER

If you have a number of related calendars, you no longer have to sort through them all individually. (Let's say, for example, that you've subscribed to calendars for your NFL team and the
other teams in your conference. Hey, there are freaks out there who care about this stuff. Like
me.) Now you can group related calendars together, which makes keeping track of them easier
and more convenient. Just press-and-hold the Shift key, then click the plus sign (+) button in
the bottom-left corner of the iCal window (its icon will change into mini-calendars with a plus
sign), which creates a collapsible Calendar group. Now just drag-and-drop your NFL calendars (within the Calendars list on the left side of the iCal window) into this group. Then, click
the group's downward-facing arrow to collapse the group, removing the clutter and bringing
some sense and order into your otherwise chaotic list of calendars.

     iCal: AUTOMATICALLY CREATE A BIRTHDAY CALENDAR

If you've been including people's birthdays with their contact info in your Address Book, then you can use iCal to automatically create a calendar of their upcoming birthdays for you. Here's how: From iCal, press Command-, (comma) to open the iCal preferences and turn on the checkbox for Show Birthdays Calendar. This adds a special calendar to your list of calendars with all the birthdays you've dutifully entered in your Address Book. Now that they're on your iCal calendar (rather than buried in your Address Book), there's a better chance you'll remember to send them a lavish gift.

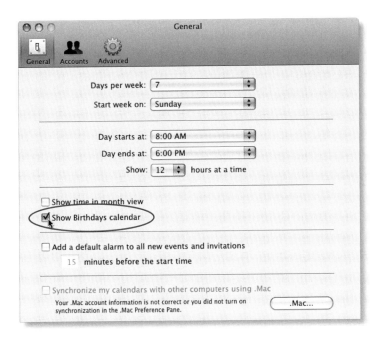

iCal: HAVING A MEETING? LET iCAL DO THE INVITES

If you're scheduling a meeting, you can have iCal send out an email invitation to the people you want to attend. First, create a new event for your meeting and click the Add Attendees link (if you want to add attendees to an existing event, just double-click on it in your calendar and click Edit). Now start to type a person's name or email address in the Attendees field. As soon as you start to type, a list of possible matches from your Address Book will open. If you see the person you want on the list, press Return and they're on the list. If you want to add additional people, type the next name and press Return again. Go crazy and add as many as you want. Invite enough people and your meeting might turn into a party! When you're done inviting, click the Send button and your emails are on their way. *Note:* This only works if you have each attendee's email address in your Address Book, so make sure you do first.

iCal: HAVE iCAL CALL YOUR CELL PHONE

If you're like me, you sometimes need "extra" reminders about things like appointments, birthdays, meetings, etc. If you do, you can have iCal send an email to your cell phone reminding you of that important meeting (provided, of course, that you have a cell phone that accepts email). The first thing you need to do is put your phone's email address in your Address Book (not in iCal—in the Address Book application), in the card that you have designated as "My Card." Then, go to iCal and double-click on a date to create a new event, and in iCal's Info panel, click None, which appears to the immediate right of Alarm. A pop-up menu of alarm notifications will appear. Choose Email. Then a new field will appear with a list of email addresses that you have in (guess where?) your Address Book application in your My Card contact (that's you).

Choose your cell phone's email address, choose how long before the appointment you want that email reminder sent, and you're good to go. As long as (a) your cell phone's turned on, (b) your Mac is still on, and (c) you have an Internet connection, it'll do it.

   KEEPING YOUR PRIVATE DATA PRIVATE

If you have sensitive information on your computer, you're probably most vulnerable to "peekers" when your computer is up and running (like at the office), or if you step away for a moment to grab a Starbucks Peppermint Mocha Frappuccino (or maybe you just go to the bathroom. Either way, for a few minutes it's "open season" for anyone with a curious mind). If that's a concern, you can keep those prying eyes away by going to the Apple menu, selecting System Preferences, and clicking on the Security icon. When the preference pane appears, click the General tab and turn on the Require Password to Wake This Computer from Sleep or Screen Saver checkbox. Of course, before you do this, make darn sure you know your password.

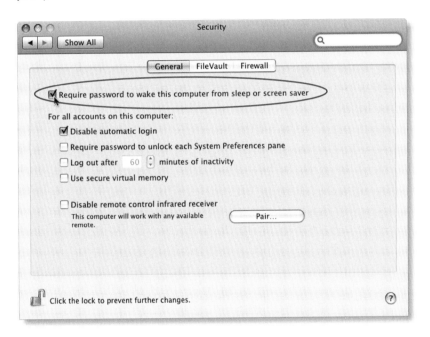

   SET A DEFAULT PRINTER

In previous versions of Mac OS X, your default printer was whichever printer you used last. This kinda stunk, because if you used the same printer every day, but changed to a different printer to print just one document, the next time you'd go to print, that's the printer you got. Well, now you can designate one printer to always be your default printer, and even if you switch to another printer temporarily, the next time you come back, your default printer will be right there waiting for you. To assign a printer as your default, go to the Apple menu and choose System Preferences. Click the Print & Fax icon, then choose the printer you want from the Default Printer pop-up menu near the bottom of the dialog (just be sure not to choose Last Printer Used). That's it!

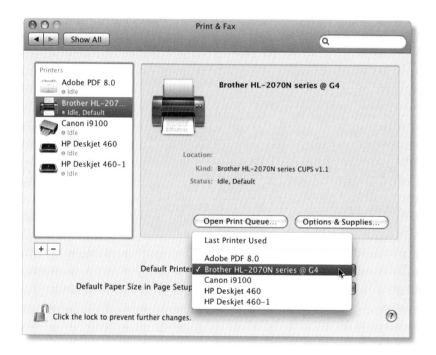

   MAKE YOUR MAC MONOLINGUAL

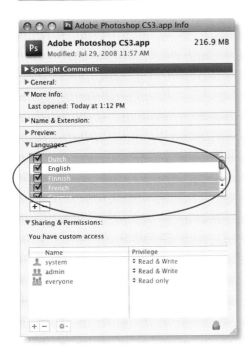

Applications install language resources so you can read menus in your native language (although it's fun to change a friend's preferences so menus show up in something like Chinese) but most also install additional language resources. If you speak 108 languages and want to use a different one every day, you'll need them all. If not, all those extra languages are just taking up space. A lot of space. Luckily, getting rid of them is easy—just click an application's icon and press Command-I to open the Info panel. You will see a number of sections (General, More Info, Name & Extension, etc.) within the Info panel. If this application has language resources installed, there will be a section named Languages. If it's not already expanded, click the right-facing triangle and you'll see all the languages installed for the application. Don't bother with the checkboxes, they just disable a language—we want to delete them. Click on any of the languages, press Command-A to select them all, and then Command-click on any language you want to keep. Now just go right below the box and click the minus sign (–) button and those extra languages will be moved to the Trash. For example, in just the default applications that install with Leopard, I just deleted over 30,000 files and reclaimed 486 MB of drive space. *Note:* You'll get a scary warning dialog asking if you're sure you want do this, so just be sure and click Continue.

THE BURN FOLDER ISN'T BURNING ALIASES

When you create a Burn folder in Leopard (which you do by either choosing New Burn Folder from the File menu or from the Action menu [that's the button with a gear icon in the toolbar of Finder windows]), if you look inside that folder, you won't see your original files. Instead, you'll see aliases to the originals (you can tell they're aliases because they have a little curved arrow on them). But don't let that throw you—when you do finally click the Burn button (in the upper right-hand corner of the Burn folder's window), it actually gets the original files and burns those to disc, so you don't have to worry about having a CD full of aliases pointing to files you no longer have. Why all
the aliases in the first place? Because it points to your files (rather than copying them into the folder), which makes burning discs much faster than in older versions of Mac OS X.

BURNING MULTIPLE TIMES TO THE SAME DISC

Generally, when you burn files to a CD once, you're done—you can't burn to that CD again. Unless you use this little trick: First create a new folder (it doesn't matter if it's a Burn folder or a regular folder) and give it a descriptive name (something like "Burn baby burn!" Kidding), then click-and-drag the files you want to burn into that folder. Now go to the Applications folder, open the Utilities folder, and launch Disk Utility. When it opens, go to the File menu, select New, and choose Disk Image from Folder. In the navigation window that opens, locate the folder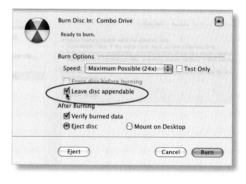
with the stuff you want to burn, select it, and then click the Image button. When the Save dialog opens, you can give the image a new name if you want, but don't change anything else. (If you started with a Burn folder, you'll be asked which extension to use. Just select Use .dmg.) In a few moments, a disk image of your folder's contents will appear in the list on the left side of the Disk Utility dialog. Click that icon, and then click the Burn button at the top left of the Disk Utility dialog. When you are prompted to insert a disc, do exactly as it says and no one will get hurt. Now click the blue downward-facing triangle on the right side of the dialog and turn on the Leave Disc Appendable checkbox. Now you can click the Burn button and your files will be burned to the disc. To add more files later, just insert that same disc and go through these same steps again (they're easier the second time around), except when you get to that final Burn dialog, the button won't say Burn—it will say Append. *Note:* Sadly, this only works with CDs, not DVDs.

   MAKING YOUR MAC VISIBLE ON A NETWORK

Networks used to be something you found only in big buildings where everyone dresses up and spends their days sitting in a cubicle slightly smaller than your average prison cell. Not anymore. My house, for example, has four people, five computers, five printers, one scanner, one VOIP phone, and three routers. Admittedly, I'm a bit of a geek, but home networks are very common these days. Leopard makes accessing other computers (Macs and the other kind) virtually automatic. The only thing you have to do to be visible on the network is to enable File Sharing. To do that, go to the Apple menu, select System Preferences, click the Sharing icon, and turn on the File Sharing checkbox in the column on the left. That's it—your computer will now be visible in the Shared section of the sidebar on any other Mac connected to your network. The next tip will show you how to grant or restrict access to your folders and files to network users.

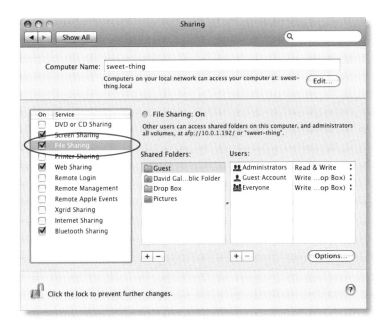

 WHAT TO SHARE AND WHO TO SHARE IT WITH

The previous tip showed you how to turn on File Sharing on your Mac so other people on your network can see you. Letting them see you on the network is one thing—letting them have access to everything on your drive is a whole different thing. People drive down my street every day and see my house, but I'm not stupid enough to put a sign in the front yard letting them know the door's not locked and inviting them to come on in and help themselves to whatever they want. The Sharing preference pane is where you decide who goes where and what they can do when they get there. There are only three things you need to decide: The first is what you want to share. Open your Sharing preferences and use the plus sign (+) and minus sign (–) buttons below the Shared Folders column to select the folders you want to share. Next, use the same buttons under the Users column to select the users you want share your folders with. Third, use the little up and down arrows next to a user's name to set how much access to your shared folders you want them to have. What about the Options button at the bottom right? Unless you have tape on your glasses and are wearing a pocket protector, don't touch it—trust me.

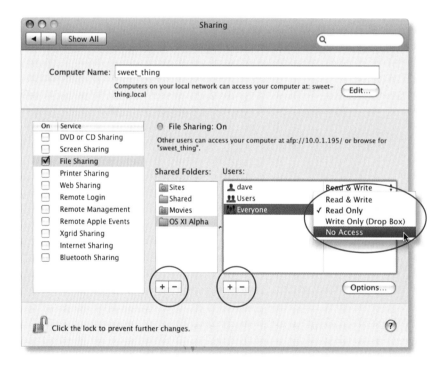

   TEMPORARILY SHARE A FOLDER

If you have a particular folder you want to share with some-one temporarily, click on the folder and press Command-I. If you look in the General section of the Info dialog, you'll see a new Shared Folder option. Turn on the checkbox (as shown here) and the folder and its contents are instantly shared. If you don't have File Sharing enabled in System Preferences, a "Hey, dummy" alert will appear to let you know that sharing the folder will work a whole lot better if you enable File Sharing in System Preferences. At least it's nice enough to include a button for you to click to open the Sharing preferences pane and rectify your embarrassing faux pas.

 JUST DROP IT IN MY SECRET DROP BOX

By default, whenever you connect to a network, you are automatically connected to every other computer on the network as a guest. As a guest, there is only one thing you can do—drop files in someone's Drop Box. If you look at your User folder (the one with the house icon), you will see a folder named Public. If there are files you want to share with anyone who happens to stop by, put them here. When other people are connected to your Mac as a guest, inside your Public folder they will see another folder named Drop Box. This is a place they can put a file they want you to have, but don't want anyone else to see. Here's the crazy thing (at least to me): I'm a guest and want to give you a file. I click your computer in the sidebar and see a folder named "Joe's Public Folder." This strikes me as odd because your name's Connie, but I go ahead and drop the file on the folder anyhow and am immediately confronted with a very rude message letting me know I'm not good enough to put a file in your Public folder. So I double-click the folder and see a "drop box." I drop the file on the Drop Box, and get another message reminding me that I'm a weak, powerless little person who doesn't have sufficient permission to see my own file once I put it in the Drop Box (as shown here). Here's my problem: First, I typically don't open folders to add files to them—I just drop them on the folder's icon. Second, if I see a folder on your computer named Public, I think it's reasonable to assume that I would be able to put a file in it. Third, why doesn't the message that lets me know I'm an idiot for thinking I would have access to your Public folder just tell me to open the folder, look for the Drop Box folder, and put the file in there? Better yet, why can't it just go ahead and put it in the Drop Box for me? It's like walking in the front door of the Pentagon to leave a file at the reception desk for a friend who works there, and being told I'm not allowed. But I'm welcome to go to the super-secret war room located deep underground and leave it for him there. It's a little thing, but it drives me crazy.

WHEN YOU LOVE SOMEONE, YOU'LL SHARE YOUR SCREEN

You'll let anyone see what's in your Public folder. You will let some people access your hard drive by setting up File Sharing. But letting someone actually see your screen and take control of your computer is something you will want to reserve for someone you're in a serious relationship with. It is actually a very handy thing to be able to do: You can use an application they have. You can watch their screen while you walk them through doing something they're not familiar with. They can watch their screen while you do something they know nothing about. You can troubleshoot a problem "in person" rather than trying to tell them what to do over the phone. Like I said—very handy. To set up Screen Sharing, go to the Apple menu, select System Preferences, and click on the Sharing icon. Turn on the Screen Sharing checkbox in the list on the left, then give access to all users (a potentially bad idea) or just certain users. If someone in your network has enabled screen sharing, their computer will appear in the sidebar of any Finder window on your desktop. To share their screen, click on their computer in the Shared section of the Finder's sidebar, then click the Share Screen button (it may look different from the example shown here, depending on which view you are using). Now just enter a username and password and their screen will open on your desktop. If you're not ready for a serious relationship, you don't have to share your screen in order to access someone else's—but you might consider getting counseling to find out why you're afraid to open your Mac to another.

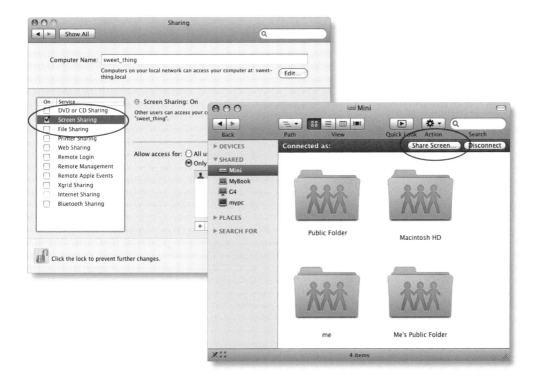

   Preview: CUSTOMIZE PREVIEW'S TOOLBAR

Like the Finder itself, Preview's toolbar is very customizable, and you can easily adjust it so that only the tools you want to see will appear on the toolbar. You do this by Control-clicking anywhere in Preview's toolbar (with a file open), and choosing Customize Toolbar from the contextual menu. A panel will slide down that has icons for various tools that you can drag right up to the toolbar and drop wherever you want them to appear. If there's a tool you don't want on the toolbar, just click-and-drag it off the toolbar. One thing that is different between Finder and Preview toolbars is that the tools available in Preview's toolbar depend on what type of file you have open. So when you customize the Preview toolbar, if you have a photo or graphics file of some sort open, the panel that opens when you Control-click the toolbar won't have any text editing icons available to drag. And if you have a text document open, you won't have any photo editing tools available. Try it and you'll see what I mean.

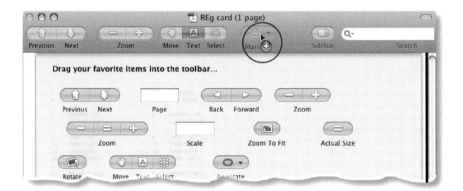

   Preview: ASSIGNING A COLOR PROFILE

Color management is big these days. You will never get a photo to look exactly the same on your camera's preview screen, computer display, and printer, but embedding a color profile in your image can help get as much consistency as possible. You can assign a profile to any open JPEG or TIFF image by going to the Tools menu, choosing Assign Profile, and then choosing one of the profiles from the pop-up menu. If your image already has a profile assigned, you can change it by choosing Match to Profile (instead of Assign Profile) from the Tools menu.

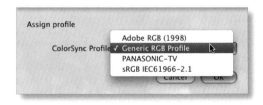

   Preview: ANNOTATE PDFS

Typically, when you need to mark up a PDF document with notes, highlighted text, etc., you use Adobe Acrobat Pro. But if you don't feel like dropping $400 to pick up a copy of Acrobat, and you just need to be able to do simple annotations, Preview can probably do it. If you don't have the annotating tools on your Preview toolbar (see tip on the previous page), you can access them from the Tools menu. While not having anywhere close to Acrobat's capabilities, you can still do things like add comments and notes, highlight text, create links, and draw ovals and rectangles to draw attention to certain features. All annotations are saved with the PDF so you can share them with others.

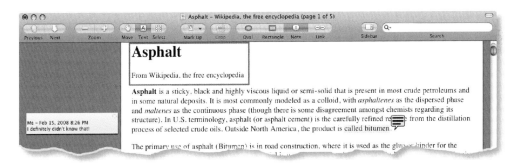

   Preview: FILLING OUT PDF FORMS

I've heard old-timers tell stories about how back in the late '70s and early '80s they had things called typewriters that were used to do things like produce documents and fill out forms. Well, I don't have one of these typewriters, so when I have to fill out a PDF form, I just have to use Preview. All I have to do is click in any form field and start typing. When I want to jump to the next form field, I just press the Tab key. When I've got everything filled in, I can print it like any other Preview document or email it to someone. It's easy, but it doesn't sound like it's as much fun as a typewriter would be. Maybe someday I'll be lucky enough to own one.

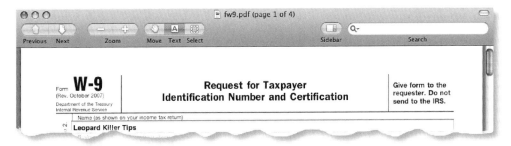

 Preview: PRINTING MULTIPLE IMAGES ON ONE SHEET

This is one sweet feature that's been added to Preview. You can print multiple images to a single piece of paper, or you can print multiple copies of the same image. Start by opening an image (JPEG, TIFF, PNG, etc.), and then click the Sidebar button in the top-right corner of the window. I probably don't need to point this out (but by now you should know that I rarely let reason or common sense stand in my way, so I'm going to go ahead and do what most people wouldn't), but open your image in Preview, or none of this will work. Now select the other files you want to include in your print, and drag them into the sidebar. Click anywhere within the sidebar and press Command-A to select all the images, then press Command-P to open the Print dialog. Finally, go to the bottom of the dialog and click the pop-up menu next to Images Per Page and select one of the options. If you prefer to print multiple copies of each image, all you need to do is turn on the checkbox next to Print X Copies Per Page. Once all your selections are made, but before you pass the printing point of no return, take a quick look at the preview of your pages to see how they look, then click Print.

DAVE GALES

   Preview: PRINT MULTIPLE DOCUMENTS TO ONE PAGE

The previous tip works great for image files, but for some reason it doesn't work with other types of files. (I would ask somebody why, but the answer would probably be unintelligible geek-speak to which I would respond with an occasional head nod, chin rub, and a few "Hmmm, interesting" interjections thrown in for dramatic effect.) Here's how you can cheat: If your document isn't already a PDF, most applications (Pages, TextEdit, Numbers, etc.) will allow you either to save or export a document as a PDF. Once you have your PDFs, simply open them in Preview, then do a "Save as" and select JPEG from the Format pop-up menu. Now you can follow the steps from the previous tip and end up with all the pages of your document printed on one page.

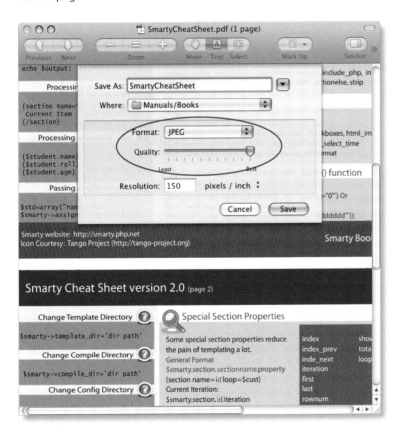

   Preview: DO SIMPLE PHOTO CORRECTIONS IN PREVIEW

I know, it sounds crazy, but Preview actually has some pretty decent image-editing controls (very much like iPhoto's new image-editing controls except, believe it or not, Preview lets you set custom White and Black Levels, whereas iPhoto doesn't). To unlock the photo-editing power of Preview, go to the Tools menu and choose Adjust Color. A floating palette will open with adjustment sliders for basic exposure and color corrections, plus sliders for White Level, Black Level, and Sharpness. Go ahead and play around with the sliders and see what they do—you can always get back to where you started by clicking the Reset All button at the bottom of the palette.

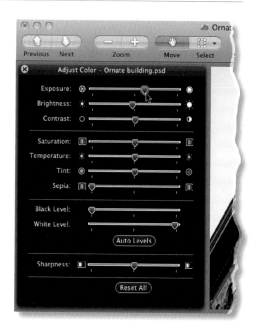

   Preview: SEEING A PHOTO'S EXIF DATA

When you take a photo with a digital camera, a boatload of background information is embedded into the file (called EXIF metadata), including when the photo was taken, the make and model of the digital camera, the exposure, shutter speed, lens focal length, whether the flash fired, and a host of other related info. Believe it or not, Preview can display all this EXIF metadata—you just have to know where to look. To see the EXIF data for the current image, just press Command-I, then click the More Info tab (the one in the middle), and then click the Exif tab. There you go—more information than you ever imagined you had.

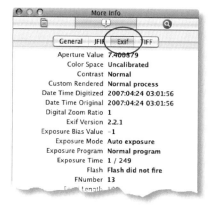

    Preview: REMOVE A PHOTO'S BACKGROUND

Believe it or not, Preview includes a couple of tools you can use to take out a background in a photo. Open the photo, and then select Instant Alpha from the Select button's pop-up menu (it's on the toolbar). Now click-and-drag in the area of the background you want to get rid of. If you accidentally select an area you don't want to remove, just press-and-hold the Option key, drag over the area, and the mask will be erased. When you like your selection, press Return. If you want to see your photo with the background removed, press Command-Option-B (or select Show Background Image from the View menu). You'll see a checkerboard pattern where the background has been removed.

DAVE GALES

   Preview: **BACKGROUND REMOVAL HINT**

Here's a tip to help you get more accurate extractions. If the color of the area you're trying to extract is similar to another color, it's going to be very difficult to select the entire area you need without having the selection spill over to other areas. Here's what you do: Don't try to make the selection in one drag—do a series of small ones. You can add to an existing selection by simply clicking-and-dragging another one. You can even adjust a selection after you've pressed Return to "lock in" your selection. Sometimes you may have to make a dozen small selections to prevent bleeding, but that's okay. Oh, and if you do drag too far and release the mouse button before you notice, just press Command-Z and try again.

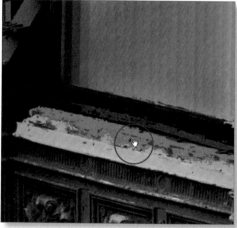

DAVE GALES

KILLER TIPS

  Preview: SEE YOUR DOCUMENT UP CLOSE AND PERSONAL

Preview has several options for zooming in and out of documents. A couple of them are on the default toolbar (Zoom In and Zoom Out). A couple more can be added to the toolbar (Actual Size and Zoom To Fit). But the one I use most often is Zoom To Selection. If you want to zoom in on a particular section of an image or document, just click your mouse button and drag a selection around the area you want to enlarge. When that's done, you can either go to the View menu and select Zoom To Selection or use the keyboard shortcut Command-* (asterisk) and your selected area will now fill the Preview window. Nice. Something else that's cool is once you're zoomed in on your selection, if you press-and-hold the Spacebar and click-and-drag your cursor, you can move your selection to other areas of your image to see them at the same level of magnification. Even nicer.

DAVE GALES

   Preview: **SORTING IMAGE THUMBNAILS IN PREVIEW**

Preview is a great application to use when you want to take a quick look at some photos or graphics files. When you open more than one image file in Preview, a thumbnail for each image will open in the sidebar. You can adjust the size of the thumbnails by using the slider at the bottom of the sidebar, and you can re-order them by simply clicking-and-dragging them into new positions. But if you click the Action button (it looks like a gear), which is just under the sidebar, and select Sort By, you will get a pop-up menu giving you the option to sort by name, size, keyword, and more. What's cool is that the details for the sort criteria you use are then displayed under the image's filename. For instance, if you sort by size, not only will the images be arranged from smallest to largest, but you can also see exactly what size they are. Sort by date and you see the date and time displayed. Doesn't sound like that big a deal, but it can be helpful.

  Preview: MAKE VERTICAL SELECTIONS IN PDFS

If you have a PDF file open, and you want to want to copy the text from that document into TextEdit so you can easily edit it, select Text Tool from the Tools menu, drag it over the text, press Command-C to copy it, then paste it (Command-V) into TextEdit. Not a real surprise there, but if you hold down the Option key while you drag over the text, you can make a vertical selection. This means that you can copy information from just one column in a table, for example, and paste it into a text file or spreadsheet without needing to edit out any extra text.

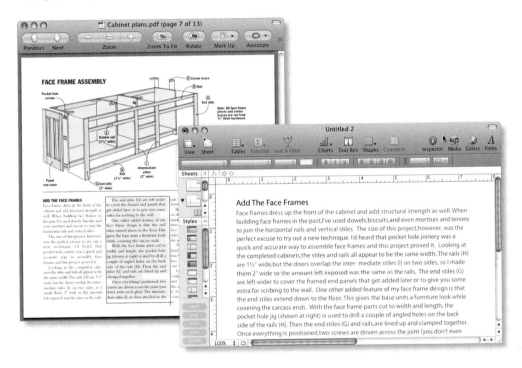

   Preview: TURN ANY SELECTION INTO A GRAPHIC

Here's another cool Preview feature that lets you select a section of a PDF document and insert it into other applications as a graphic. From the Tools menu, choose the Select Tool and drag it over the area of the document you want to use as a graphic, then press Command–C to copy it. Now go to the document where you want to use the graphic, and press Command–V to paste it in. Now you can move it around, resize it, and add effects like drop shadows, etc. If you're using Photoshop, your selection comes in on its own layer as a Vector Smart Object. This is a really handy way to make illustrations if you are producing proposals, reports, manuals, or other exciting and creative documents.

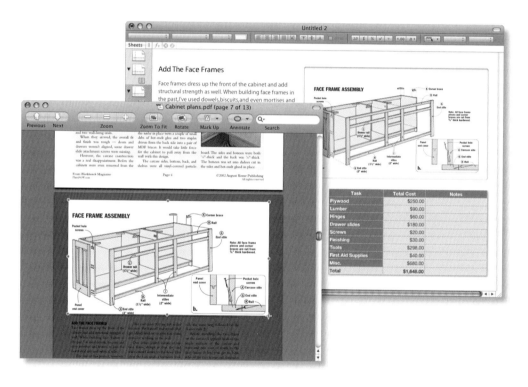

   Stickies: A CURE FOR A BAD MEMORY

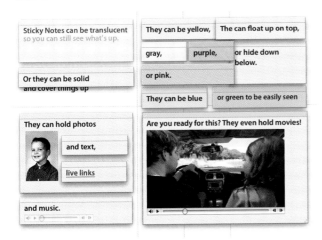

I forget things. I'm not talking just little things like taking out the garbage (though I do forget that), I'm talking appointments, deadlines, bank deposits, bill payments, trips—big stuff. Stickies don't do anything to improve my memory, but they have saved my neck on many occasions.

   Stickies: CREATE THEM FROM JUST ABOUT ANYTHING

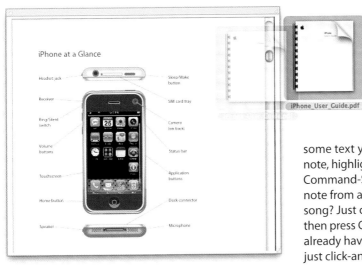

One thing that makes Stickies so useful is that they are so easy to make. If you're in a Finder window, just press Command-Shift-Y and start typing. If you are reading some text you want to put on a note, highlight the text, then press Command-Shift-Y. Want to create a note from a PDF, image, movie, or song? Just click on the file's icon, then press Command-Shift-Y. If you already have a note open, you can just click-and-drag files onto it. If your image or document is bigger than the Sticky, you can either click the bottom-right corner of the Sticky and drag it to make it bigger, or you can use the arrow keys, or the Page Up and Page Down keys, to navigate the content. If you use a PDF to create a Sticky, scroll bars will appear that you can use to move around the document.

⬤ ⬤ ⬤ **Stickies: ARRANGE YOUR STICKIES AUTOMATICALLY**

Stickies are so handy that they can end up scattered all over the screen. For some reason, you can't Shift-click, Command-click, or draw a selection around multiple Stickies to select them all at once. If you want to move them, you have to do it one at a time. But if you go under the Window menu and choose Arrange By, a submenu will open, giving you several options. The nice thing is that when they are arranged, they are all collapsed and aligned nicely. They still might not be where you want them to be, but it's a start.

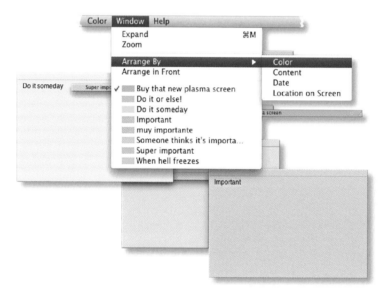

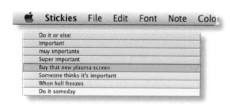

  TextEdit: FONT CONTROL CENTRAL

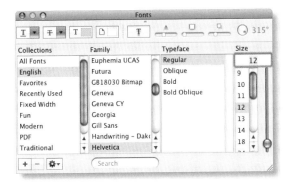

Press Command-T to open the Fonts panel and you'll see that TextEdit gives you surprisingly robust control over your font formatting. You can choose the font family, typeface style (bold, italic, etc.), and point size, and then you can see your choice in a large preview at the top of the Fonts panel (just choose Show Preview from the Action button's pop-up menu in the bottom left-hand corner of the panel). Just under the preview is a toolbar where you'll find everything from controls for colorizing your text to adding drop shadows.

   TextEdit: ADJUSTING THE SPACE BETWEEN LETTERS

Wacky (Normal)

Wacky (Kerned)

Kerning is the act of adjusting the space between letters. (When it's called kerning, that usually refers to adjusting the space between only two letters. If you're adjusting more than two letters at once, it's usually called tracking.) At standard text sizes like 10, 11, and 12 points, you don't normally worry about kerning, but when you start creating display-sized type (like 72-point type), sometimes wide gaps appear between letters. (The space between a 72-point capital "W" and the small letter "a," as shown here, is a perfect example.) To tighten the space between letters, highlight the two letters (or highlight an entire word if you want to tighten the whole thing), then go to the Format menu, select Font, select Kern, and choose Tighten. This is a very slight adjustment, so you'll probably have to run it more than once (okay, probably more than five or six times). Since it's a pain to go through all those menus, I went to the Keyboard & Mouse preferences and set keyboard shortcuts to tighten (Option-Right Arrow key) and loosen (same, but with the Left Arrow key) the kerning.

   TextEdit: HAVE TEXTEDIT DO THE WORK WHEN CREATING LISTS

If you're creating a list (with bullet points, numbers, etc.), you can have TextEdit do most of the work for you. Just enter the items in your list with a simple Return between each item. Then highlight the items you just typed, go to the Format menu, select Text, and then choose List from the submenu. Now, you simply choose which type of bullet you want from the Bullet/Number pop-up menu. I usually adjust the spacing as well. To do that, just highlight the entire list, then drag the Tab stops (the little triangles in the Ruler, as shown here) until you like what you see.

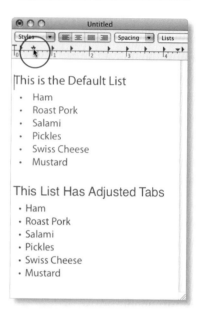

   TextEdit: POP-UP SPELL CHECKER

TextEdit makes use of the same spell-checking features as most of the other applications in Leopard. If you want to check the spelling in your TextEdit document, save yourself a trip to the menu bar. Simply Control-click the word in question. When the contextual menu opens, if your suspicions are confirmed and the word is indeed misspelled, the correct spelling (or Spell Checker's best guess at what word you might be trying to spell) will be at the top of the list of menu options. Scroll up the list to highlight it, then click to have it replace your original attempt.

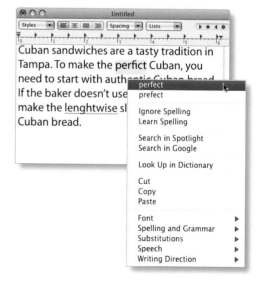

    TextEdit: SAVING FILES AS WORD DOCUMENTS

If you love TextEdit, but routinely send text files to people on other platforms who don't have TextEdit, but surely have Microsoft Word, you can make things easy for them by saving your TextEdit files in Word format so they can easily read them. Here's how: When you go to save your file in the Save As dialog, the default file format is Rich Text Format (RTF), but if you click the File Format pop-up menu, you'll see that you can also save the file in Word format. Choose one of the Word formats, and your worries are over. (Well, you'll still have worries, just not about how other people will open your text files.)

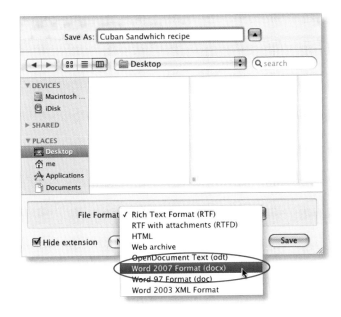

Chapter 10

COOL & THE GANG

WAY COOL TIPS

I know, I know, it's supposed to be "Kool
& the Gang" (with a "K") not "Cool & the
Gang" with a "C." Okay, Mr./Ms. Smarty-Pants—

Cool & the Gang
way cool tips

you know so much about the band, which
one is Kool? The lead singer? Wrong! That's JT.
Kool is actually the bass player—the guy who
originally formed the band. Okay, now what was
their first million-selling single? "Ladies Night"?
"Celebration"? "Too Hot"? "Fresh"? Nice try. It
was "Jungle Boogie." Geez, I don't know where
you got all this attitude, because apparently
aside from spelling their name, you really don't
know that much about the band. Now, what
does all this have to do with Mac OS X? Plenty.
Anyway, here's a "celebration" of tips that were
"too hot" to be contained in any other chapters.
(I know—they're lame puns, I don't care—I'm
using 'em.)

 WHEN YOU'RE NOT QUITE SURE HOW IT'S SPELLED

This is a very cool feature when you're typing and you're not exactly sure what word you're looking for or how it's spelled. It's not really a spell checker and it's not a thesaurus—it's more like the predictive text you use for text messaging on your cell phone. So if you type in as much of the word as you know, then press either F5 or Esc, a list of words that begin with those letters will pop up. If you see the word you want, click on it and it will be inserted automatically. If it's not there, press F5 (or Esc) again and you're back where you started. For example, despite the fact that I have been a photographer for more years than many of you reading this book have been alive (not to mention the fact that I was usually the spelling bee winner every Friday in my third grade class), I have some sort of mental block remembering if that thing I use to take pictures ends in "ara" or "era." Luckily, I'm sure of the first three letters, so when I type in "cam" and press either F5 or Esc, right there on the list of words that start with "cam" is camera. Perfect. I love anything that makes me look smarter than I really am. *Note:* This really sweet feature doesn't work in Microsoft Word. Yet another reason to get iWork and use Pages!

LEFT-HANDERS FINALLY GET A BREAK!

I've often secretly wished I were left-handed because it just seemed so cool. Well, I have a left-handed son and you know what? It would be a lot cooler to be left-handed if it weren't such a right-handed world. Simple things like scissors, spiral notebooks, and two-button mice are not left-handed friendly. But if you're a Mac user who uses a two-button mouse, this tip will make your computing life a bit easier. Go to the Apple menu, select System Preferences, then click on the Keyboard & Mouse icon. Now click the Mouse tab and select whichever one of your mouse buttons is the regular click (the Primary Mouse Button) and which is Right-click, which will now be a Left-click (yippie!).

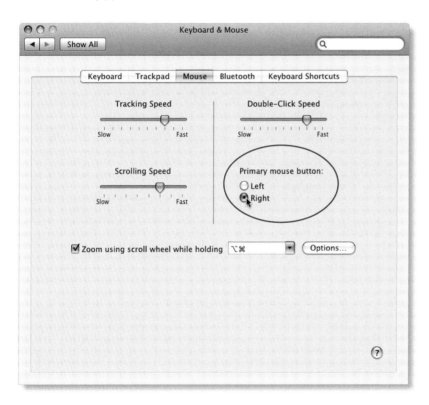

   CALCULATOR'S BEEN HIDING ITS POWER

I can't really blame people for thinking the calculator included with Mac OS X is lame because, to be honest, it looks lame. But under its rather plain exterior is a calculator Stephen Hawking might use (if he ever needed to use a calculator, of course). To put this baby into action, go to the Applications folder and open Calculator. Now go to the View menu and select Scientific. See what I'm talking about? Heck, I bet you don't even know what all the keys do! I know, of course, and would love to explain their functions to you, but my editor says that's got nothing to do with this book. I want to, really, but my hands are tied. So, the next time you hear someone trashing the calculator, you can feel all smug and snooty while you chuckle quietly at their naiveté.

 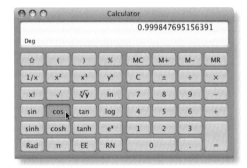

   HAVE A CONVERSION EXPERIENCE WITH CALCULATOR

Besides doing all sorts of calculations most of us don't understand and will never use, Calculator does one thing that's really useful— conversions. It does your basic, everyday conversions like acres to hectares, calories to joules or ergs, and kilowatts to horsepower. It even does some less common ones like miles to kilometers, Fahrenheit to Celsius, U.S. dollars to British pounds (or Hungarian forints). Just open Calculator and enter a number. Now go to the Convert menu, select the type of conversion you want to perform, and then use the pop-up menus that open to choose the specifics. In the example shown here, I converted days to minutes to see how many minutes a year I waste playing with the cool Leopard features. Wow! Good thing it wasn't a leap year.

  TAKE A SCREEN CAPTURE OF YOUR SCREEN

Leopard includes a screen capture utility called Grab (it's in the Utilities folder, inside the Applications folder) that does a good job of taking screen caps (as they're known in "the biz"). But if you just need a quick capture, there are some keyboard shortcuts you can use so you don't need to open Grab. If you want to capture the whole screen, just press Command-Shift-3. You'll hear a sound effect of a camera's motor drive (this is about the only place you hear one of those babies anymore) and your capture will be saved to the desktop. If you don't need to capture the entire screen, press Command-Shift-4, then click-and-drag the crosshair to select the area you want to capture (anything in the dimmed-out area will be captured) and then release the mouse button.

 TAKE A SCREEN CAPTURE OF ONE WINDOW

The previous tip showed how to take a quick screen capture of your screen or a portion of your screen. Let's say you want to get a capture of a Finder window or a dialog. You could use the Command-Shift-4 shortcut to drag out a selection, but here's a much easier way. After you've pressed Command-Shift-4, instead of dragging out a selection area, press the Spacebar. The crosshair cursor changes to a large camera, and as you move it around, every object it touches gets highlighted. When the object you want to capture is highlighted, just click your mouse. Want to know something freaky? Here it is: If the cursor touches any portion of an object, it will highlight it. So if you want to get a capture of something that's behind something else, if the camera cursor can even touch just a small corner of it, you can capture it. I mean capture the whole thing, not just the tiny corner you can see. Told you it was freaky.

DAVE GALES

  CREATE A PDF FROM A SCREEN CAP WITH ONE CLICK

Okay, the previous tips have shown you how to take a screen cap that is saved automatically as a graphic file (a PNG to be exact) on the desktop. But there are lots of times you need a PDF that you can easily share with other people. You can always open the PNG file with Preview and save it as a PDF, but there's a faster way. If you take a capture using Command-Control-Shift-3 (captures the entire screen) and Command-Control-Shift-4 (captures a selected part of the screen), instead of creating a file on your desktop, the capture will be put into your Clipboard memory. So what about the PDF-with-one-click thing? After you take the capture, launch Preview and press Command-N to create a new file. There it is—your screen capture. Preview created the new file directly from the contents of your Clipboard (in this case, it was your screen capture, but it will do the same thing with any file you have copied to your Clipboard). All you need to do now is press Command-S and select PDF from the Format menu in the Save As dialog. That is absolutely the fastest way I know to create a PDF of a file.

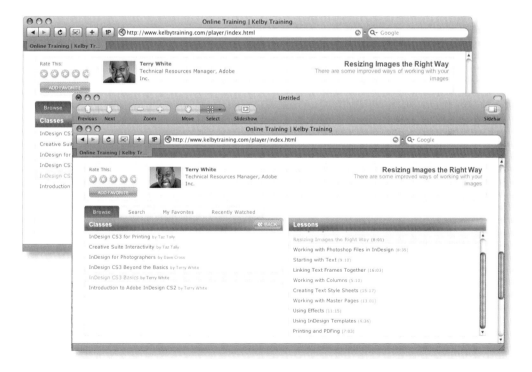

   CREATE A PDF OF ANY DOCUMENT

Remember back in the day when you wanted to give someone a file to look over, they had to have a copy of whatever application the file was created in? It was crazy. Then Adobe came up with a file format that could be read with a free reader they made available and, even better, the same file could be read by either a Mac or a PC. There was just one catch: the reader was free, but the application needed to convert documents to PDFs wasn't—not by a long shot. Fortunately, that's changed and now you can create a PDF from virtually any type of file for free. Open the document you want to convert to PDF, and press Command-P to open the Print dialog. When it opens, go to the bottom-left corner, click the PDF button and select Save as PDF. Give your file a name in the dialog that opens, press Return, and you now have a PDF you can share with anyone.

  ADD WEB PHOTOS TO YOUR iPHOTO LIBRARY WITH ONE CLICK

If you're on the Web and you see a photo you'd like, with just one click you can add it to your iPhoto Library—just Control-click directly on the photo, and choose Add Image to iPhoto Library from the contextual menu.

DAVE GALES

   USE QUICK LOOK TO PREVIEW AUDIO CLIPS

This is especially handy if you are looking for a sound effect to use for some project and don't feel like opening several hundred clips—one at a time—in iTunes to find the one you're looking for. Go to the folder containing the files you want to listen to and Shift-click to select a chunk of them. Now press the Spacebar, then press the Play button, and Quick Look will treat you to a little sound effects concert. When you hear one you think you might want to use, pause the slide show (I know it doesn't seem like a slide show, but that's what it actually is), make note of the filename so you can open it later, then resume your concert. (By the way, you can also preview video files. Just click on the video file, then press the Spacebar. The video, complete with audio, will start playing.)

   USE AN RSS FEED AS YOUR SCREEN SAVER

If you're a news junkie, you can set your screen saver to display RSS news feeds. Here's how:
Go to the Apple menu, select System Preferences, and click on the Desktop & Screen Saver
icon. When the preference pane opens, click the Screen Saver tab, click the triangle next to
Apple under Screen Savers on the left, and then click on RSS Visualizer. Unless you sit in front of
your screen all day eagerly awaiting morsels of information from Cupertino (Apple Hot News),
click the Options button and select the RSS feed you'd like to use. If you're a news junkie, enter
the address of your favorite news feed. Now every time your screen saver kicks in, you'll get
a continuously updated stream of information for you to absorb, thus ensuring that you never
have a moment of uninterrupted tranquility in your life.

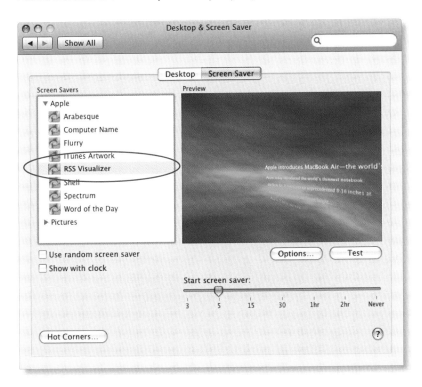

 THE COOLEST SCREEN SAVER EVER

If you choose a folder containing pictures to use as your screen saver, you have a choice of three ways to display them. The first one, "Pictures inhaling and exhaling," is the one you're used to from previous versions of Mac OS X. There are two new effects in Leopard: the "snap-shots being thrown on the table" effect and the "big pictures shrinking and hooking up with other shrinking pictures" effect. I think the real names are something like Slideshow, Collage, and Mosaic, but I prefer something a bit more descriptive. To use them, go to the Apple menu, select System Preferences, and click on the Desktop & Screen Saver icon. Now click the Screen Saver tab and select any folder in the Pictures category from the list on the left. To choose the Display Style for the images, click one of the three buttons directly under the Preview window. The last of the three is the one you want to click if you want to see the coolest screen saver ever. I can't really describe it to you, and I sure as heck can't begin to explain how it works. But I'm telling you, I could easily waste hours watching it if I weren't the focused, disciplined, "unable to be distracted by the least little thing" person I am.

  iTUNES ARTWORK SCREEN SAVER

This one I love, and a lot of people (even cool people like yourself) don't know about it. This particular screen saver looks through your album artwork in iTunes and creates a tiled wall of album covers. One by one these tiles flip to reveal other albums. You set it up by going to the Apple menu, selecting System Preferences, and clicking on the Desktop & Screen Saver icon. Now click the Screen Saver tab (if it's not already selected), go to the list of Screen Savers, and choose iTunes Artwork (if you don't see a list, click the little right-facing triangle next to Apple and the list will open). Click the Test button and you'll see what it's going to look like when it runs. If you want to make the album covers bigger or smaller, click the Options button and change the number of rows that will be displayed. If you haven't tried this one yet, give it a shot.

   ONE MORE SCREEN SAVER TIP

There are some other files hidden away in your System folder that can be used as screen savers. Messing with stuff in the System folder isn't usually a good idea if you don't know what you're doing. Don't worry, I will guide you on this brief foray into nerd territory. Stick with me and you'll be fine. First, you need to get the files. Make sure you're in Finder, then press Command-Shift-G and type in the following path exactly as it appears here (but leave off the quotes): "/System/Library/Compositions". Next, press Command-N to open another Finder window. Click on your home folder in the User folder, select Library, and then choose Screen Savers (if there isn't a folder by that name in your Library, go ahead and make one). Now, click back on the Compositions folder, select all the files in it, and Option-drag them into the Screen Savers folder (this makes copies, leaving the originals intact and in place). You can close the Finder windows now, and open the System Preferences and click on the Desktop & Screen Saver icon. When the pane opens, click the Screen Saver tab at the top, then click Other from the Screen Savers list on the left. Now you can just start browsing through the list to see what they do. Not all of them will work (you can go back to the Screen Savers folder in your Library and delete them if you want), and the ones that do work will need some tweaking. If you click the Options button under the Preview window, you will be able to change colors (most of them have lovely shades of gray as the default) and add an image or images to make the effect more dramatic. So some day when you are looking for something to do, have some fun and play around with these now "unhidden" screen savers.

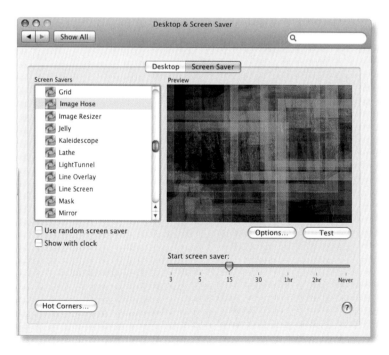

   PHONE NUMBER WIDGET TRICK

Dashboard is one of those things you use multiple times every day. For one thing, you can access it instantly from anywhere on your Mac by simply pressing the Dashboard or F12 key. Another reason it's so useful is the huge number of widgets available. Here's a trick to try the next time you use the Address Book widget. Pull up someone's contact info using the Address Book widget, click on his or her phone number and it will appear in *huge* numbers across your screen (as shown here). This also works in the regular Address Book, but for some reason it seems cooler using it in Dashboard.

813.POUTINE

  GOOGLE MAPS WIDGET TRICK

This one is a variation of the phone number trick. Once you've pulled up the contact information (see previous tip), instead of clicking on the phone number, click on the address. Safari (or whatever your default browser is) will launch, go to Google Maps, and open a map for the address. That is over-the-top coolness!

USE THE SAME WIDGET MORE THAN ONCE

Sometimes it's handy to have multiple copies of the same widget open. For example, I keep several Weather widgets open to keep tabs on the weather in the cities I'll be traveling to in the next couple of weeks. I'm a Florida boy and am your basic wimp when it comes to cold weather. So if it's going to dip below 70°, I want to know so I can get mentally prepared to freeze. To open multiple copies of a widget, press the Dashboard or F12 key to open Dashboard, then click the Open (+) button in the lower-left corner of the screen to open the Widget Bar. Click the widget you want as many times as you want. Now just drag out all those copies (they're all on top of each other) until you've cleared out the stack. Customize each one as needed, and you're good to go.

USE PREVIEW TO CONVERT IMAGE FILE FORMATS

If you need to convert an image from one format to another, Preview does a beautiful job. Say you have a photo that's saved as a TIFF (Tagged Image File Format, in case you've ever wondered) that you want to upload to a website. But the site requires you to send it as a JPEG (Joint Photographic Experts Group) file. Not a problem, just open the TIFF file in Preview, go to the File menu, and choose Save As. When the dialog opens, click the Format pop-up menu to select the format you want to save the image in. As you can see from the example here, you have a lot to choose from.

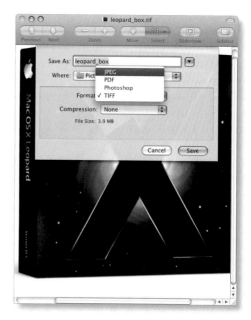

  CHECK YOUR EMAIL FROM ANY FINDER WINDOW

This tip is going to show you how to create a Smart Folder that will let you check for new emails from any Finder window. It takes a few steps to set up, but trust me, it'll be worth it. Plus, you'll move up a bit on the Nerd Scale upon successful completion of this exercise.

STEP ONE: Press Command-Option-Spacebar to open Spotlight and click the plus sign (+) at the far right-hand side of the window to add another search criterion.

STEP TWO: In the new search criteria bar, click the Kind pop-up menu, select Other, and scroll through the list of options until you see Spotlight Items. Select it, then click OK.

STEP THREE: Click the plus sign again to add another search criterion. This time, click on the Any pop-up menu, scroll to the bottom of the list of options and select Other, and then type "mail" (no quotes) in the text field that appears to the right. Since Spotlight updates on the fly, you'll see all your email messages in the results box. But you don't want all of them, so you need to add one more search criterion.

STEP FOUR: Click the plus sign again, click the Kind pop-up menu, and select Created Date. Since you want to see new emails, choose Today from the second pop-up menu. Now press the Save button, give your Smart Folder a name, and make sure Add to Sidebar is checked.

Pheeww, you're done. Your new Smart Folder will be in the sidebar of every Finder window from now on. So whenever you want to see what new emails have come in, just click on it. Congratulations on your Nerd Scale promotion. Put an extra layer of tape on your glasses—you deserve it.

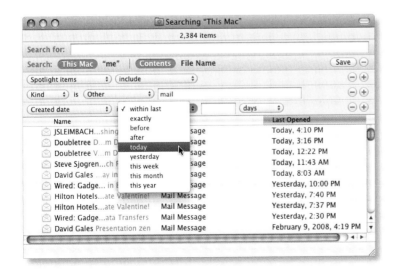

   PREVIEW YOUR NEW EMAILS WITH QUICK LOOK

But wait, there's more! If you set up a Smart Folder to automatically search for new email (see previous tip), when the list of emails is displayed in the search results window, click on any one of them and press the Spacebar. Quick Look will open a preview of the email, allowing you to read it without switching to Mail. Now use the Up and Down Arrow keys to preview other emails in the list. Sweet, huh? Gotta love it.

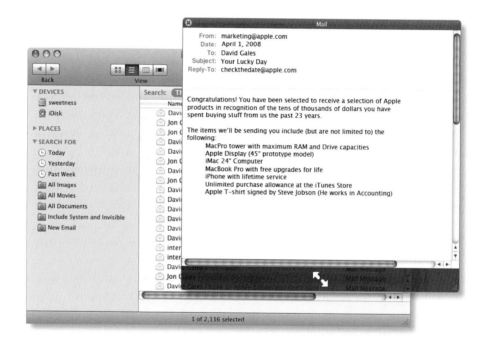

     SET UP A GUEST ACCOUNT FOR "THE OTHERS"

This feature will come in really handy if your plane ever crashes on a weird island populated with some spooky people. Sometimes you want to let other people do something on your Mac: check email, visit questionable websites, shop, or whatever. You're happy to let them use it for a few minutes, but you really don't want them to have access to your stuff. It's not that you don't trust them; it's just that you don't want them accidentally messing something up (or leaving something inappropriate on your desktop. Prevent the embarrassment and set up a guest account for others to use that will give them limited access to your Mac. Go to the Apple menu, select System Preferences, and then click on the Accounts icon. By default, the Guest account is already set up, but only allows guests to connect to shared folders. To give them a little more room to roam, turn on the checkbox next to Allow Guests to Log Into This Computer. Parental Controls will also be enabled automatically. If you feel lucky, go ahead and disable them. If you have common sense, open Parental Controls and set up any restrictions you want. All a guest has to do now is click on Guest from the login screen. They'll get a blank desktop, default Dock, and no access to your vital information. Here's another reason to use a Guest account—when they log out, everything they have done will be erased, including emails, browsing history, cookies, etc. That's good for them as well, because they don't really want to leave their private information on your Mac.

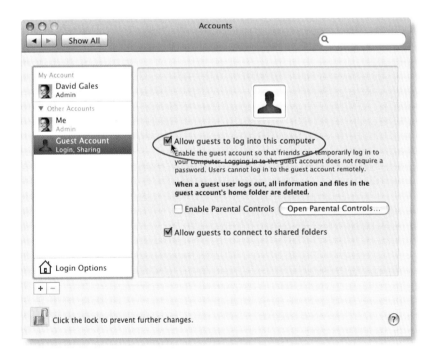

   COMBINE SEPARATE DOCUMENTS INTO ONE PDF DOCUMENT

Preview gives you the ability to combine multiple TIFFs, JPGs, or other supported files to create a single PDF document. Locate one of the files you want to use, click on it to select it, and then press Command-C to copy it. Now, switch to Preview and press Command-N to create a new document with the copy you just loaded into your Clipboard. Before you add your other images, you need to save the new document as a PDF. From the File menu, choose Save (or, better yet, just press Command–S). The important thing is to make sure you choose PDF from the Format pop-up menu in the Save dialog or this won't work. So now you have a PDF document containing one image—time to add some more. First, open Preview's sidebar by pressing Command-Shift-D. Next, locate the images you want to add to this document and simply drag them into the sidebar and drop them wherever you want. You can always drag them to new positions later. Finally, press Commmand–S again to save your document and you're done.

   WAS IT KAL-IB-RA OR KAL-EEB-BRA?

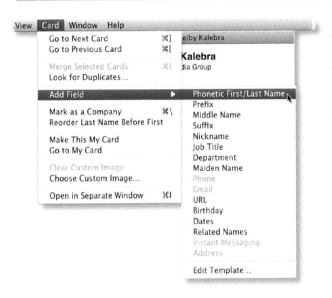

If you enter a new contact and you're concerned that when you call them again, perhaps months from now, you won't remember how their name is pronounced, Address Book can help. Just go to the Card menu, select Add Field, and then choose Phonetic First/Last Name. This adds a field right above your contact's name where you can enter the phonetic spelling of their name, so when you do call them back, you sound like a 'jēn'yəs (genius)— or at least someone with a good memory.

   FINE TUNE YOUR VOLUME

If you want to adjust your Mac's speaker volume from the keyboard, you can just press the Volume Up and Volume Down or F4 and F5 keys. Each time you press one of the keys, the volume goes down or up one step of the 16-step scale. If you want to make more subtle adjustments, press-and-hold Option-Shift while you press the F4 and F5 keys. Now one press of the keys will increase or decrease the volume by one-quarter of a step on the scale. In other words, you now have 64 increments instead of 16. *Note:* If you're using a laptop and have selected the standard function key option in the Keyboard & Mouse preferences, you will have to press-and-hold the fn key (the one in the bottom-left corner) along with the Option and Shift keys for this to work.

Chapter 11

SPEED
THRILLS

Mac OS X
Speed Tips

If I could show you some Mac OS X speed tips that would make you more productive at Mac OS X than you ever dreamed

Speed Thrills
mac os x speed tips

possible, how much would you be willing to pay? 50 bucks? 75 bucks? 100 bucks? Easily. So basically, by paying a list price of about 35 bucks for this book, I figure you're ahead by at least $15 (if you said 50 bucks) and possibly as much as $65 (if you said 100 bucks). Well, if you think about it, only this particular chapter is on speed tips, so in reality, you were willing to pay between $50 and $100 for just the tips in this chapter, so technically, you should've paid extra for the other chapters. Now granted, they won't all make you faster, so I'm willing to give you a discount—$10 a chapter—so add 10 bucks for each chapter. Now, if you ordered this book from Amazon.com, and got 30% off the list price, you're just flat-out taking advantage of the situation, and I expect you to feel a level of guilt that is commensurate with the value actually received.

   ESSENTIAL KEYBOARD SHORTCUTS

1. **COMMAND-C, COMMAND-X, COMMAND-V**
Command-C will copy any text you have selected to the Clipboard. Command-X will delete the selected text and copy it to the Clipboard. Command-V will insert the contents of the Clipboard at the point where the cursor is positioned. I know, that's three shortcuts, but they're right in a row on the keyboard and work together, so I consider them a "shortcut family." (Plus, it's a legitimate way I can slip in a couple extra shortcuts.)

2. **COMMAND-N, COMMAND-SHIFT-N**
These are two shortcuts you will use every day. Command-N opens a new Finder window. When you're dragging files from one folder to another, sometimes it is easier if you open two or three Finder windows. Command-Shift-N will create a new blank folder in the current window.

3. **SHIFT-CLICK, COMMAND-CLICK**
Shift-click on two items in a folder and all adjacent items between them will be selected. If you want to select multiple items that are not contiguous, Command-click on each of the items.

4. **COMMAND-DELETE**
Command-Delete moves any items you have selected in the Finder to the Trash.

5. **COMMAND-S, COMMAND-SHIFT-S**
To save a file and keep the same filename, use Command-S. If you want to save a copy of a file, use Command-Shift-S and you will get a chance to give it a new name and/or location.

6. **SPACEBAR**
In the Finder, select a file you want to preview, press the Spacebar, and Quick Look will show you a nice big, beautiful preview. I use this all the time to see a file without needing to open its application, look at emails without opening them, and preview short sections of video or audio files.

7. **COMMAND-SPACEBAR, COMMAND-OPTION-SPACEBAR**
To find something fast, press the Spacebar to open the Spotlight search field. To find all instances of something or to do more complex searches, use Command-Option-Spacebar to open the Spotlight window.

8. **COMMAND-W**
Closes the active window. In the course of a day, I would guess I open and close a couple hundred windows. That means there would be a whole lotta clickin' going on if I didn't use this shortcut.

9. **COMMAND-A**
In Finder windows, this shortcut selects every item in a folder. In most applications, it will select everything in the document.

10. **COMMAND-P**
The universal command for Print.

   LOOKING FOR HELP?

In most applications, just press Shift–Command–? (question mark) to open that application's Help resources. As soon as you start to type in the search box, you'll see a list of possible matches. Select the one you want and a menu will open with a giant blue arrow pointing to the menu item you need. A little life preserver in front of one of the items in the results list means that it's an explanation, not a menu item. Click on it and you can read all the details. With any luck, you'll find an answer.

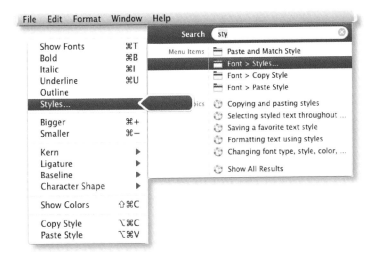

   ORGANIZE (OR DISORGANIZE) YOUR ICONS FAST

If you have a folder set to Icon view, and if you have set the Arrange By pop-up menu in View Options (Command–J) to Snap to Grid, then you will always have neatly arranged icons. But if you're sitting around one day and decide it's time to get a little crazy, press-and-hold the Command key while you click-and-drag an icon (or group of icons) and they will ignore the Snap to Grid setting. It works the opposite way as well. If you're a free spirit—unfettered by the constraints of organization (in other words, a slob)—and have set your View Options to None, then if you press-and-hold the Command key and click-and-drag an icon or icons, they will line up on the invisible grid and make you look like a neat freak—at least temporarily.

   QUICK WAY TO ADD WORDS TO YOUR DICTIONARY

If you're typing a message in almost any application and run across a word that should be in your Spell Checker's dictionary (such as your name, your company's name, etc.), you can quickly add it so it won't get flagged as misspelled in the future. Here's how: When you come to a word you want added to your dictionary (such as the name "Kelby"), Control-click on it and choose Learn Spelling from the contextual menu. Now it's added, and it will no longer be flagged as unrecognized (unless you really do misspell it).

   YOU CAN GO EVERYWHERE FROM ANYWHERE

If you're in a Finder window and want to trace your path backwards, you can use Command-Left Bracket key ([ ). But if you want to go back further than that, it will be faster (it's all about speed, right?) to Control-click the window's title (at the very top of the window). The complete path from the current file all the way back to your Mac's root level will be displayed, and you can instantly go back as far as you like by simply scrolling down to the location you want and clicking. But here's the best part: This works in application windows as well as Finder windows. So no matter where you are, you can get wherever you want to go with two clicks. That's fast.

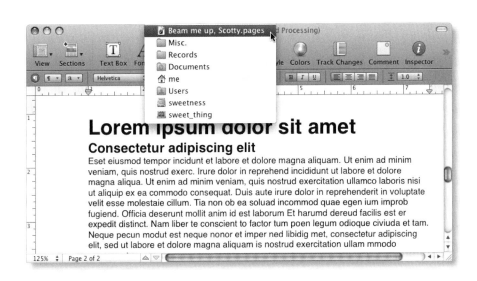

   DROP TEXT ON DOCK ICONS FOR FAST ACTION

Here are a couple of tips that can save you a bunch of time. Let's say you find a picture or some text in a document, and you want to email it to a friend. Don't do the copy-and-paste thing. Instead, just click-and-drag your cursor over the text to select it (or just click on a photo or a graphic) and drag-and-drop it right on the Mail icon in the Dock. Mail will open and put the text or graphic into a new mail message. And here's another drag-and-drop trick: If you run across something in a document, and you want to get more information about it, select a key word or phrase from the text and drag-and-drop it onto the Safari icon in the Dock. Safari will open, go to Google, run a search on the text you selected, and display your results. Sweet! Unfortunately, these tips don't work with all applications, but they work with many of them. Very useful.

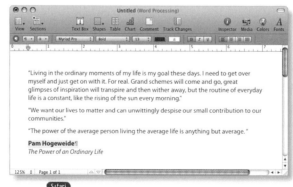

    LOAD APPLICATIONS AUTOMATICALLY WHEN YOU LOG IN

If you'd like a particular application to open every time you log into (or start up) your Mac, now all you have to do is Control-click (or click-and-hold) the application's Dock icon and choose Open at Login from the contextual menu. Now restart your Mac and the application will launch automatically. If you want to hide the application after it automatically launches (so it stays hidden from view until you click on it in the Dock), here's how: Go to the Apple menu (or to the Dock) to System Preferences. In the System Preferences pane, click the Accounts icon, select your user account, then click the Login Items tab. Now turn on the Hide checkbox next to the application's name. Close the window and your application's set.

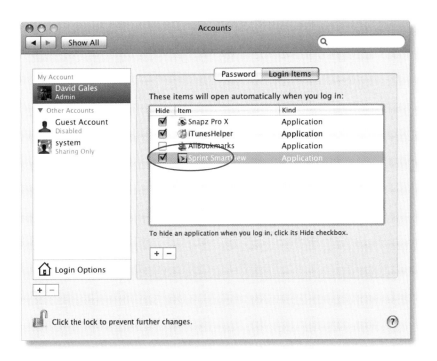

   OPEN DOCUMENTS WHEN YOU LOG IN

You can take the previous tip a step further and have Leopard automatically open particular documents every time you log in. My wife read the title of this tip and couldn't imagine anyone ever wanting the same file to open every time they log in. I pointed out that I have several documents set to open automatically. I then told her I do it because it saves time which I can then spend talking with her. She believed the first part. If you want to have more time to spend with your spouse, go through the same steps you used in the previous tip, but select a document rather than an application to open.

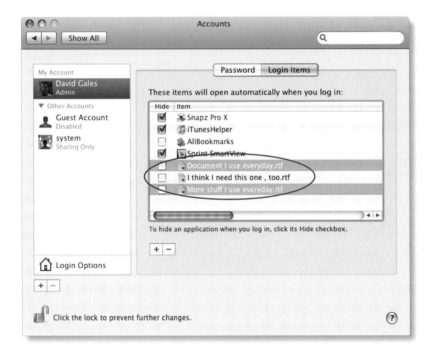

   SAVE FILES TO THE DESKTOP IN A FLASH

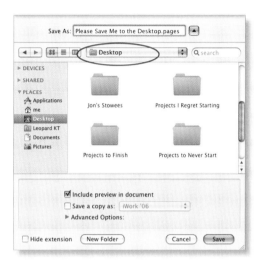

When you're in the Save As dialog and you want to save a file to the desktop, just press Command-D and the save location will switch to Desktop (as shown here), so all you have to do is name your file and click Save. Another alternative is saving in the Documents folder (like the OS really wants you to), so get to your Home folder by pressing Command-Shift-H, and Home (your user folder) will appear as your destination. Now just click the Documents folder in the window.

SAVE TIME WHEN YOU "SAVE AS"

Here's a fairly wild Mac OS X tip for saving a file (this is a great one to show at parties. Well, at least parties where there are lots of Mac-heads). If you're going to save a document using Save As, and the folder you want to save to is visible in a Finder window or on the desktop, you can drag-and-drop the folder to one of the columns in the Save As dialog. If you can't see the columns in the Save As dialog, click the blue button with the down-facing triangle next to the Save As naming field. This is one of those things you have to try once yourself, but once you do, you'll use it again and again to save time when saving documents.

DAVE GALES

   NAVIGATE THE SAVE AS DIALOG AT TURBO SPEED

By default, when you press Command-Shift-S (the keyboard shortcut for Save As), the current filename of the document you're saving is entered and highlighted in the Save As naming field so all you have to do is type in a new filename. But if you want to save the renamed file to a different location, you can speed things up by using the keyboard (specifically the Tab and Arrow keys) to get around. When you're in the Save As dialog, each time you press the Tab key the focus shifts to the next interface component. When the focus moves to the sidebar, you can press the Up/Down Arrow keys to move to a particular folder. If you press the Tab key again, it won't look like anything has happened, but the focus has moved to the first column of the folder's contents. Don't believe me? Press one of the Arrow keys and you'll feel bad for doubting me. (It's okay, I understand.) Now you can use the Arrow keys to navigate through the folder structure until you get to the one where you want your renamed document to be saved. When you get there, press the Tab key again to highlight the Save As naming field so you can name your file, and then press the Return key or click Save. It seems a bit convoluted at first, but do it a couple of times and you'll see how fast and easy it is. *Note:* If you don't see the sidebar or viewing modes, click the little blue down-facing arrow button to the right of the Save As field.

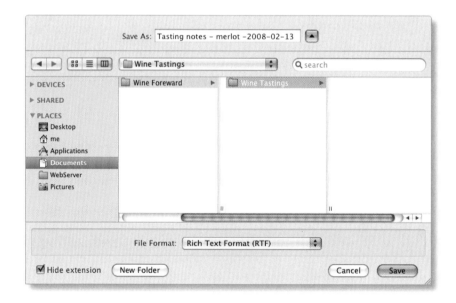

   USE THE FINDER'S PATH BAR TO NAVIGATE FAST

To make this work, you have to have a Finder window open first. Now go to the Finder's View menu, and choose Show Path Bar. Now at the bottom of every Finder window there is a bar with icons of folders starting with your hard drive and ending with the file you are currently viewing. That alone is cool because you can tell where you are at any time. But here's the best part of the path bar: you can access any folder along the path just by double-clicking it. This means if you want go back three levels of your drive structure, you only have to click once (well, twice since it does take a double-click). And, guess what else you can do? You can move any file from anywhere on your drive into any of the folders in the path bar by simply dragging it from its current location and dropping it onto the folder (in the path bar) that you want to move it to. You sacrifice a small amount of screen space by adding the bar at the bottom of windows, but you gain a lot of navigation speed.

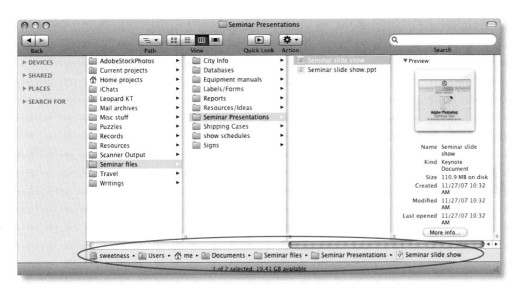

   SWITCH TO GRID VIEW IN QUICK LOOK

Here's a tip that will make Quick Look even quicker: One of the things I do all the time is use Quick Look to view a whole folder of photos. By default, they open up in slide show mode, which is nice if I only have a few images to look at. But most times I'm looking at hundreds of images, so I want to view them as thumbnails. No problem, just click on the thumbnail button (it looks like four tiny TV screens) at the bottom of the preview window. But if you're a keyboard shortcut kinda person and want to avoid using your mouse, just press Command-Return when Quick Look is in slide show mode and you've got your thumbnails. If there's an image you want to see full-size, just move to it using the Arrow keys on your keyboard (or, if you must, click on it), then use the same Command-Return shortcut. It's a beautiful thing.

KILLER TIPS

   OPEN SIDEBAR ITEMS IN THEIR OWN WINDOWS

My buddy Terry White found this cool tip: If you click an icon in your sidebar, it just opens in the current window, but if you Command-click an item in the sidebar, it leaves the current window alone, and opens that item in its own separate window. Option-click a sidebar item, and it closes the old window while opening a new one. Very handy stuff.

   THE FASTEST WAY TO QUIT MULTIPLE APPLICATIONS

If you want to quit just one program, press Command-Q. But if you have several you want to quit, the absolute fastest way to do it is to press Command-Tab. You can quickly quit any program without even going to that program. Press-and-hold the Command key and press the Tab key. Every time you press the Tab key (keep the Command key pressed) the next application icon will highlight. If this is one you want to quit, press the Q key (so now you are using the normal Command-Q shortcut) and it will instantly obey. Still pressing the Command key, press the Tab key again until the next application you want to quit is highlighted, then press Q again. As long as you keep the Command key pressed, you can move right down the line of applications alternating the Tab and Q keys. If you get mixed up and release the Tab key by accident, your hard drive will be erased and reformatted—just kidding. All that will happen is the Application bar will close and you'll have to press Command-Tab again to open it.

   SET A NEW DEFAULT APPLICATION TO OPEN A FILE

When you double-click on a file to open it, how does your Mac know what application to launch? I have it from a some-what unreliable source that a group of Leopard developers got together over beers at a local establishment, grabbed a stack of napkins, and came up with a list of what applica-tion would open each type of file. Most of the time they did pretty well: Photoshop opens Photoshop documents, Safari opens HTML documents, TextEdit opens text documents, etc. But knowing that a few pitchers can make even a bad idea seem brilliant, they figured they needed to give you a way to override the defaults they came up with, especially the ones they thought of after things started getting a bit fuzzy. For example, by default, JPEG files open with Preview. That's okay, but if it were me (and it is) I would rather use Photoshop to open them. To make Photoshop the default application for opening JPEGs, find a JPEG file on your drive, click on it, and press Command–I to open the Get Info dialog. Go about halfway down the dialog, to the Open With section. Click the pop-up menu, then choose Photoshop (or whatever application you want to use to open the file). If you close the Get Info dialog now, your change will only apply to this one file. To apply it to all files of this type, click the Change All button (as shown here) before closing the dialog. From now on, when you double-click on a JPEG file, Preview will leave it alone and let Photoshop take over.

DAVE GALES

    INSTANTLY HIDE EVERY OPEN WINDOW ON THE DESKTOP

Pay careful attention to this tip—it may save you a "heap of hurt" someday. Imagine your anniversary is coming up soon (let's say…tomorrow) and you're doing some last-minute online shopping when you hear your spouse coming up behind you. You don't want them to see what you're doing because you know they'll connect the dots and bust you for not remembering your anniversary. Here's what you do: Command-Option-click anywhere on the desktop—instantly, every open application window will be hidden. But what if you have a very observant spouse who knows there must be some shenanigans going on because you're just sitting there staring at a blank desktop? Again, there is an easy solution. Keep a "decoy document" (something boring like a spreadsheet, database file, HTML document, etc.) open and visible while you're shopping. When you hear the footsteps behind you, Command-Option-click on your decoy. Instantly any open windows for every other application will be hidden. Oh, I forgot to tell you how to "unhide" the windows. I haven't a clue. You might try clicking on their applications' icons in the Dock.

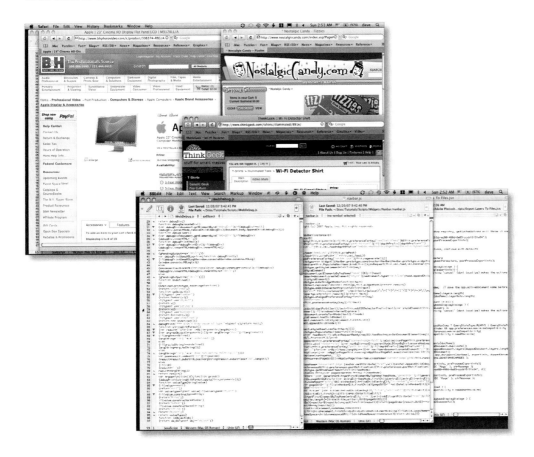

   KEEP A TEAM ADDRESS BOOK CURRENT

If you're part of a team at work, church, athletics, etc., it can be a major ordeal to keep every-body up to date on contact information for each other. Here's a tip that will eliminate the heartburn: Whenever someone changes any of their information, or when someone new joins the team, have them contact the person who has the privilege of keeping the contact list up to speed (assume for the moment it's you). Once you've made the changes in your Address Book, go over to the Group column, click on the name of the group, and drag it on top of Mail's icon in the Dock, then release the mouse button. Mail will open a New Message window with the vCards of the contacts already attached. All you have to do now is enter the group name in the address field, type in a subject and any message you want to include, and then click Send. Now any of the recipients can just click on the attachment and import the vCards. If there are any duplicates (which, obviously, in this situation they will mostly be dupes), Address Book will ask what you want to do with them. Of course, the weak link in this process is getting people to let you know when there's a change. If you figure out how to do that, you will become the patron saint of team moms the world over.

    SEND AN EMAIL TO EVERYONE IN YOUR GROUP

If you've created a group (like friends, or co-workers, or perhaps total Mac freaks) in Address Book, you can send that entire group an email with just one click. Simply Control-click on the group (in this case, we'll Control-click on our group named "Seminars"), and then choose Send Email to "Seminars." Your default email client will open a New Message window with the group name (instead of separate addresses for each person) already in the address field. Just add a subject, write your email, and click Send. Just like that, everyone in your Seminars group will receive the email. Not bad, eh?

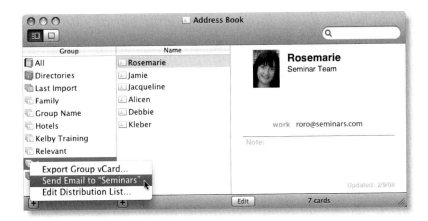

   UNLEASH YOUR MAC'S POWER WITH SCRIPTS!

Wouldn't it be cool if there were extra built-in automation power already on your Mac, and all you had to do was turn it on. Yeah, that'd be cool. Well, you can unlock this automation by just doing a little digging. Start by opening your Applications folder, and then look inside your AppleScript folder (don't worry, you're not going to be doing any scripting—the scripts are already written for you). Now double-click on the AppleScript Utility icon, and in the resulting window, turn on the Show Script Menu in Menu Bar checkbox. Quit AppleScript Utility, and then go to the menu bar and click the Script icon—a list of all sorts of cool automatic functions are now just a click away.

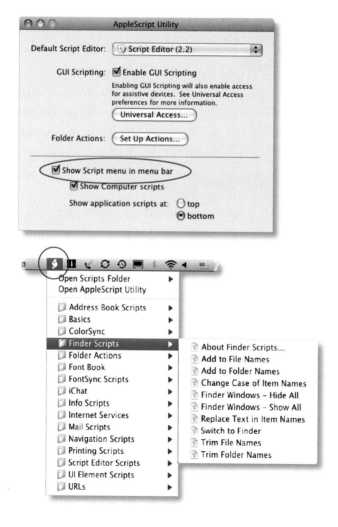

   OPEN COMMONLY USED PREFERENCES FAST!

There are three preferences you will be using fairly often: Display, Sound, and Keyboard & Mouse. Apple kindly provided keyboard shortcuts you can use to open these preferences fast.

Option-F3	Sound	(F4 or F5 keys also work)
Option-F1	Display	(F2)
Option-F8	Keyboard & Mouse	(F9 or F10)

Some keyboards may be a little different (like the mini-Bluetooth one I'm using, or the new flat keyboards), so you might need to experiment a bit. Also, if you're using a laptop you may also need to press the Function (fn) key, depending on how your keyboard preferences are set.

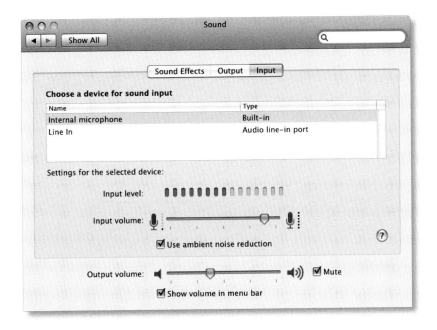

MOVING A FILE OUT OF A FOLDER IN LIST VIEW

Moving files from one folder to another in List view is easy—you just click-and-drag it. But what if you just want to take a file out of a folder and keep it in the window instead of inside a folder? Sounds simple, doesn't it? Try it, I'll wait. Not as easy as you thought it would be, huh? Here's the trick: Expand the folder containing the file you want to move, click on the file, then drag the file's icon on top of one of the headers at the top of the window (Name, Date Modified, etc.) and release your mouse button. That's it—your file is now free from the confines of the folder that once held it.

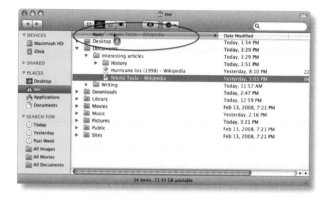

CHANGE FINDER WINDOW VIEWS FAST

If you want to switch your Finder view without clicking the buttons on the toolbar, use the following keyboard shortcuts:

Icon view	Command-1
List view	Command-2
Column view	Command-3
Cover Flow view	Command-4

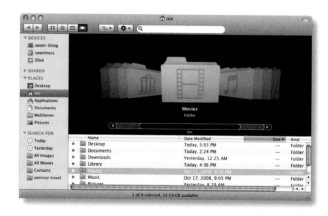

    CREATE A LIST OF FAVORITE SPECIAL CHARACTERS

If you find you need to use special characters (things like ©, ™, °F, ®, £, ÷, ä, ¼) frequently, you can save yourself some time by collecting the ones you use into a Favorites category in the Character palette. Open the Character palette (see page 218) and select one of the categories from the list on the left-hand side of the palette. When you find a symbol you want to add to your favorites, click on to select it, then click the Action button (the little gear-like thingy) in the lower left-hand corner of the palette and choose Add to Favorites from the menu. Add as many characters as you want from any category. Don't worry about what font is selected in the Collections window when you add a character to your favorites. That window is only there to let you know what fonts include the character you've selected and show a preview of what it looks like. Whenever you insert a character into a document, it automatically matches the formatting of the document. To use the characters in your Favorites collection, you do what you normally do to add a special character (select Special Characters from the Edit menu), but instead of selecting from the categories list, click the Favorites tab located just above the preview window in the palette and make your selection. It's still a bit of a pain, but it's a lot easier than sifting through all the categories to find what you're looking for.

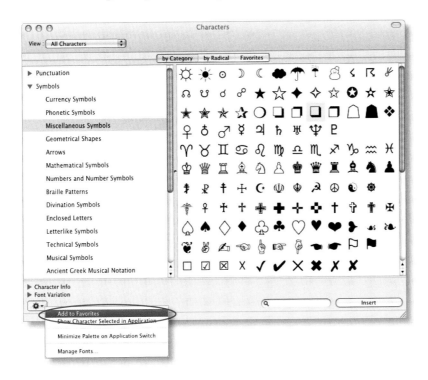

   DON'T SHUT DOWN YOUR COMPUTER

This tip is mainly for people who have switched from a PC to a Mac. The next time you're hanging out in a place where public WiFi is available, notice how many times you hear the familiar startup chime for a certain operating system. I guarantee that 90% of the people using PC laptops will open their computer case and start up their laptop. I don't mean wake it up, I mean start it up. Why? Because they never put their laptops to sleep; they shut them down instead. Why? Because the operating system they use has a well-deserved reputation for not waking up from sleep very well. So if you're an escapee from the dark side (don't worry, it won't be long before you, too, are a Mac elitist) here's a tip: you don't need to shut down your Mac when you're done doing whatever you're doing. I know it sounds crazy, but all you have to do is close the lid. You heard me right, close the lid. It will instantly go to sleep until you lift the lid again, at which time it will instantly wake up. This may seem odd to you, but many Mac users of the geek persuasion take great pride in their "uptime." Sleep is a wonderful thing—enjoy it.

```
Terminal — bash — 166×54

In the world of Mac, it's all about uptime, baby.
Uptime is status. It's coolness (At least as cool
as geeks can be). Uptime is POWER!!! At the end
of the day, the geek with the longest uptime
walks away with the spoils of victory:  three new
pocket protectors, a new calculator beltclip
and a random assortment of Klingon memorabilia.

So what's my uptime?

Last login: Sun Oct  6 19:34:19 on ttys001
You have new mail.
sweet-thing:~ me$ uptime
19:56  up  23:4:27, 2 users, load averages: 0.

sweet-thing:~ me$ █

Twenty-three days. Cool.
```

SET THE WARNING BEEP VOLUME FAST

Here's a hidden little tip that lets you adjust the volume of your warning beep sound right from the desktop. At the top of your screen, on the right-hand side, are several menu extras. One of them is a volume control (if it's not there, select Show Volume in Menu Bar in the Sound preferences). When you click on it, a volume slider opens, which you can use to adjust the master volume for your computer. But if you Option-click on it, the slider now controls the volume of your system's warning beep.

TAP INTO THE COLLECTIVE INTELLIGENCE OF WIKIPEDIA

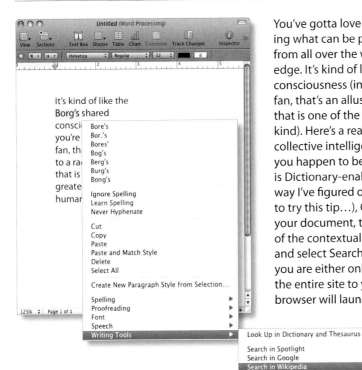

You've gotta love Wikipedia. It's truly amazing what can be produced when people from all over the world pool their knowledge. It's kind of like the Borg's shared consciousness (in case you're not a Star Trek fan, that's an allusion to a race of machines that is one of the greatest threats to humankind). Here's a really fast way to tap into the collective intelligence we call Wikipedia. If you happen to be using an application that is Dictionary-enabled (honestly, the only way I've figured out how to tell if you are is to try this tip…), Control-click on a word in your document, then scroll to the bottom of the contextual menu, to Writing Tools, and select Search in Wikipedia. Assuming you are either online or have downloaded the entire site to your hard drive, your Web browser will launch, go to Wikipedia, perform the search, and show you the page with the information you're looking for—all automatically. For example, if I wanted to know more about the Borg, I would just Control-click on the word "Borg" in the earlier sentence, scroll down to Writing Tools, select Search in Wikipedia, and find the following entry: "Borg (Star Trek)—a fictional race of cyborgs in the Star Trek universe." Fictional?

  CLEAN UP THE SIDEBAR

If your sidebar is getting a bit crowded, it may be time to get rid of some items. If there is an item you don't need to keep in the sidebar, just click-and-drag it out of the sidebar. Poof, it's gone. If you change your mind, just find the item on your drive and drag it back onto the sidebar.

   SELECT THE SECONDARY OPTION IN DIALOGS

When you do something like open a file and make some changes, then close it without first saving it, a warning message will open saying, "Hold it just a second, pal. I'm thinking it's a bad idea to close this puppy without saving the changes you just made." If you want to accept the advice, just press Return.

But if you know what you're doing and don't want to save the changes, there are two other options: Don't Save and Cancel. Instead of using your mouse to click one of the alternates, just press the letter D (it doesn't have to be uppercase) to carelessly disregard the warning or C to rethink your planned course of action. *Note:* Some applications will put a heavy stroke around the Don't Save option. In these cases, you have to press Command-D to choose it. If you want to choose Cancel you're going to have to do it with your mouse. It's just another one of those "features" that make things harder.

   A FASTER WAY TO VIEW THE WIDGET BAR

I really like Dashboard widgets because they are so handy. The problem is, they can suck up a lot of memory if you keep a lot of them open. Well if you're in Dashboard (press the Dashboard key or F12 if you're not) and want to peruse your entire collection of Dashboard widgets, rather than clicking that big plus sign (+) button in the lower left-hand corner of your screen, next time try pressing Command-plus (+) and the Widget Bar will pop right up. You can use the same shortcut to hide the bar when you're done.

   COPY & PASTE A STYLE

I use this tip every single day. Say you're working on a document and paste in some text you have copied from another document. In the example here, I copied some flight information from an online itinerary and pasted it into an itinerary template I created in Numbers to use when I travel. I could leave the big orange text from the website in my carefully laid out template, but only if you threatened to make me watch *Brady Bunch* reruns for 48 hours straight. Here's how you can get rid of non-conforming formatting fast: First, select some text that has the formatting you want to use and press Command-Option-C. Unlike Command-C (which copies the text), when you add the Option key, only the format of the selected text is copied. Now select the text you want to change and press Command-Option-V. That's it—faster than Marsha and Jan can get into a fight over a boy, your text is now the correct font, size, and color.

SCRUB THROUGH VIDEO

Just in case you haven't yet been persuaded to buy a multi-button mouse with a scroll wheel, here's another reason you should hop online right now and order one. The next time you're watching a video with QuickTime Player and want to skip ahead or go back to something you missed, all you have to do is move the scroll wheel on your fancy mouse and you'll be scrubbing through your movie with the simple roll of one finger. If you're using a laptop and have enabled two-finger scrolling, you can skip the mouse and let your fingers do the scrolling.

  OPEN MULTIPLE INSPECTORS IN AN APPLICATION

This isn't new to Leopard, but not many people know about it. If you are using an application that has an Inspector (like most of the iApps) and click on one of its buttons, whichever panel was already open closes. For instance, you're working on a table in a Pages document. You open the Inspector and click the Table button to set the borders for the table. Next, you click the Text button to center the text within a cell. When the Text panel opens, the Table panel closes. So if you want to merge two cells or change the background color, you have to click the Table button again, which closes the Text panel. It gets a little annoying—okay, it gets a lot annoying. But, if you Option-click one of the buttons in the Inspector, the new panel will open in its own panel. Ahhhh. Much nicer. Feel free to go crazy and open a separate panel for every button. Or, if you really want to live on the edge, open multiple panels for the same button. Oh yeah, you can do it. Can't think of a single reason you would need to, but that's never stopped me before.

OPEN AN APPLICATION'S PREFERENCES FAST

If you want to check your preferences settings for the application you are working in (most of them anyhow), just press Command-, (comma) and the preference window opens instantaneously. You might think that pressing the keyboard shortcut again would close the preferences window. You might think it, but you would be wrong. Being the power user you are, however, you know to just press Command-W to close the window.

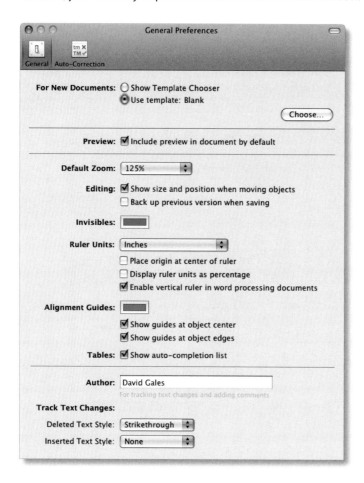

   DUPLICATE SMART MAILBOXES

Smart Mailboxes (it probably goes without saying that they're used in Mail, so I won't say it) make it easy to keep your emails organized and accessible. No doubt, most of the Smart Mailboxes you set up are simple, like messages from a certain person. But if you're the type of person who likes to make things really complicated, you can create a Smart Mailbox like the one shown here. In the unlikely event that you want to create another Smart Mailbox just like this one, except you want it to contain emails from Gales instead of Kelby, the easiest way is to duplicate the existing one and edit the one field that is different. To do that, open Mail, then Control-click on the Smart Mailbox you want to duplicate (it's in the sidebar), and choose Duplicate Smart Mailbox from the contextual menu. Now all you have to do is double-click the new mailbox, make any changes you want to the selection criteria, and give it a new name. Then you might consider getting some therapy to explore this need to complicate things unnecessarily.

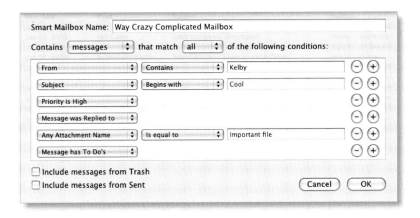

   PREVIEW A DOCUMENT RIGHT IN THE PRINT DIALOG

How many times have you sent a document to the printer clear on the other side of the building, hiked over to pick it up, and discovered you printed it horizontally instead of vertically? I'm big enough to admit that I've done it, but I'm not big enough to tell you how many times. One of my favorite new features in Leopard is the ability to see a preview of a document in the Print dialog so you can make sure you have your page layout settings correct, you are printing the right document, etc. When you press Command-P to open the Print dialog, you'll see the preview on the left-hand side. If you are printing a multi-page document, you can scroll through it using the arrow buttons under the preview. When you're satisfied everything is correct, just click Print. Printing without surprises is a wonderful thing. *Note:* If you don't see a preview when the Print dialog opens, click the blue triangle to the right of the name of the selected printer to expand the Print dialog.

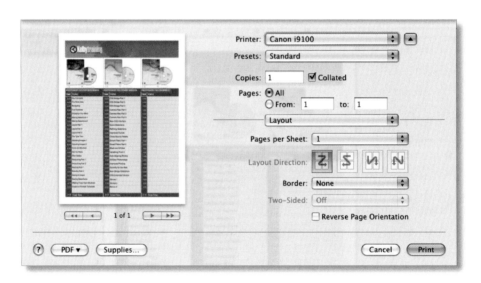

  ● **YOUR DEFAULT PRINTER FOLLOWS YOU**

If you have a laptop and use printers in multiple locations, Leopard detects your current location (spooky, isn't it) and changes the default printer to the one you used the last time you printed there. When I'm at home, I have two printers to choose from, so I can usually remember which one I want to use. But when I print something at my office, about 60 printers show up on the list of available printers, which means the odds of my remembering the one I am supposed to use are pretty darn slim. But now I don't need to because Leopard remembers.

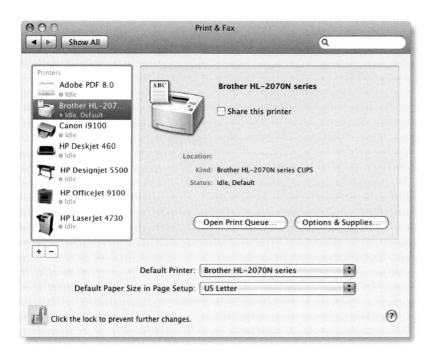

   FASTER WIDGET CLOSING

Want a faster way to close any open widget in Dashboard? Just press-and-hold the Option key and move your cursor anywhere over the widget you want to close. The Close button will appear (that little X in the upper left-hand corner), and you can click that X to close the widget.

   DISABLE A WIDGET

Widgets are great and allow you to keep fun stuff, cool stuff, and even useful stuff one keystroke away. But if you keep a lot of them open, they can take up some substantial processor power and more than their share of memory. It's not enough to matter if you're a rich, elitist snob who keeps extra processors and RAM chips lying around for your kids to play with, but for the rest of us who always need just a bit more RAM than we have, it can be an issue. You can save some of your precious memory by pressing the Dashboard key or F12 to open Dashboard, then clicking the plus sign (+) in the bottom-left corner to open the Widget Bar. If you click the Widgets icon at the far-left end (or click the Manage Widgets button), the Manage Widgets dialog (shown here) will open. Now you can select the widgets you want to be active. Anything not selected will be disabled, but not deleted from your drive. If you find you need one of them, all you have to do is open the Manage Widgets dialog again and select it. If

you downloaded a widget, and then decide that you want to get rid of it, you can remove it from Dashboard by going to your Home folder and looking inside your Library folder. Inside that you'll find a folder named Widgets, which holds all the widgets you've downloaded (from Apple's site and elsewhere). To delete one of those widgets, just click it and press Command-Delete to send it to the Trash. That's it—it's gone!

   OPEN ALL IMAGES IN ONE WINDOW IN PREVIEW

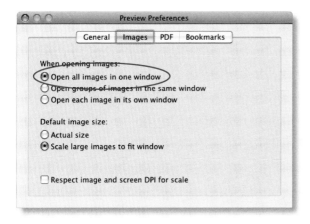

If you have multiple images you want to look at in Preview, instead of having each of them open in a separate window, you can have Preview open them in one window with thumbnail previews visible in a sidebar. Launch Preview if it's not already open, go to the Preview menu, and select Preferences. Now click the Images tab and click on the Open All Images in One Window radio button. From now on, if you have an image open in Preview, any additional images you open will open in the same window.

   BATCH RESIZE IN PREVIEW

DAVE GALES

Here's another great time saver you can do with Preview. It's fairly common to have a large number of photos you need to resize. Preview can do it for you with just a couple of clicks. Select your images and click-and-drag them onto Preview's Dock icon. Now that they are open in Preview, press Command-A to select all the thumbnails in the sidebar, go to the Tools menu, and select Adjust Size. When the sheet opens, you can enter a size, click OK, and Preview will do the rest.

   BATCH ROTATE IN PREVIEW

If you have a lot of photos you need to rotate, here's the fastest way to do it: Open the images in Preview, press Command-A to select all the thumbnails in the sidebar, then press Command-R to rotate them 90° to the right or Command-L to…I don't think I need to go there. There you go. Told you it was fast. *Note:* If you find yourself needing to rotate images frequently, you might want to Control-click on Preview's toolbar, select Customize Toolbar from the contextual menu, then drag the Rotate icon onto the toolbar. That way, you can rotate images with just one click.

DAVE GALES

   CREATE LIVE INTERNET LINKS FROM TEXT AUTOMATICALLY

In many applications, if you type an Internet address in your document, it will automatically change to a live link. For instance, I can type "www.apple.com" and, as shown here, the text changes and it's now a link. You'll just have to trust me on this, but I didn't do anything at all to turn the text I typed into a link. The same thing works for email addresses. Type an address (such as "dontsendmeanything@ mac.com") and it will change to a "mailto" link that will launch Mail and open a blank email, ready for you to compose a message. As long as a Web address is in a valid format (such as "www.something.com"), an application such as Pages thinks it's real. Crazy, huh?

   CREATE SIMPLE WEB ADDRESSES IN MAIL

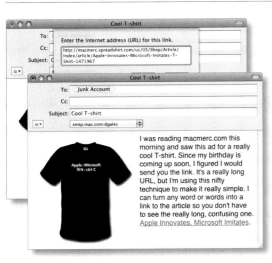

When you are sending someone a link to something cool you found buried in a website, the address is likely going to be very long and filled with cryptic language that only a few humans can decipher. I know—all the person getting your email has to do is click on the link, but it destroys the Zen and creates inner tension for me. Fortunately, there's an easy solution that allows you to send the link while maintaining inner balance. Here's how: Go to the webpage you want to link to in your email and copy (Command–C) its address from the address field. Next, go to Mail and compose the message to your friend. Now, Control–click on the word (or select multiple words and Control–click on them) you want to use as the link, select Link from the contextual menu, choose Add, then paste (Command–V) the web address you copied into the text box, and click OK. Now you have a nice, clean, short link instead of 200 seemingly random characters. My erudite instructions make it seem exceedingly complex (kind of like this sentence), but trust me—it's easy and will take you about half a second to do.

   DISPLAY MORE INFORMATION ABOUT FILES IN ICON VIEW

In the Finder's Icon view, the only information you can usually see about a folder or file is its name. But there is an option you can select that will add a line of unobtrusive light-blue, 9-point type just below the name of the file or folder that will give you some more information. For instance, for folders you'll see how many items are in the folder. If the file is an image, its dimensions will be shown. On audio or movie files, the length of the song or movie is shown. It's really pretty helpful. To enable it, make sure you're in Icon view, then press Command-J to open the View options. Go about halfway down the dialog and select the Show Item Info option. *Note:* Any new windows you open will display the information, but you will need to enable it for any existing folders individually.

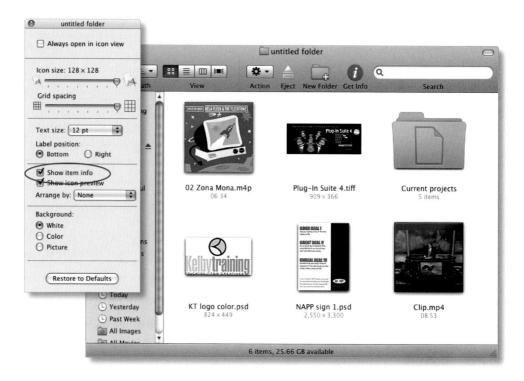

She Drives Me Crazy

How to Stop Annoying Things

Mac OS X is an amazing operating system. Yet it can also be an annoying operating system. So, depending on what you're

She Drives Me Crazy
how to stop annoying things

doing with it—it's either annoyingly amazing or amazingly annoying. Okay, I'm not really being fair, because in reality it's not the operating system itself that's annoying; it's things in the operating system—aspects of it (if you will)—that are annoying. This chapter is about how to quickly make some of the most egregious annoyances go away. But make no mistake about it—Mac OS X isn't the first Apple operating system to include wildly annoying features. Remember Balloon Help—Apple's attempt at coming up with a better form of onscreen help, which could have been devised only by the Prince of Darkness himself (not Darth Vader—El Diablo!)? There's a hint, just a hint, of that type of stuff in Mac OS X, but this chapter will help you exorcise those demons fast!

HIDE YOURSELF WHEN YOU'RE VIDEO CHATTING

When I do a video chat with someone, I find it very annoying to have to see myself. For some reason I never look
as good onscreen as I do in my imagination—go figure.
Fortunately, iChat will enable my denial by letting me
take myself off the screen. Just go to the Video menu and
choose Hide Local Video. Now I'm lookin' good.

   SLEEP LESS—WORK MORE

Have you plugged your
laptop into an AC outlet,
but it's still going to sleep
on you every 5 or 10 min-
utes? Honestly, that drives
me nuts, and if you're like
me, once you plug in, you'll
want to go to the System
Preferences (in the Apple
menu) and click the Energy
Saver icon. When its pane
appears, click the Sleep tab
(if you don't see the tab,
click the Show Details button at the bottom left), and
then click-and-drag the top
slider over to a reasonable
amount of time (like 30
minutes or more). That way,
if you do call it a night and
forget to put your laptop
to sleep, eventually Energy
Saver will kick in.

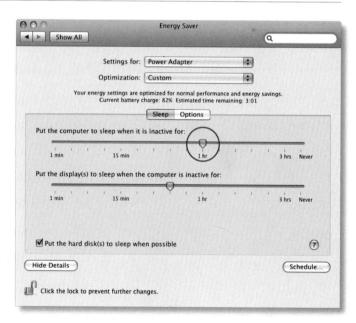

    ENTERING A PASSWORD TO USE MY OWN COMPUTER

If you're the only person who uses your Mac, it's very annoying to have to enter a password to do simple things like move files or install applications. Unfortunately, there isn't a way to prevent Leopard from asking for a password. Fortunately, if you leave the password field blank when you set up (or edit) your user account, all you have to do when you're asked to enter your password is press the Return key. Unfortunately, anyone who gets access to your Mac can do the same thing, giving them full access to things like credit card account numbers, PINs, usernames, passwords for websites (like the iTunes Store and Amazon, where I enjoy the convenience of one-click purchasing), financial information, medical information, and personal writings.

Then there's the whole wireless network thing. I like having access to the other computers on my wireless network at home. I love using Back to My Mac to access my home network from the road; no matter what city I'm in, when I open my Mac and look in the sidebar, I'll see my home machines. But when I take a seat at Tampa International Airport, log into the free WiFi, and look at my sidebar, I see what you see in the image shown here. I'm not the paranoid type when it comes to wireless security, and I realize that making myself visible on a shared network doesn't mean that other people have access to my files. But there are plenty of 14-year-olds out there who love trying.

I have always been an I-don't-need-a-password kind of guy, but I've recently converted and I now have my Macs protected with secure passwords. Is it a pain sometimes? You bet. Is it a bigger pain than someone having access to all my personal information? Not even close.

CHAPTER 12 • How to Stop Annoying Things   321

   DISABLING THE CAPS LOCK KEY

For some people, this tip alone will be worth the price of the book (and frankly, I love those people). You can completely disable the Caps Lock key on your keyboard by going to the System Preferences (in the Apple menu), then clicking the Keyboard & Mouse icon. When the preferences appear, click the Keyboard tab. At the bottom of the Keyboard preferences is a button named Modifier Keys. Click that button, and the first pop-up menu is for the Caps Lock key. From its pop-up menu, just choose No Action, click OK, and that's it. Life is good.

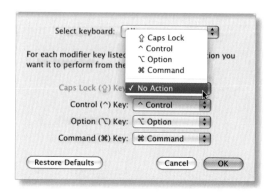

   SHUT DOWN WITHOUT THE WARNING

When you choose Shut Down from the Apple menu, a dialog appears asking if you really want to shut down. Yes, it's annoying. To make it go away, just press-and-hold the Option key as you choose Shut Down, and your Mac will just shut down (without insulting your intelligence by asking you if what you chose is really what you want to do).

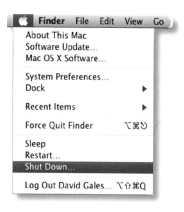

     THE SILENCE OF THE BEEPS

If you have a keyboard that has volume controls right on the keyboard (like most MacBooks), then you're probably used to hearing a little "confirmation" beep each time you press one of these volume controls. If those little beeps get on your nerves (who needs more things beeping at them?), then just press-and-hold the Shift key and this will silence the beeps as you press the volume keys. If you want to turn these sounds off permanently, go to the Apple menu, and choose System Preferences, then click on the Sound icon (or just press-and-hold the Option key as you press a sound key to open the Sound preferences). Click the Sound Effects tab, then turn off the Play Feedback When Volume Is Changed checkbox.

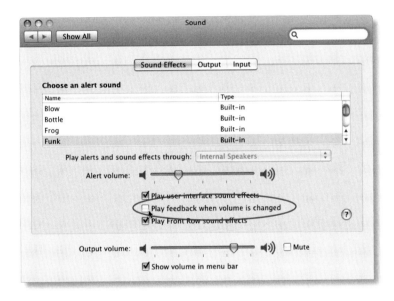

   GENIE'S CUTE AND ALL, BUT SHE'S JUST GOTTA GO

The Genie Effect that occurs when you send a document to the Dock sure looks cool the first few times you see it, but it doesn't take long before you want to put the genie back in the bottle for good. To turn off the Genie Effect and use the faster Scale Effect, Control-click on the vertical Dock divider bar, and from the contextual menu, under Minimize Using, choose Scale Effect.

   STOP THE BOUNCING, I BEG YOU!

Every time you launch an application, its icon starts bouncing up and down in the Dock like a three-year-old hyped up on sugar. I know applications launch a lot faster now than they used to, but it still drives me crazy. If you like to count the bounces for some weird reason, just ignore the rest of this tip. The rest of you can click on the Apple menu, select System Preferences, then click on the Dock icon. Now all you have to do to get rid of one more annoyance in your life is turn off the Animate Opening Applications checkbox.

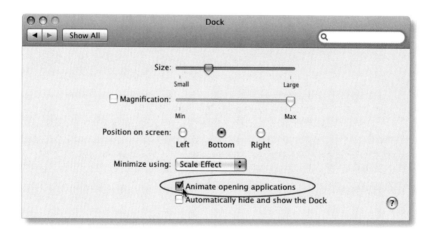

   HOW TO STOP THE QUICKTIME PLAYER BLUES

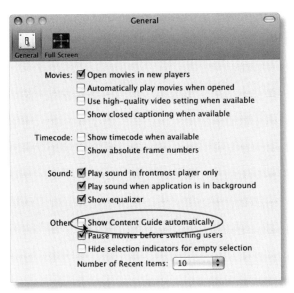

If you launch the QuickTime Player while you're connected to the Internet, before you can do anything else, it goes to the Web, downloads a little advertising clip (usually for a new album or movie), and plays it in your QuickTime Player. It's called the Content Guide, which is a euphemism for "unsolicited advertisement." The good news is that you can turn off this annoying "feature." Just launch the QuickTime Player, then go under the Menu menu, and select Preferences. Now in the General pane, turn off the Show Content Guide Automatically checkbox. Ahhhh, now isn't that better?

   HOW TO STOP MAGNIFYING YOUR DOCK

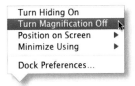

This may be a very embarrassing subject for some of you, so I'll try to handle it with the utmost sensitivity. If you have a very small Dock (and you know who you are), the Magnification feature is almost a necessity. However, if you leave your Dock icons at their default size (which many people do), magnification can be wildly annoying, and because the icons are so large to begin with, magnification is totally unnecessary. When my wife first saw large Dock icons being magnified even more, the first thing she said was, "Is there a way to turn that awful thing off?" There is: Control-click the Dock's vertical divider bar and select Turn Magnification Off from the contextual menu.

   STOPPING THE SOFTWARE AUTO-UPDATING MENACE

The idea is great—Leopard phones home every morning to see if there have been any software updates (system software or any of the iApps) while you were sleeping. If there have been, a window pops up to tell you what they are and offers to download and install them for you. If you have a fast Internet connection, it's not a problem—they download in the background and you never notice it. The problem is the installing part. Somehow, Apple knows when I'm slamming to meet a deadline or am five minutes from packing up for the day, and picks that time to let me know about the updates. Of course, they word it so only a loser would decline to take them up on the offer, so being insecure and desperately wanting Apple's approval, I tell it to go ahead. So what if I miss the deadline, lose my job, and end up a heroin addict on the streets—I'll have the latest software. If you don't want to risk ruining your life, you can take control of the software updates and decide when you'll check for them. Go to the Apple menu, click System Preferences, and then click on the Software Update icon. Now just go to the bottom and turn off the Check for Updates checkbox. If you don't feel comfortable taking such a bold step, instead of turning off the update option, you can click the pop-up menu and choose to be interrupted at the wrong time only, say, once a month.

  YES! I'M SURE I WANT TO EMPTY THE TRASH

There's nothing like executing a simple command and having the OS ask, "Are you sure you want to do this?" By default, every time you go to empty the Trash, it asks this annoying question (and it has for years upon years). Disabling the Empty Trash warning is a little different in Mac OS X than it was in previous versions. Now you go to the Finder menu, choose Preferences, and click the Advanced icon. Then turn off the checkbox for Show Warning Before Emptying the Trash.

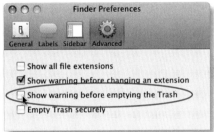

  CLOSE THE PRINTER ICON IN THE DOCK AFTER PRINTING

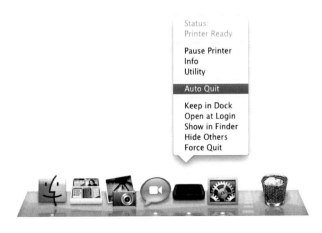

When you print a document, the printer icon shows up in the Dock. No problem. But what's really annoying is when you're finished printing, it stays there. Here's the solution: the next time you print something, click-and-hold on the printer's icon in the Dock, select Auto Quit from the pop-up menu, then click-and-hold on the printer's icon in the Dock again, and select Quit. From now on, the printer's icon will close after it's done printing and you can stop muttering under your breath.

   SHUT OFF THE WARNING BEFORE CHANGING A FILE EXTENSION

Let's say that for some reason you want to change the extension (the dot followed by three letters at the end of filenames) for one of your files. It seems so easy. You click on the file's name to highlight it, take off the existing extension, then type the new one and hit Return. The nasty warning dialog shown at the bottom here opens just to let you know you might be about to destroy civilization as we know it if you make the change. In an attempt to be politically correct and not offend anyone, Leopard offers a compromise—why not use both extensions? Brilliant. I have a better suggestion. Press Command-, (comma) to open the Finder preferences, then click the Advanced icon. Go down to the second item in the list and turn off the checkbox next to Show Warning Before Changing an Extension.

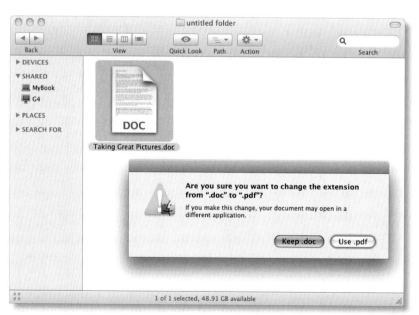

   CHANGE THE FONT MAIL USES FOR NOTES

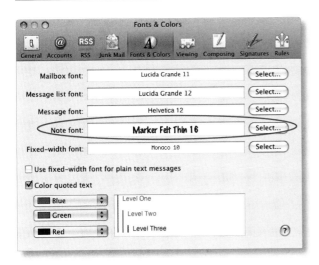

I like the ability to write quick notes and To Do items. But the default font, Marker Felt, makes it look like a 12-year-old girl wrote it. The only thing missing is the little heart above the letter "i". If you want a font that looks more normal, open the Mail menu, select Preferences, and then click on the Fonts & Colors icon. The one you want to change is Note font. When you click the Select button, the Fonts panel will open so you can choose your favorite.

   REARRANGE SYSTEM PREFERENCES ICONS

Every time I have to do something in the System Preferences window, I waste a lot of time looking for the preference I need. That's because, by default, they are arranged in five categories: Personal, Hardware, Internet & Network, System, and Other. I can never remember what category something like Sound or Energy Saver is in (Hardware, in case you're interested) and end up looking for the preference pane I need by its icon. But the next time you open the System Preferences window, go to the View menu, and choose Organize Alphabetically. Now, unless you goofed off in preschool and never quite mastered the alphabet, you will be able to locate the item you need easily.

Chapter 13

Living the iLife

Tips for Using iLife Applications

"Agna consed tatie dolorperit am, sum iore dolorercilla feummy nummy nim dunt dolenisim dolore feuipit nullum

Living the iLife

tips for using ilife applications

dolore." These lyrics from the 12th century band "Gregory and the Chants" talk about that spark of creativity, the "feummy nummy" as Gregory called it, that lies within each of us. It's this inner burning to create that inspired Michelangelo to sculpt, Mozart to compose, Monet to paint, and Me to write this chapter intro. Wait, it might have been a different inner burning that's responsible for this intro. Luckily my wife got me a new bottle of Tums just yesterday. But if you have that inner burning to create , iLife will provide you with the tools you need to express yourself. If you just have an inner burning, CVS has a great sale on Tums this week.

GarageBand: THE 10 MOST ESSENTIAL SHORTCUTS

Like most Apple applications, GarageBand has a host (okay, a bunch) of keyboard shortcuts and there's no sense in memorizing them all, because you won't use them all (some you won't even want to use—ever), but there are a few essential shortcuts you'll want to start using now, before you pull your hair out:

1. Press the Spacebar on your keyboard to start/stop your song.
2. Press the letter Z to jump back to the beginning of your song.
3. To delete the current track, press Command-Delete.
4. You can mute the current track by pressing the letter M.
5. Isolate (solo) just the current track (which mutes all the others) by pressing the letter S.
6. Press the letter C to turn cycling (looping of your song) on/off.
7. Press Command-U to turn the built-in Metronome on/off.
8. Command-L shows/hides the Loop Browser.
9. Start/stop recording by pressing the letter R.
10. Press Command-D to duplicate any track.

Learn these shortcuts and it will make your GarageBand life much easier.

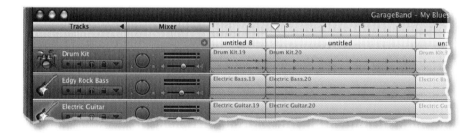

   GarageBand: TAKE YOUR PICK OF KEYBOARDS

When you need to play a Software Instrument to do some recording, but don't have an external keyboard available to connect, you can either use GarageBand's onscreen keyboard or you can use your computer keyboard using Musical Typing. To start, open an onscreen keyboard by pressing Command-K (don't worry about it being too small to use, the next tip tells you how to fix that). To switch to the computer keyboard, click the button in the top-left corner of the pretend "pretend keyboard" (even if it were big enough to use, it's still a "pretend keyboard." But it's not really a real "pretend keyboard," which makes it a pretend "pretend keyboard") that looks like a computer key. Now you can use the designated keys on your Mac to play the corresponding notes on the Software Instrument. It's a bit clunky to use at first, but it won't take you long to get pretty good at it. Even if you have an external keyboard available, it might be good to give this a try. You never know when you might get inspired and want to get something recorded before you forget it.

   GarageBand: SUPER SIZE THE KEYBOARD

You're ready to do some recording, so you create a new track, select a Grand Piano for your instrument, lean back and crack your knuckles to get ready to play, then press Command-K to open a keyboard on the screen to use to input the notes. You know how when you hear a person on the radio all the time, you develop a mental picture of what they look like? They've got this deep, rich voice—like the one you hear on NFL highlight films. But then you see this person at some event and the body just doesn't even come close to matching the voice? That's what you're going to experience when you open the default keyboard. Obviously, you weren't expecting a full 88 keys, but something bigger than a stick of gum would be nice. So when the "keyboard" opens, click the resize button in the lower right-hand corner, and drag it out to a size you can actually use.

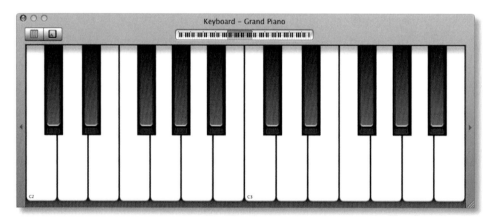

   GarageBand: PRINT YOUR MUSICAL NOTATION

If you have been using previous versions of GarageBand, and went through all the workarounds to be able to print a copy of the musical notation for one of your Software Instrument tracks, you are going to love this new feature. All you have to do now is click the header of the track you want to print, then press Command-P to print it. Oh yeah. No screen shots. No cutting and pasting. Command-P. Not only does it print the notation, it prints it beautifully. Enjoy.

   GarageBand: CREATING REGIONS IN YOUR SONG

Typically, any piece of music can be broken down into regions, depending in large degree on its genre. A typical country or rock song will have at least an intro, verse, chorus, and close. They might also throw in a bridge, a turnaround, and a hook just for fun. GarageBand lets you define regions within your song that you can then use to create arrangements. Here's how you do it: Press Command-Shift-A to show the Arrange Track (it will appear just above the track for the first instrument), then click the Add button (the nearly impossible to see plus sign [+] just to the left of the Arrange Track) to create a new region. Now grab the edge of the new region and drag out a selection that includes all the measures you want to include in the region. To name the new region something more meaningful than "untitled," just double-click the default name and type in your own. Repeat these steps to create as many regions as you like.

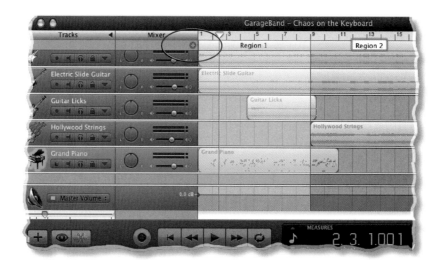

   GarageBand: USE REGIONS TO CREATE ARRANGEMENTS

Once you have divided your song into regions (see previous tip), it's time for the fun part—
creating an arrangement. Let's say your song contains the following regions: Intro, Verse,
Chorus, and Close. These are arranged like so: Intro / Verse / Chorus / Close. Basic, but boring.
You decide to add a second verse, so you click on the Verse region in the Arrange Track, press-
and-hold the Option key, drag a copy, and drop it after the Chorus region. You don't want to
end with the verse, so you click-and-drag a copy of the chorus and drop it between the Verse
and Close regions. Better, but still not destined to be a hit. You add another verse and chorus,
but now it's going back to boring. So you click on the last verse you created and press the
Delete key to get rid of it, and create another copy of the chorus. Better, but three choruses in
a row doesn't work. No problem. You write a quick turnaround and a bridge, which you wrap
in new regions. You click on the Bridge region and drag it (no Option key this time) between
the last two choruses. Then you put the Turnaround region between the bridge and the last
chorus. Perfect. You can Option-drag, move, or cut-and-paste regions to your heart's content.
The real beauty is when you move a region, all the tracks in the region move as a group. That
means you don't have to worry about leaving the drum track behind. But then again, it's just a
drummer. If we were talking guitar player, now that would be a different story.

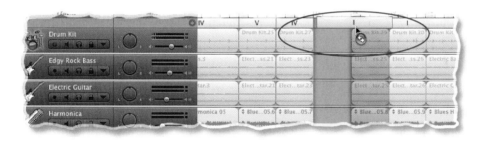

   GarageBand: DEMYSTIFYING THE LOOP BROWSER

At first glance, the Loop Browser can be confusing. But once you understand how it works, you'll find it a rather ingenious method of searching. The keyboard shortcut to open the Loop Browser is Command-L (of course you knew that because you read a tip about it at the beginning of this chapter). When the browser opens, you will see 30 keyword buttons that are used to search for loops. It's not immediately apparent, but the three search categories are Genre, Instrument, and Mood (plus Favorites if you've marked any). To search, just select any keywords that fit. The more keywords you select, the more focused your search will be. For example, here I wanted some Country loops (something to drive my daughter nuts) with a single clean acoustic guitar playing something cheerful and relaxed. The browser sorted through thousands of loops and narrowed it down to four possibilities. It doesn't make any difference what order you select the keywords in. If you select one then change your mind, just click it again to deselect it. If you want to start all over again, just click the Reset button in the top-left corner. One more thing: don't worry if my browser doesn't have the same buttons as yours or has them in a different order. Read the next tip and you'll see why.

   GarageBand: CHANGE THE ORDER OF LOOP BROWSER BUTTONS

If you don't like the order of the loop buttons in the Loop Browser, you can easily change them. For example, if you want the Percussion loop button up top, just click directly on that button and drag it to the top row. You can also rename the loop buttons. So if instead of the All Drums loop button, you'd like it to show just snares, Control-click on the All Drums button, select Instruments, then All Drums, and choose Snare. You can use this same trick to change any Instruments button into either a Genre button or a Descriptors button.

   GarageBand: USING THE BUILT-IN TUNER

GarageBand has a built-in digital tuner that you can use to make sure your real guitar, bass, etc., is perfectly in tune. To use this tuner, first create a new Real Instrument track (go to the Track menu and choose New Track). Then click the up and down arrows at the left side of the LCD display until you see the Tuning Fork icon. Now just play a note on your instrument and make any adjustments necessary based on what the Tuner display shows.

   GarageBand: SEEING THE REST OF THE LOOP BROWSER BUTTONS

By default, you can see 30 keyword buttons. But there are more buttons available (even some blank buttons waiting to be customized), but they're kind of hidden. To make them visible, click anywhere on the dark, brushed metal bar above the Loop Browser and drag it up.

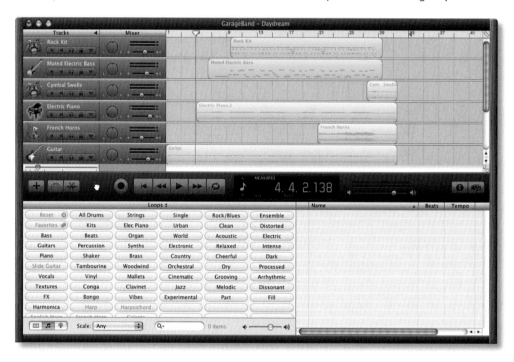

     GarageBand: YOU WON'T BELIEVE ALL THE EFFECTS

You will be blown away by the number of effects available to you. I used to work in the audio field and I can't imagine how much it would cost to load up effects racks with all the digital processing equipment that is available with just a couple of clicks. To access the effects, press Command-I to show the Track Info. If you click the Software Instrument tab at the top of the Info panel, you will see a list of instrument categories in the left-hand column. Click on an instrument category, and you will see all the specific instruments available in the right-hand column. If you go to the bottom-left corner of the Track Info panel and click on Details, you will see a list of the most common types of effects on the left and the preset that is applied to the instrument that's currently selected. Here's the thing: There are dozens of presets available for each of the dozens of instruments. If you can't find a preset you like, you can adjust each of the effects manually. I don't think even Stephen Hawking could figure out how many possible combinations are available for shaping your sound. Personally, I think presets are one of God's greatest creations.

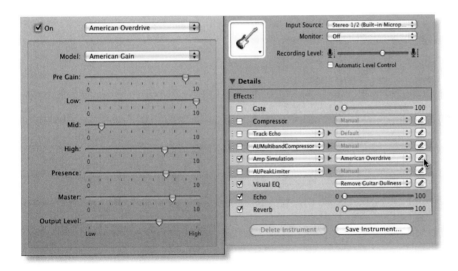

   GarageBand: ADD AUTOMATION TO INDIVIDUAL TRACKS

Bands made up of bad musicians subscribe to the belief that every member of the band should play every note of every song at maximum volume. That's why they are painful to listen to. Good musicians understand that songs need to "breathe," and are very careful to vary different dynamics throughout a composition. They vary the loudness and intensity. There are sections when every instrument is playing, and others when there is only one. GarageBand has the capability of automating dynamics changes multiple times for each track. To view the automation for a track, click the Automation button (the little triangle located at the far-right end of the row of buttons under the track's name). The default param- eter is volume. You'll notice there is a green shaded area visible in the track now. Click on the top of the shaded

area at the horizontal point where you want to change the volume. A green ball will be set at the point you clicked. Now you can click the green ball and drag it up or down to increase/ decrease the volume of this one track. Now go to the next point along the track where you want the volume for the track to change again and, just like before, click the top border of the green shaded area. You can add as many points as you like in any track. You can also add addi- tional parameters for individual tracks. Just click the pop-up menu again, select Add Automa- tion, and then make a selection from the list that appears.

  GarageBand: ADD EFFECTS TO ALL TRACKS AT ONCE

Typically, there are certain effects you want to apply to an entire song. To do that, Press Command-B to show a Master Track at the bottom of the Tracks window. If the Track Info panel isn't visible, press Command-I, and then click the Master Track tab. In the left column there is a list of various general musical styles. When you select one of the options, a list of presets for that style appears in the right column. Click on one of the presets and you will see the default settings for each of the effects parameters in the Details section at the bottom. If you are a sound engineer (or a wannabe), feel free to click the little pencil to the right of each preset and edit that effects parameter manually.

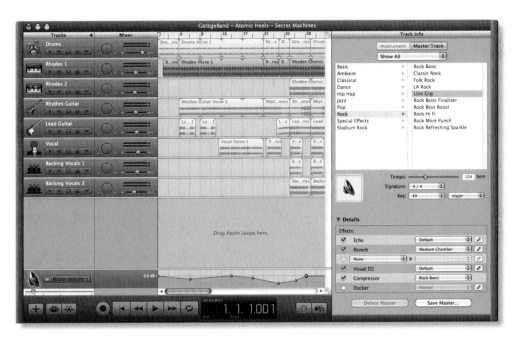

GarageBand: MAKE FINE ADJUSTMENTS WITH PANNING KNOBS

Every track has a panning knob in the Mixer column (if
you don't see the Mixer column, press Command-Y) that
is used to place the audio output of the track in the left
speaker, the right speaker, or somewhere in between.
If you adjust it by clicking on the outside edge of the
knob, it snaps to preset increments. For example, as
you "turn" to the right, it jumps to +16, then +32, then
+48, then +63. But if you click the center of the knob
and scroll up and down, you can make adjustments in
1% increments. Here's another fine tuning tip: if you're
using the volume slider to adjust the volume for a track,
press-and-hold the Shift key and you'll be able to make
finer adjustments.

   GarageBand: FADING OUT AT THE END OF A SONG

If you can't come up with a good ending for your song, do what the pros do—fade out. To do
that, press Command-B to make the Master Track visible, then select Track and choose Fade
Out. You'll notice that some points have been added to the Master Volume curve to create a
10-second gradual fade at the end of the song. If you want to adjust the time or shape of the
fade (make it more or less gradual), all you need to do is click on one of the points and drag it
until the volume curve is the length and shape you want. Here's the thing to remember: the
steeper the curve, the faster the fade.

  ● **GarageBand: TRY OUT A LOOP BEFORE COMMITTING TO IT**

Sometimes a loop sounds great by itself, but when you drag it up into your Timeline and play it with everything else, it just doesn't fit. Well, here's a great tip for trying out loops with your song, without having to add them to your song first: Just click the Play button for your song, then click on the loop you want to try out (in the Loop Browser). In a second or two, you'll hear both your song and the loop, which is automatically synced to the song. So if you like what you hear, you can drag the loop to a new track, but if it just doesn't fit with the other tracks (who would have dreamed that the Tennessee Twister loop I tried out wouldn't blend with the French Horns and Hollywood Strings?), you just saved yourself the work of adding it and then deleting it.

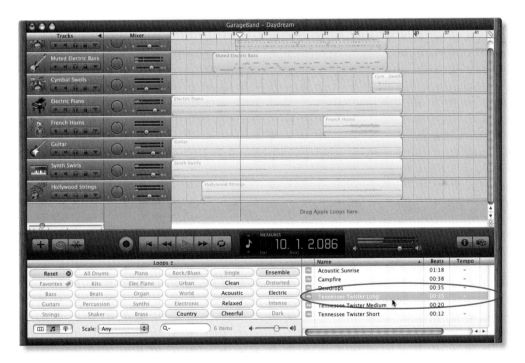

   GarageBand: IT'S NOT JUST FOR MUSIC

The number of podcasts available has exploded in the past couple of years, but unfortunately the production quality of many of them hasn't been a top priority with the podcasters. Obviously, the persons responsible for these weapons of mass distortion don't use GarageBand, which, in addition to being such an amazing application for producing music, is loaded with tools to produce kickin' podcasts. When you launch GarageBand, choose Create New Podcast Episode from the options on the splash screen and start playing around. Even if you don't use all the features of GarageBand for production, you should consider using it to record your audio tracks. Bad audio in a podcast is like a neon sign flashing "cheesy amateur." But if you take advantage of the plethora (gosh, I love that word. It makes me feel like I have a plethora of IQ points—or is it a dearth?) of effects, it will give your sound the professional quality that will set your podcast apart from the pack.

   GarageBand: PUT TOGETHER YOUR OWN MAGIC BAND

When I was learning to play the blues, I would buy CDs that were basically recordings of a blues band without the lead instrument. I would pull out my guitar, put on the CD, and pretend I was in a smoky club in Memphis playing the blues. Now I can form my own Magic GarageBand to help enable my musical fantasy. To form a band, launch GarageBand and select Magic GarageBand from the options on the splash screen. When the stage window opens, select the style of music you want to play and click the Audition button in the lower-right corner. The curtain will open and your band is there waiting to rock the house. Once the applause dies down, press the Play button. While the band plays a loop, if you click on an instrument, you'll see a row of other instruments available to play this part. So if you're playing Slow Blues and want to hear what it would sound like with a Gritty guitar playing the Melody, walk over to the horn players on the stage and tell them to take a break (in other words, click on their picture). Now select the Gritty guitar from the row of instruments sitting in front of the stage, and in just a couple of seconds you'll swear Stevie Ray has just joined the band. Pretty cool—especially if you're not a musician. When you have the right players on the right instruments and things are really starting to groove, click the Create Project button in the lower-right corner and you can save your song for an encore performance.

   iMovie: IT'S NOT ALL BAD

If you're new to Macs and have never used previous versions of iMovie, you probably think iMovie '08 is a great application. iMovie '08 does a good job doing what it is intended to do—serve as a place to store and access all your videos (like iPhoto does for photos) and allow you to put together short videos very quickly using techniques you use in other applications (like selecting clips the same way you select text in other apps), and share them online (YouTube or MobileMe) with the click of a button. But if you believe Apple when they tell you it's an upgrade to iMovie and try to use it like the previous versions, you're going to start cussing, throwing things, and sending off nasty emails to Steve Jobs. So here's my advice:

- Accept the fact that it's not iMovie HD and don't try to make it do things that an application named iMovie ought to do.
- Embrace its simplicity to do those "quick and dirty" videos you get sucked into doing by family and friends.
- Keep iMovie HD on your drive to use when you need to edit video (not just put together some clips). If you don't have a copy, Apple has made it available as a free download for registered owners of iMovie '08. Interesting, huh?

DAVID GALES

   iMovie: SKIMMING ROCKS

Despite my rants, iMovie '08 does have a couple of really cool features. One of them is skimming. Open any event in your Video Library, and it will be displayed so it looks like a filmstrip (if the word "filmstrip" doesn't stir up memories of sitting in a darkened elementary school classroom watching images from a wound-up roll of 16mm film projected onto a screen that pulled down in front of the chalkboard…your video will open up as a row of thumbnails in the source video window). If the part of the clip you want to use doesn't happen to be at the beginning of the strip, move the cursor (technically, it's called a pointer in iMovie) to its approximate location. As you move the pointer, you'll see the video play in the Preview window. But it doesn't really play, it skims through the video and shows you the frames that are under the pointer. It's a huge time saver that you'll find yourself using a lot.

   iMovie: PLAYHEAD INFORMATION WILL DRIVE YOU CRAZY

As you no doubt noticed while you were skimming through some video with the previous tip, an annoying (that doesn't even come close to describing it, but my children might actually read this) box that gives you insanely detailed and utterly useless information about when the clip that is under the playhead was created appears. It does provide one helpful piece of information: a time read-out showing you exactly what frame the playhead is over. If you find the Playhead Information feature as annoying as I do, go to the View menu, scroll to the bottom, and click on Playhead Info to deselect it (better yet, just press Command-Y and end your misery faster).

   iMovie: SPLIT DAYS INTO SEPARATE EVENTS AUTOMATICALLY

Let's say you just took a 10-day vacation to New Zealand and want to put together a video that will have a different section for each day. You can, of course, import all the video into a "Dream Vacation" event, then split it apart later. But you don't need to work that hard. When you import the video, click the Create New Event radio button, then turn on

the Split Days Into New Events checkbox. iMovie will read the information that's embedded in your video and split it up for you, thus freeing you from the chore of having to look at hours of video of breathtaking natural beauty.

   iMovie: JUST IMPORT THE VIDEO YOU NEED

Your children's school programs are always more interesting when you're watching them in person than when you're reliving the entire thing—all 83 minutes of it—on video. Fortunately, you don't have to import the entire thing into iMovie, just the three-minute clip that has your little girl's class singing their song. Here's how:

STEP ONE: Set the switch on the left side of the Import window to Manual (shown here, circled in red).

STEP TWO: Use the playback controls in the Import window to rewind, fast-forward, and review your tape. After you've reviewed your video, rewind the tape to the point where you want to start importing.

STEP THREE: Click Import. The video begins importing from the point where you had queued it.

STEP FOUR: Click Stop when you want to stop importing. Each time you stop importing, iMovie takes a few minutes to generate thumbnail images of your imported video.

STEP FIVE: To import additional video, repeat steps 2 through 4.

Here's another tip for you: Next time, don't set the camera on a tripod, press Record, and let it run, and run, and run. Just tape the highlights—that would be anytime your daughter is on stage.

   iMovie: MERGING EVENTS CAN BE A DRAG

If you shoot a lot of video, you will end up with a lot of events. To keep things a bit neater, you can merge multiple events. For example, if you have separate events for every birthday in your family for the past year, you could merge them into one "Birthdays" event. There are two ways to do the merge: (1) click on one or more events in the Event Library and drag them on top of another event; or (2) select multiple events, Control-click, and choose Merge Events from the contextual menu. If you ever change your mind, click the event that contains the clip you want to unmerge, then click the clip itself and select the portion you want to split out (or press Command-A to select the whole thing). Now, from the File menu, choose Split Event Before Selected Clip.

   iMovie: PREVENT STORAGE SPACE THEFT

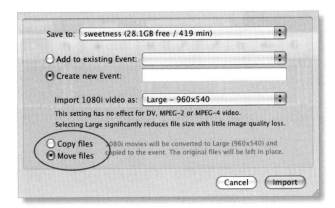

Video sucks up hard drive space—gigabytes and gigabytes of space. Every five minutes of video will cost you around 1 GB of storage space. The good news is, drives are constantly getting bigger and cheaper. The bad news is you have to keep stacking up external drives on your desk as your storage needs increase. Here's a tip that can save you some drive space. iMovie '08 only uses video that is stored in its Video Library. So if you want to use a piece of video you put onto your drive without using iMovie '08, before you can use it in a project, iMovie must perform a purification ritual to make sure it is worthy of admittance to the Video Library. Here's the thing: when you go to the File menu and select Import Movies, iMovie will give you the option to either move the existing movie file into your iMovie project folder or copy it there. Unless you have a compelling reason to keep two copies of the video on your drive, having iMovie move it into the Library will save yourself a lot of drive space. Waste a gigabyte here and a gigabyte there, and pretty soon you've wasted some serious space.

   iMovie: ALL SELECTIONS CAN BE CREATED EQUAL

If you're putting together a video where you want different clips of the same length to show in sequence, you'll love this tip. By default, whenever you click on a video clip in the source video window, four seconds of video are selected, starting at the point you clicked. So all you have to do to assemble your clips is click the source video to create the selections, then drag them into the Project window. If you want to change the length of the selections, go to the iMovie menu, and select Preferences. Halfway down the dialog, you'll see a slider (just under Clicking in Events Browser Selects) you can use to set a new selection default.

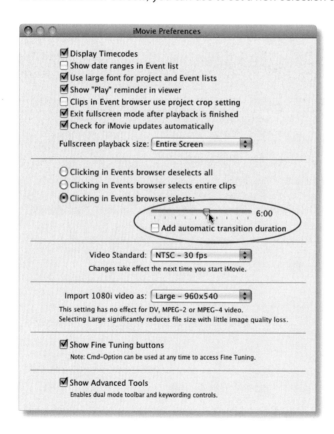

   iMovie: **SOME QUICK TIPS ON SELECTIONS**

Here are a couple of quick tips for selecting a portion of a clip:

- To change the beginning or ending point for a selection, just Shift-click where you want the new point (either beginning or ending) to be.
- Another way to adjust a selection is to click the left or right edge of the yellow selection box and drag it until it's the size you want.
- If you want to set the in/out points more accurately, slide the clip thumbnail slider (it's in the bottom-right corner of the window) to the left before you make your selection.

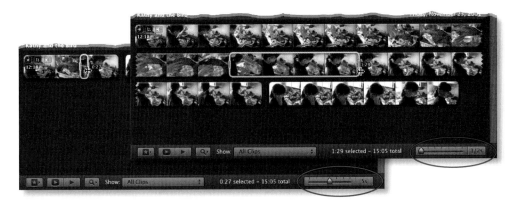

  iMovie: **RIGHT SIZE—WRONG PLACE**

What if you have a selection that is the length you need, but it's not selecting the part of the clip you want to use? All you have to do is get your video gear, put the family on the plane and head back to the Grand Canyon to reshoot the whole thing. Or, a less time-consuming option would be to go to the source video window and move the cursor until it is over the top or bottom edge of the yellow box that's around your selection. When the pointer changes to a hand with two little arrows, simply click-and-hold the mouse and drag the selection wherever you want it. The key to this tip is the hand with two arrows. If you don't see arrows, you're not over the selection box, and it won't work. No arrows—no work.

   iPhoto: IMPORT PHOTOS FROM YOUR CAMERA

If you're importing photos from a camera or memory card, when you connect your camera or memory card reader to your Mac, by default iPhoto launches and shows you thumbnails of the photos on the card. Now, you can either select particular photos (by Command-clicking on them) you want to import to your Mac and click the Import Selected button in the lower right-hand corner, or just click Import All to grab them all. You can always delete the bad ones later.

iPhoto: IMPORT PHOTOS FROM YOUR DRIVE INTO iPHOTO

Apple's iLife and iWork applications all work together and make it easy to access resources between different applications. If I'm working on a spreadsheet in Numbers (one of the iWork applications), I can click the Media button on the toolbar and access any audio, photo, or movie file on my Mac. It's easiest to browse them if they are in one of the iLife or iWork applications, which is one of the advantages to having all your photos in your iPhoto Library. To import them, go to the File menu and choose Import to Library. Now simply navigate to the location of the photos you want to import and click the Import button.

   iPhoto: RATE PHOTOS FAST BY BATCHING

In iPhoto you can rate photos on a scale of one to five stars, but unless you really love performing mind-numbing tedious tasks, here is how you can rate your photos in batches. Locate the first photo you want to have a five-star rating and click on it. Then Command-click on other photos you feel are deserving of the elite status of five stars. When you have all of them selected (or at least a good chunk of them), press Command-5 and every photo you selected will instantly be rated with five stars. Now just do the same thing for four-star photos, three-star photos, etc. *Note:* If you don't see the stars under your photos when you rate them, press Command-Shift-R to display them.

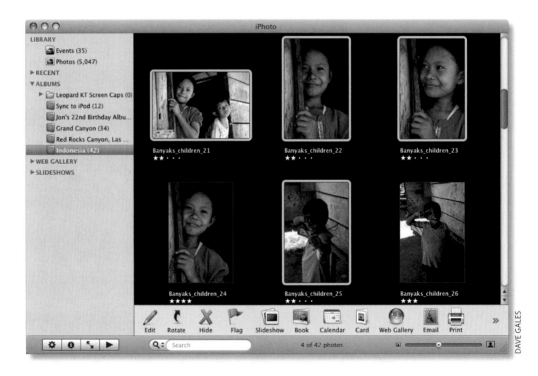

DAVE GALES

   iPhoto: AUTOMATICALLY ORGANIZE YOUR PHOTOS BY EVENT

Our lives are marked by events, not random dates. I remember teaching my daughter to ride a bike, backpacking with my son and having the bears get all our food during the night, my youngest son's first flying lesson, and my youngest daughter's first violin solo. But I couldn't even get close if you asked me the dates of when these things happened. So it only makes sense to organize photos the same way. It figures that if it works for my brain, it should work for my pictures. The easiest way to organize your photos by event is to let iPhoto do it automatically when you import photos. iPhoto assumes that if you took 73 photos on February 3, and another couple of dozen on February 13, they were different events and will organize them accordingly. To adjust the time period that triggers a new event, go to the iPhoto menu, select Preferences, and click the Events icon in the Preferences dialog. Now click on the Auto-split Into Events pop-up menu and pick a time period.

iPhoto: CHOOSE A NEW PHOTO FOR YOUR EVENT THUMBNAIL

When you view your events in iPhoto, they have nice big, beautiful thumbnails—most of the time. Occasionally, a really bad photo will come up as the Key Photo (as it's officially known). Fortunately, it's easy to change. All you have to do is move your cursor back and forth over the event to skim through all the photos. When you find the one you want to use, Control-click on it and choose Make Key Photo from the contextual menu.

DAVE GALES

   iPhoto: COMPARE PHOTOS SIDE BY SIDE

Sometimes when you are making corrections to photos, it's helpful to be able to see them in the same window so you can compare the results. Here's how: Select the thumbnails of the images you want to compare (you can view up to eight at once), go to the View menu, and choose Full Screen (or click the Full Screen button in the bottom-left corner of the thumbnail window). That's it. If you want to replace one of the previews with a different photo, click it once to make it active (you'll know it's active when it has the white frame around it), then use the Arrow keys on your keyboard to scroll through other photos (if you want to go directly to a specific photo, move your cursor to the top of the screen and select the image you want from the thumbnail strip). Now you can move the pointer to the bottom of the screen and use the image correction tools to make adjustments to the photos.

DAVE GALES

  iPhoto: ROTATE A GROUP OF PHOTOS AT ONCE

There is a law that clearly states that all photos must be taken horizontally. Think about it. Ever go to a movie and see the screen set vertically? Me neither. Ever tried to buy a television with a vertical screen? Good luck. Computer screens? Horizontal. Even the walls in your home and/ or office are most likely horizontal. So when iPhoto imports your photos, it brings them in horizontally. Sure, you can rotate a thumbnail by selecting it and clicking the Rotate button. But if you just got back from a trip to New York City, I'm thinkin' you have more than a couple of photos that violate the horizontal law. Here's an easy fix: slide the thumbnail size adjustment slider to the left so you can see a lot of thumbnails at once. Just make sure they're big enough to see if the image is vertical or horizontal. Next, Command-click on each of the thumbnails you want to rotate. When you have them all selected, click the Rotate button and the Empire State Building will be pointing in the right direction in all your photos.

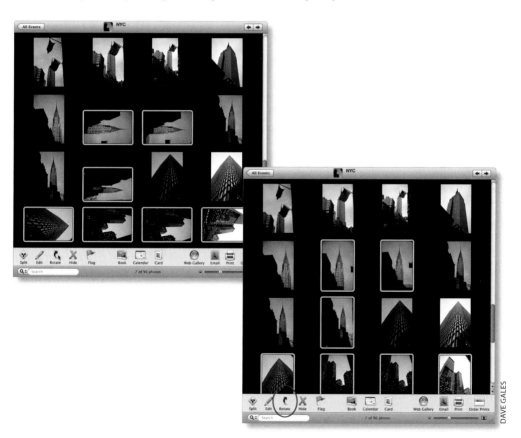

DAVE GALES

   iPhoto: ROTATING IN THE OPPOSITE DIRECTION

When you click the Rotate button, by default it rotates your image counterclockwise. If you want to rotate your image clockwise, just press-and-hold the Option key before you click the Rotate button (you'll notice the arrow on the button is now pointing to the right, not the left). If you want to make this a permanent change, press Command-, (comma) to open the preferences, click the General icon, and choose your default Rotate direction.

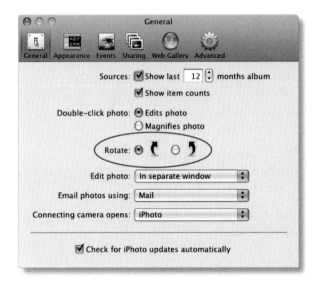

   iPhoto: PHOTOGRAPHERS' BASIC BLACK

There's a background that's very popular with photographers for organizing their photos—basic black. Using black as your background gives you that "artsy photographer" look that artsy photographers love. To get that look, go to the iPhoto menu and choose Preferences. Click the Appearance icon and drag the Background slider to the far left (to Black). Then it's up to you whether you want your thumbnails to appear with a white border (turn on the Outline checkbox under Border section) or without (by turning off all Border checkboxes).

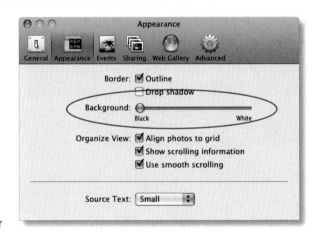

   iPhoto: CORRECT THE COLOR BALANCE (AND OTHER PROBLEMS)

This is a bad picture. Well, it's not really a bad picture, it's an old picture that has had a color shift. Okay—it's a bad, old picture that has had a color shift. Everyone has photos packed away in boxes or photo albums in the back of a closet that have developed a color cast (usually it's yellow or magenta). You'll be happy to know that you can fix them with just a couple of clicks in iPhoto. Once you have your photos scanned and imported into iPhoto, double-click on one of them to switch to Edit mode. (If you've changed iPhoto's preferences to edit photos in another application when you double-click on them, here's how you can edit the photo in iPhoto: click once on the photo to select it, then click the Edit button in the lower-left corner of the Preview window.) Once you're in Edit mode, click the Adjust button (if you don't see it, make the window wider). Many times a photo will have multiple problems that need to be fixed. In the example here, both the exposure and the color balance needed to be corrected. Legally, it doesn't matter which you do first, but I usually work on the color balance before exposure. There are two steps to correcting color balance: First, click on the Eyedropper tool. Second, move the crosshair cursor to a spot in the picture that should be a neutral gray color. Something white that is in a shadow would be an example. When the crosshair is in position, click. How's that for dramatic effect?

DAVE GALES

It's not perfect, but it's a whole lot better than what it was before. Since this procedure is so complicated, let me run through it once more: click, click. If the colors really whack out when you perform the second click, it just means you weren't over a neutral color. Just move the crosshair to another spot and click again. Now you can correct other problems such as exposure, sharpness, etc.

   iPhoto: COPY & PASTE CORRECTIONS

Once you have made corrections to one of your photos, you can copy-and-paste the corrections to as many other photos as you want. When you have a photo adjusted to your liking, go to the lower-right corner of the Adjust palette and click the Copy button. Now, double-click another image to open it, click the Adjust button from the toolbar along the bottom of the window, then click the Paste button. Instant correction—it's a wonderful thing.

  iPhoto: **SOMETIMES LESS IS MORE—SO CROP YOUR PHOTO**

We did a Photoshop seminar in Ottawa last summer and had a couple of days to hang out before going to the next city. This young man was part of the changing of the guard ceremony at the Tomb of the Unknown Soldier, which was right across the street from our hotel. How could you walk past this guy and not take his picture? I like a lot of things about this shot, but to me, the bayonet sticking up is distracting. But if it wasn't sticking up, I wouldn't be able to show you the Crop tool, so it's all good. Double-click the image you want to crop to open it in Edit mode, then click on the Crop tool. If you have a particular size you want your photo to be, click the pop-up menu that's at the bottom center of the photo and select the size you want. While there, scroll to the bottom of the list and select an orientation for your image. By default, the Constrain checkbox is turned on, so when you click anywhere on the edge of the cropping border and drag, the size of the border will change, but it will keep the correct proportion for the print size you selected. You can always turn off the Constrain checkbox and make your print any proportion you want. If you click inside the border, the cursor changes to a hand, which allows you to click-and-drag the entire cropping border to position it where you want it. The grid lines are there to help you compose your photo using the rule of thirds. When you have everything the way you want, simply click the Apply button.

DAVE GALES

   iPhoto: REMOVE BLEMISHES AND DUST SPOTS

If you have ever owned stock in the company that makes Clearasil, I think you owe me a huge "Thank you" for the thousands of tubes I've purchased in my life. When I was a teenager I used to dream of the day when I would outgrow my complexion issues. I haven't been a teenager in a lot of years and I'm still dreaming. Fortunately, blemishes are a whole lot easier to get rid of in iPhoto than in real life. Open the photo with the blemish you want to get rid of, then click the Retouch tool. The trick to using this tool is you want to have the brush slightly bigger than the spot you want to remove. As you slide the Size adjustment slider back and forth, you will see a circle indicating the size of the brush tip. Center the brush over the blemish, and then click. Presto! No more blemish. You can also use the Retouch tool to fix dust spots, reflections from bright objects, or scratches. For things like scratches, click-and-drag the brush along the length of the scratch.

iPhoto: MAKE YOUR PHOTOS POP

iPhoto '08 has added some surprisingly sophisticated image editing tools that typically are only available in higher-end applications. To access them, open one of your photos in Edit mode, then click the Adjust button at the bottom of the window. Don't let all these options scare you. Most of the adjustment sliders' functions are self-explanatory. The best advice I can give you is just to slide them and see what they do to your image. No matter how bad you end up making your photo look, you can always go down to the lower-left corner and click Reset to go back to the default settings—or, if you press-and-hold the Option key, Reset changes to Revert (as shown here), which will roll things back to the settings you had the last time you saved the image. Typical adjustments that you will make are correcting exposure, lightening faces and opening up detail in shadow areas with the Shadows slider, and adding some sharpening. Often, seemingly slight adjustments will make your photo just pop. It's difficult to explain, but you'll know it when you see it.

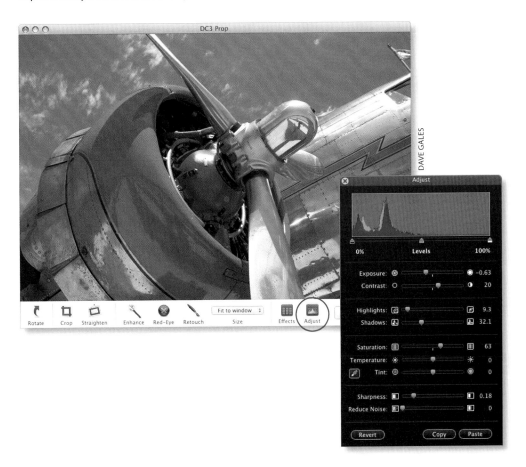

   iPhoto: DEFEATING DA DOUBLE-CLICK DEFAULT

Many authors would never even think of butchering the English language like I did in the title of this tip just to preserve alliteration. Frankly, it doesn't bother me. And if you're reading this, that means it must not have bothered the editors too much either. So here's the deal: Depending on how you have your preferences set, double-clicking a thumbnail in iPhoto will either display a large preview of the image, or open the image to be edited (either in iPhoto or an external editor [see the next tip]). But you can temporarily override the default by pressing-and-holding the Option key when you double-click. If you want to switch the default, just press Command-, (comma) to open iPhoto's preferences and select the other option for Double-click Photo.

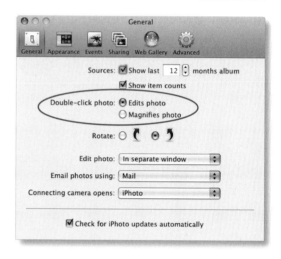

   iPhoto: EDIT PHOTOS IN ANOTHER EDITING APPLICATION

iPhoto lets you adjust a variety of aspects of your image, from tonal adjustments to removing red eye, using iPhoto's built-in image editor. However, you can have iPhoto launch the editing application of your choice (such as Adobe Photoshop or Photoshop Elements) when you double-click on the image inside iPhoto. Go to the iPhoto menu, choose Preferences, and then click the General icon. Now, under Double-click Photo, click on the Edits Photo radio button, and then use the Edit Photo pop-up menu to select the application you want to use to edit your photo. Now whenever you double-click a photo, it will open in your favorite image-editing application.

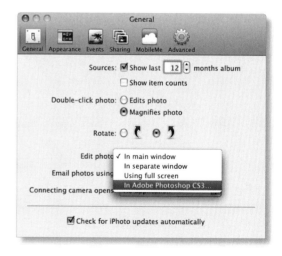

   iPhoto: HAVE FUN WITH SPECIAL EFFECTS

Some photos are boring. That might be a little harsh. However, there are some images that are okay, but they just need a little something extra. If it were professional baseball, you could just use steroids (that one is definitely harsh), but iPhoto has something even better—effects. Double-click an image in your iPhoto Library (unless you have set up double-clicking to open photos in an external editor, in which case you will need to Control-click on the image in the Library and choose Edit from the contextual menu), and then click the Effects button located just below the preview window. (If you don't see the Effects button, make the window wider and you'll see it.) Now just click on one of the effects to see how it looks on your photo. When you click on some of the effects, you will see a number between two arrows at the bottom of the effect's thumbnail. If you click on the arrows, you can increase or decrease the intensity of the effect. You can also combine effects (the image shown here has Sepia, Edge Blur, and Vignette applied) to create different looks. If at any point you're not feeling a good vibe about how things are looking, just click the thumbnail in the center of the Effects palette and you'll go right back to your original.

DAVE GALES

   iPhoto: CREATE ALBUMS OF SPECIAL PHOTOS

Remember the photo albums that people used to get that had the sticky pages with the plastic sheet that covered your photos? If the glue from the page didn't destroy your photos, the chemicals in the plastic page did. We have some photo albums packed away somewhere that we never look at. But I have some albums in iPhoto that I sync with my iPod. This means I can look at them any time I want, I can change the pictures with a couple of clicks, and there is no glue to destroy them. Here are some different ways to create albums.

OPTION ONE: Browse through your photos and select the ones you want to collect into an album. When you have them all selected, go to the File menu and select New Album from Selection.

OPTION TWO: When you are collecting photos from multiple events to put into an album, after you select a photo you want to add, press Command-. (period) to flag it and move on to the next one. You don't have to worry about keeping photos selected, and if you flag one accidentally, just press Command-. again to "de-flag" it. Once you have your flags set, go to the sidebar and click on the Flagged category and you'll see your photos. Press Command-A to select them all, and then go to the File menu and select New Album from Selection.

OPTION THREE: Go to the File menu and select New Album. Give your album a name (maybe something like "My Favorite Pictures of Myself") and start browsing your photos. When you find one you want to add to your new album, just click on it and drag it on top of the album's icon in the sidebar. When you see the green plus sign (+), release the mouse button. You can also select multiple photos and drag-and-drop them all into the album at once.

    iPhoto: **PUBLISH AN ALBUM TO THE WEB WITH TWO CLICKS**

For the past several years, Apple has been coming up with ways to make it easy to put your photos and movies on your own website. We're not talking cheesy sites—the templates they have come up with make them look better than a lot of "real" sites you visit. But I've gotta tell you, they have absolutely blown me away with the online capabilities you have with iPhoto '08 and the ease with which you can use them. You know the photo album you put together in the last tip? You can put it on the Web with two clicks. Here we go:

CLICK ONE: Click the Album icon in the sidebar to open it, then press Command-A to select the photos.

CLICK TWO: Click the Web Gallery button at the top, enter a name for your gallery, and press Publish.

Easy enough? Now as you probably noticed, there are some options that you can select, but they'll require some additional clicks. Now that your gallery is up, the next tip will show you some things you can do with it.

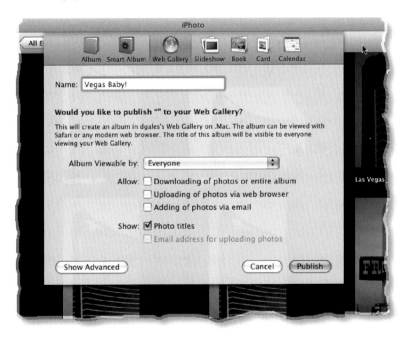

   iPhoto: MAKE YOUR WEB GALLERY A COMMUNITY EFFORT

In the previous tip, I mentioned some options that are available (I downplayed them, as you no doubt noticed, since I didn't want to mess up the two-click thing. Somehow saying, "You can publish your own Web gallery with only eight clicks!" doesn't have the same pizzazz.) But now that I've backed up my two-click claim, here are some other options you can use that will take your Web gallery to the next level of coolness:

- Turn on the Downloading of Photos or Entire Album checkbox if you want visitors to be able to download the photos.
- Turn on the Uploading of Photos Via Web Browser checkbox: I'm guessing you've got this one figured out.
- Turn on the Adding of Photos Via Email checkbox. This is very cool. If you select this option, you will have an email address you can use yourself—and can give to other people—that will allow you to send photos to the gallery and have them added automatically. If you turn on this option, you can choose to have the email address appear on the gallery (by turning on the Email Address for Uploading Photos checkbox from the Show section), so anyone who visits can use it.

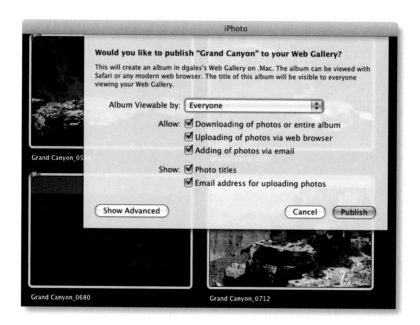

   iPhoto: CONTROLLING ACCESS TO YOUR WEB GALLERY

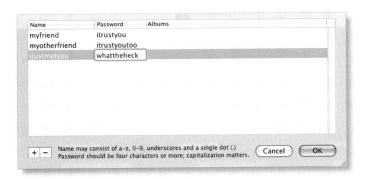

If the idea of allowing anyone who has the Web address of your gallery to have this level of access (see the previous tip) seems a bit scary—that's because it is. You need to be careful, or you might end up with a lot of pictures on your gallery that will require some serious explaining. But there is something you can do to limit access. At the top of the dialog with all the publishing options, instead of selecting Everyone from the Album Viewable By pop-up menu, select Edit Names and Passwords. This allows you to basically set up accounts for those people that you trust. Any gallery set up like this won't even appear on your public site. It will have a special address you can give to the people you have set up a password for. One nice thing is that all your galleries don't have to be set up the same way. *Note:* You can change access for an existing Web gallery by selecting it in the sidebar, then clicking the Settings button located at the left end of the toolbar under the preview window.

   **iPhoto: ADD NEW PHOTOS TO iPHOTO AUTOMATICALLY**

To a computer, a photo gallery is no different than a news story—in the end it's all just ones and zeros. That means that, in the same way that you can subscribe to RSS feeds in Safari to get updates to a website automatically sent to you, people can do the same thing with your Web galleries. To subscribe to a feed for your albums, all anyone has to do is click the Subscribe button at the top of the album's gallery window. Now your friends can either get a regular RSS feed, letting them know new images are available, or they can have iPhoto automatically download the new photos directly to their copy of your album on their Mac. How cool is that?

Chapter 14

GLOATING ISN'T A SIN

SHOWING OFF LEOPARD'S SEXY SIDE

I remember back when Windows 98 was introduced, a friend who was a PC user almost started hyperventilating while he was

Gloating Isn't a Sin
showing off leopard's sexy side

telling me about all the cool new features the whiz kids at Microsoft had dreamed up. I felt so sorry for him because Windows users have so little to get excited about—so I let him go on for a while. I even threw in an occasional "Wow, really?" or "That's pretty sweet!" to make him think I was truly impressed. When he finished, I reached in my pocket and pulled out a button someone had given me that simply said, "Windows 98 = Mac 84." Most of the time, Mac users show remarkable restraint when Windows users brag. But Leopard has so many "over the top" cool features that restraint is going to be tough. Okay, some are eye candy (nothing wrong with that), but most are raw power in a pretty wrapper. So gloat, it's okay. God understands—He's a Mac user, too.

    HERE'S TO THE CRAZIES

One of the things that makes Apple different from other computer companies is their obsessive (in a good way) attention to design. It's not just evident in the design of the computers, it's evident in their peripherals (compare any Apple power supply to any Dell power brick), cables (white cable? Must be Apple), packaging (the only boxes I keep), and even the bags at the Apple stores. This attention to detail shows up in some very subtle ways in Leopard—the icons, for instance, are tiny little works of art. One of my favorites is the TextEdit icon. You can see that it has some writing on it, which you might assume is just Greeked text. But when you blow it up, you'll notice that it's the text from the voiceover (by Richard Dreyfuss) for Apple's first two "Think Different" television ads. (Here's some trivia for you: the original ad was a 60-second spot. A 30-second spot was also created and was aired only once—during the final episode of *Seinfeld* in 1998.) The commercials were titled "Crazy Ones," and this text was taken from *On the Road,* a novel by Jack Kerouac (kind of a crazy guy himself. He typed the original manuscript on a 120-foot roll of paper, which is currently owned by Jim Irsay—the owner of the Indianapolis Colts). In case you can't read it off your icon, here's the text:

Here's to the crazy ones. The misfits. The rebels. The troublemakers. The round pegs in the square holes. The ones who see things differently. They're not fond of rules. And they have no respect for the status quo. You can praise them, disagree with them, quote them, disbelieve them, glorify or vilify them. About the only thing you can't do is ignore them. Because they change things.

TextEdit
Application

    BLUE SCREEN OF DEATH ICON

Here's my other favorite icon. When you share a network, you see icons for each of the other connected computers. Leopard is pretty smart and matches the icon with the type of computer that's connected. Pretty cool, actually. Well, if a PC has somehow crashed the party, this is the icon that is displayed. Yes, it's every Windows user's nightmare—the infamous Blue Screen of Death. Now most of the tips in this chapter are things you can show to your PC friends and watch them drool. If you show them this one, they are more likely to break out in a cold sweat and start to tremble. I don't know who at Apple came up with the idea, but they rock with a funky beat.

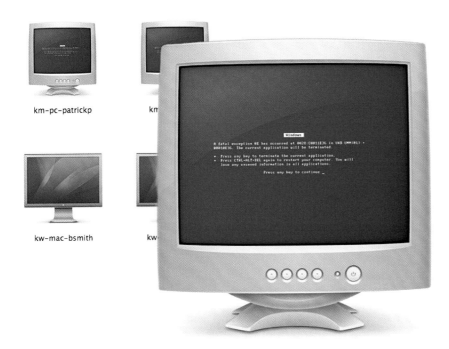

   GET A FULL-SIZED GRAPHIC OF ICONS

I'm not sure the title fully describes what this tip does, so let me explain. The icons in Leopard are highly detailed, but when you see them at the normal sizes, you can't appreciate them fully. Here's how you can see them full-size: Click the icon you want to look at to select it (it doesn't matter if you select it while you're in Icon view, Column view, etc.), and press Command-C to copy it. Now launch Preview and press Command-N to create a new file. Preview will create the file using the contents of the Clipboard, which is, in this case, the icon you copied. When the file opens, you will see a large preview of the icon on a transparent background, along with thumbnails of various sizes. Now you can admire the work of the anonymous persons who developed the icons that make Leopard so easy on the eyes.

DVD PLAYER: PUTTING CAPTIONS IN THEIR OWN WINDOW

Imagine having the ability to put captions in their own separate windows. Then imagine why in the world anyone would want to do this. Not coming up with anything? Me either. Nevertheless, here's how to do it: Go to Features, select Closed Captioning, then choose Separate Window. Obviously, you will have to also select Turn On before they will work, but then I suppose you already figured that one out. Actually, I did just think of why you might want to use this feature. If you had two displays, you could put the movie on one and the captions on the other. I'm still not sure what that would do to enhance your viewing experience, but it's just nice to know it's possible.

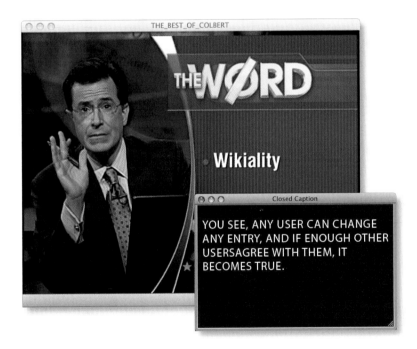

   SPOTLIGHT'S HIDDEN CALCULATOR

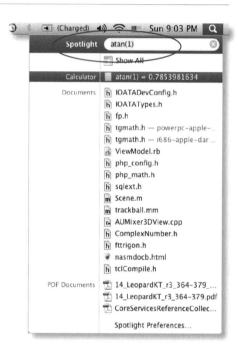

I'm not sure how often I'll use this feature, but it's pretty neat. If you need to do some quick calculating, press Command-Spacebar and type a formula into the Spotlight field (as shown here). When you're finished, the answer will be displayed in the search results list. If you want to explore your calculations further, just press Return and Calculator will open. Don't be fooled by the simplicity of Spotlight's calculator. It's actually a fairly powerful calculator that will handle things like grouping, square and cube roots, logarithms, and even trigonometric functions. So if you are hanging out at a party and want to impress your friends, fire up your Mac and type "atan(1)" into the Spotlight search field and announce authoritatively that the arc tangent of one radian is .785 (rounded to the nearest thousandth, of course). Then, while they're still reeling from wonder, close your Mac and get the heck out of there before someone asks you what an arc tangent is.

   DASHBOARD SUPER SLO-MO WIDGET TRICKS

The next time you're ready to close Dashboard (you close it by pressing the Dashboard or F12 key, or clicking on anything or anywhere other than a widget), and you're not working on a tight deadline or trying to work on your legacy, try this: Press-and-hold the Shift key, then click on something other than a widget (or press the Dashboard or F12 key again). Instead of closing the normal way, Dashboard shifts into super slow motion and your widgets slowly zoom toward you. If you are just closing one widget, you can get a different (but equally cool) effect (as shown here). Just press Option-Shift and click the Close button for the widget. One more: Press-and-hold the Shift key and click the Open the Widget Bar button (the big white plus sign in a circle in the bottom-left corner of your screen). I particularly like the way the plus-sign-in-a-circle rotates as the bar appears. (I never noticed it did that at regular speed.) So why did Apple include slo-mo effects in Dashboard? Because they know we're suckers who just love stupid stuff like that.

  EXPOSÉ SHOW OFF TRICK #1

Exposé not only has a huge "wow" factor, it's useful as well! But don't let that stop you from showing it off. For maximum effect, get a bunch of windows from several applications open on the desktop, then press F9. Wait a few seconds for your friends to get their heart rate under control, then press the Tab key several times to show how only the windows from one application will be highlighted each time you press the Tab key.

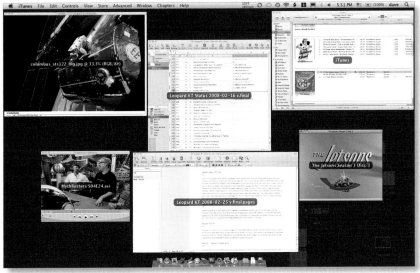

   EXPOSÉ SHOW OFF TRICK #2

After you've shown your friends the first Exposé trick, finish them off with this one. Press-and-hold the Shift key while you press F9, and the Exposé effect will go in super slow motion, which is so cool that it is very possible your friends will be rendered speechless. *Note:* This "press-and-hold the Shift key to go in slo-mo" trick works in other places, too. Try minimizing a window to the Dock while pressing-and-holding the Shift key. Again, totally for show, but "the show must go on!"

   EXPOSÉ—SPACES COMBO TRICK

You know how in boxing, a fighter will hit his opponent with a couple of jabs to the head, then come in with a right-left combo to finish him off? Here's the combo: This will take a little advance preparation to get the full effect. Make sure you have several windows from different applications open in each of three or four spaces. There's nothing magical about the number of spaces; it totally depends on how much setup you feel like doing. Now press F8 to show all your spaces at once. If your friends aren't impressed, it's because they just saw you do this a few minutes ago. They don't know that they've just been set up, so now it's time to deliver the second part of the combo: with the separate spaces still on screen, press F9. You now have Exposé within each of your Spaces. You also have some friends ready to run out to the nearest Apple Store.

   ADDRESS BOOK PHOTO EFFECTS

You can apply some cool effects to your contacts' photos in Address Book. With Address
Book open, click on a contact's name (obviously, one with a photo) to highlight it, and click
the Edit button at the bottom of the window,
then double-click on the photo thumbnail.
Just above the Cancel button at the bottom
of the dialog, you'll see two buttons: a camera
and a swirly thing. Click the swirly button and a
preview dialog will open showing the original
photo surrounded by eight thumbnails of available effects. If you want to see more options,
click the arrows in the bottom corners of the
preview to scroll through all 48 effects that
are available. When you've found the one you
want, click on it, then click the Set button. In
the whole scheme of things, it's a pretty useless
feature. But it's perfect for showing off or pulling a prank.

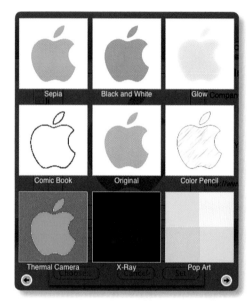

   FIND STUFF YOU NEVER KNEW YOU HAD

The Spotlight window lets you refine your searches to a ridiculous degree. Want to search for a RAW photo you took of your daughter Autumn on August 5, 2006, with a Nikon D200 set in Aperture priority mode at ISO 350 using manual focus, a focal length of 173 mm, 1/300th of a second at f/19 at 2:38 p.m. on a cloudy day (search for white balance set to Cloudy) whose dimensions are 2800x3600 pixels? No problem. Press Command-Option-Spacebar to open Spotlight window. If you click on the Kind pop-up menu, you'll see some of the more common types of files you can search for. Skip those and get to the good stuff by going to the bottom of the list and selecting Other. A list of 157 (sadly, I counted them) additional criteria you can include in any search will open. Just click the plus sign (+) button (at the far right) and select your next search criterion from the list. With each item you add, your list of results will get smaller. So go ahead and get a little crazy seeing how narrow a search you can build and still find something. Geeks do some strange stuff in an attempt to replicate the experience others call "fun."

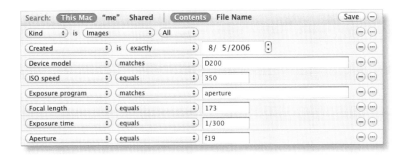

   COLORSYNC SHOW OFF TRICK

I'm sure there's an important reason for this feature; I just can't figure out what it is. But it sure looks cool, and therefore it's a perfect tool for showing off to your PC friends (which may be the real reason it's in the Mac OS in the first place). Here's how it works: Look inside your Applications folder, inside your Utilities folder, and double-click on ColorSync Utility. When ColorSync opens, click the Profiles icon up top, then click the gray right-facing triangle beside System to display a list of profiles. Click on Generic RGB Profile and to the right a Lab Plot color graphic will appear. Here's the show-off part: it's a 3D object—click your cursor right on it, drag upward, and the object will rotate in 3D. Totally cool. Totally useless. I love it!

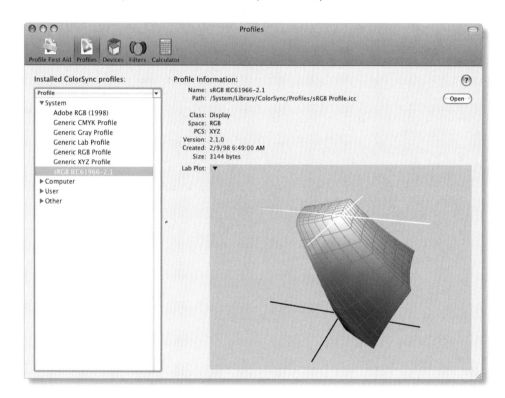

   USE CUSTOM SOUNDS FOR MAIL

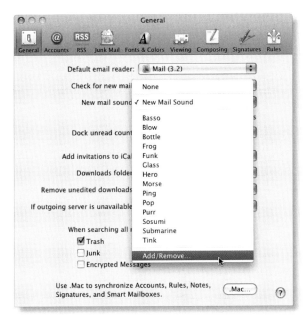

If you don't like Apple's built-in Mail alert sounds, you can use your own custom sounds (I downloaded the AOL classic You've Got Mail.aiff). Once you've got the audio file you want to use for your alert, go to your Home folder, open your Library folder, then open your Sounds folder and drop it in there. Then, go back to Mail, and in the Mail menu choose Preferences. In the Preferences window's toolbar, click the General icon. In the New Mail Sound pop-up menu, you should see your new sound at the bottom of the list. If not, choose Add/Remove (as shown here). This opens your Sounds folder, where you'll find the alert sound you put there moments ago. Click on it,

then click Done, which adds your sound to the New Mail Sound pop-up menu. Now that it's in the list, you can choose it as your new mail sound. Dig it.

   RELOADING A DASHBOARD WIDGET TRICK

Okay, although this one is more of a trick just for the sheer fun of it (because the onscreen animation is pretty cool), it actually has a practical side as well. Just click on an open widget in Dashboard, then press Command-R on your keyboard and the widget kind of twirls away (for lack of a better term) and then reappears. It looks cool, but beyond that it does actually reload the widget (as if you had just clicked-and-dragged it out from the Widget Bar), which refreshes any data that the widget calls upon. Try it once (although it's nearly impossible to do it just once, because the animation is cool enough that you'll have to do it a few times to get it out of your system). *Note:* Pressing this shortcut too much on one widget could cause Dashboard to crash (I'm being serious here).

   GET THE FULL DASHBOARD WEATHER EXPERIENCE

If you've used the Dashboard Weather widget, you've probably already noticed that Apple went to great lengths to design some really cool-looking visuals to let you know in a split second what the weather condition is for the city you're monitoring (including whether it's currently day or night in that city, and it shows the current phase of the moon). But if you live someplace that doesn't get much variation in its weather (for example, I live in Tampa, which means I only see basically sun and thunderstorms), you don't get the full Dashboard weather experience (which includes things like snow, ice, hail, locust plague, etc.). But you can have the Weather widget cycle through all its different weather graphics by pressing-and-holding the Command and Option keys, and then just clicking on the Weather widget (avoiding the city's name, as that will launch your Web browser showing more weather details). This takes you to a hypothetical town called "Nowhere," which apparently experiences a new weather phenomenon with every Command-Option-click (much like Seattle).

IF I COULD TURN BACK TIME

This tip is just for fun, because honestly, it's not tremendously practical, but it looks pretty cool. The next time you're changing the time—using the Date & Time pane in your System Preferences (found under the Apple menu)—and one of your friends or co-workers is watching you, try this: Turn off the Set Date & Time Automatically checkbox, and then instead of typing in the desired time, just grab an hour or minute hand on the preview clock and move it to set your time. Again, it serves no real purpose, but every time I set my clock like this with someone looking, they're always amazed by it. Unless they're Swiss, of course.

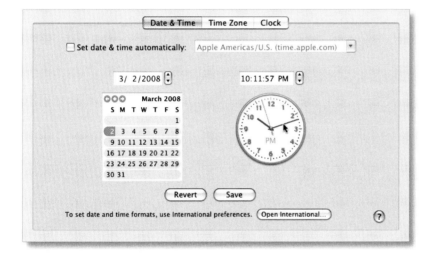

iMOVIE SLOW MOTION SWAP

The iMovie interface has two main windows—the Event Library and the Project Library—and it gives you the option to swap their locations. But as you would expect, it's a cool swap, not just an ordinary one. To make the swap, just click the Swap button (it's the second button from the left in the row of buttons that separates the top and bottom portions of the iMovie window) and the windows will get sucked into their new locations. Like all the other cool effects in Leopard, if you press-and-hold the Shift key when you click, the swap will take place in super slow motion.

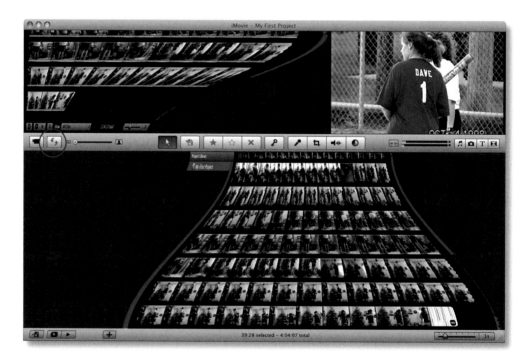

   PHOTO BOOTH IS HOURS OF FUN

Photo Booth is one of the applications that comes with Leopard, and just between you and me, it's a lot of fun. It has a couple of practical uses, like taking pictures to use for your account login, Mail, and iChat. Honestly, I think these were added as an afterthought so grown adults could justify leaving an application targeted for the 13-and-under crowd on their Macs. So get somewhere where no one will see you and start playing. Pretend you're a reporter in front of the Eiffel Tower, an outdoor type in Yellowstone, or a seasoned roller coaster rider. But since this is a book on tips, here are a couple for using Phone Booth. If the flash bothers you when you take a picture (actually, sometimes it wipes out some of the effects), just press-and-hold the Shift key when you click the Shutter button. For those of you who are too busy to wait for the three-second countdown between the time you click the Shutter button and when the shutter actually snaps, press-and-hold the Option key when you click the Shutter button and it will take your picture immediately.

Chapter 15

CHEAP TRICK

MAC OS X
Pranks

Although this is a pretty short chapter, it may be (a) the most fun, (b) the most cruel, or (c) a delightful combination of the two.

Cheap Trick
mac os x pranks

(The difference between "fun" and "cruel" is the difference between "reading the pranks" and "perpetrating them.") The original outline for this book didn't have a "pranks" chapter at all, but as I was writing tips for the other chapters, I'd sometimes think, "Boy, if you didn't know about this, and somebody who did know it wanted to mess with you, they could pretty much bring your Mac life crashing down around you." I imagined this could create a new brand of Mac heroes—people who would pull these pranks in secret on the machines of unsuspecting co-workers, then show up later to offer to "take a look at the problem," and with a few clicks, fix it—winning the respect and admiration of the victim and other office co-workers. I feel pretty safe in sharing these pranks, because I know you're not the type of person to use or abuse these little gems. Right? Right? Hello…

MESS WITH THEIR iCHAT ALERTS

Annoyance Factor: 6
Difficulty to Fix: 7
You can set iChat so it will automatically make an audio announcement of any event that occurs (a buddy becomes available, a new message is received, etc.). Launch iChat on their computer, go to the iChat menu, choose Preferences, then click on the Alerts icon. Click the Event pop-up menu and select an event, then turn on the Announce When Event

Occurs checkbox. You can do this for as many events as you want. The next time they open iChat, it will drive them nuts. It probably won't take them too long to figure out how to shut up the voice, but it will be good for a few minutes of laughs at their expense. If you want to take it a step further, turn on the Run AppleScript checkbox instead of Announce When Event Occurs. Then go to the Applications folder, to AppleScript, and select a script from the Example Scripts folder. Just be nice and pick one that will do something innocuous (remember, it is a friend), like hide all the Finder windows, print the current window, or reset the system volume to maximum.

   SHIFT-BEEP. OPTION-BEEP. COMMAND-BEEP. BEEP-BEEP!

Annoyance Factor: 7   Difficulty to Fix: 6
Would it drive you crazy if suddenly every time you pressed Shift, Option, Command, or Control it would make an annoying typewriter sound and then giant icons (that represent those modifier keys) appeared on the upper-right side of your desktop? Sure it would. Wouldn't it be funny if that suddenly happened to a friend's or co-worker's machine? Sure it would. Go to the System Preferences under the Apple menu, click the Universal Access icon, click the Keyboard tab, and turn on Sticky Keys. Will they know where to go to turn the sound and giant icons off? I doubt it. One of two things will happen: (1) they'll learn to live with it, or (2) they'll do a reinstall.

This is guaranteed to induce certain behaviors from the recipient of your System modifications. These include, but are not limited to, keyboard banging, muttering, and comments about the parentage of their Mac.

   GIVE THEIR CDS AND DVDS SOME NEW "FEATURES"

Annoyance Factor: 6   Difficulty to Fix: 7

If you know a friend or co-worker listens to music CDs on their Mac, this is going to be music to your ears. Currently when they insert a music CD, iTunes probably opens automatically so they can play it. Makes sense. But that seems so routine. Wouldn't it be more fun if, instead of launching iTunes when they inserted a music CD, the Mac would quickly go to the Web, download the latest U.S. weather map, and then launch Preview and display this map? No music. Just a map. If they pop it out and try again, they get another map. And another and another. It's map mania! Here's how it's done: Go to the System Preferences under the Apple menu, and click on the CDs & DVDs icon. When those preferences appear, from the pop-up menu where it says When You Insert a Music CD, choose Run Script. Then, in the resulting dialog, navigate to the Applications folder, click on the AppleScript folder, and inside of that click on Example Scripts. Then click on the URLs folder where you can finally click on Download Weather Map.scpt and click the Choose button. Of course, this is just a start. Tomorrow, try a different script. Maybe a printing script or a mail script. The mind reels.

SPEAK TO ME, BABY

Annoyance Factor: 6   Difficulty to Fix: 7

VoiceOver is an amazing tool that makes it possible for visually impaired people to use their Macs. Every time you click a menu item, open a window, roll your cursor over an option in a dialog—basically, whenever you do anything—it tells you what you can do from your current location or what you just did. It's indispensable for those who need it. But for those who don't rely on it, it can be incredibly annoying. An added bonus is that since it's not one of those features that is used frequently, most people don't know it's there, let alone how to activate or (for your purposes) deactivate it. Imagine the fun your friend (co-worker, evil nemesis, etc.) will have when everything they do is spoken aloud by a voice that belongs to someone who's clearly one sleeve short of a straightjacket? Here's how to make it happen: Go to the System Preferences in the Apple menu and click on the Universal Access icon. First, at the top of the pane in the VoiceOver section, click the On radio button. Next, click the Open VoiceOver Utility button. You are now a kid in a candy store of pranks. The first thing you need to do is click the General icon on the left and either delete or change the text in the Login Greeting field so they won't know VoiceOver is on. Next, for this prank, click on the Speech icon and change the default voice from Alex to Deranged. Want to make it a little eerier? Lower the Pitch to around 20. Then close this dialog, close the System Preferences, and call Nurse Ratched, because it's time to pass out the "happy pills." If they've been using a Mac for a while, they may go straight to the Speech preference pane to see if Speakable Items is turned on, but it won't be. By the way, if they're working late and you want to freak them out, lower the lights, then do this same trick, but instead of Deranged, try Whisper and set the master volume to 100%. If you try this one, better keep a mop nearby. *Note:* Make sure you check out the other quasi-evil options available by clicking the other buttons in the VoiceOver Utility sidebar.

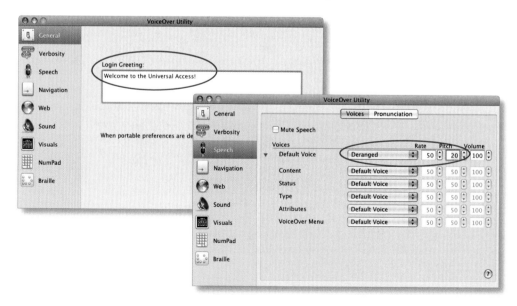

   MAKE THEIR KEYBOARD BILINGUAL

Annoyance Factor: 6   Difficulty to Fix: 7

This one can be as subtle or as infuriating as you'd like. For example, changing a U.S. keyboard to a U.K. keyboard is subtle. In fact, they might not even notice it that much until they go to type in a # symbol (which is Shift-3) and they get a British pound sign (£) instead. What throws them is that the # symbol is right there printed on their keyboard (right above the number 3), yet every time they press Shift-3, they get the British pound sign. Again, this is subtle, and the pound sign does give them a hint. Or you can go for something a bit more disconcerting, like changing the keyboard layout to Hungarian, which works fine until they type the letter Y, because it types the letter Z (and vice versa). Also, it really starts to get fun when they use any punctuation whatsoever. To start this international keyboard fest, go to System Preferences under the Apple menu and click on the International icon. Click the Input Menu tab, and now simply turn on the checkbox beside one of the installed foreign keyboard layouts from the long list of languages. Then, before you close the System Preferences, turn off the checkbox for Show Input Menu in Menu Bar at the bottom of the Input Menu pane (or they'll see up in their menu bar that you've changed the keyboard), and then just walk away. *Note:* Just be sure you don't try this out on your own Mac late at night when you're tired. The next morning you might go through three restarts, reset the PRAM, and repair the permissions before you realize what the problem is. Not that I would ever do that, but I have a friend....

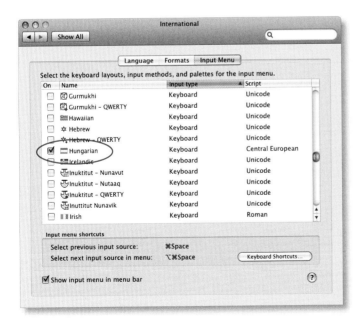

   CREATE A TERRIFYING FAKE DIALOG

Annoyance Factor: 10+   Difficulty to Fix: 8

Picture this: Your co-worker comes back from lunch, double-clicks the folder that holds the project she's been working on for three weeks, and a dialog appears telling her: "Alert: There was a fatal read/write system IO error and the contents of this folder are permanently damaged and cannot be restored." Sound like fun? It's easy to pull off, because the ability to create your own custom message that appears when a folder is opened is built right into Leopard. Here's how it works: First, click on the folder and then press Command-I to open the Info dialog. Then, click the right-facing triangle next to Spotlight Comments. In the field, write a scary-sounding warning (feel free to use the one here or make up your own. Messages mentioning how a virus has attacked the folder also work nicely). Collapse the Spotlight Comments section by clicking the arrow again, then close the Info dialog. Now, Control-click on the folder, scroll to the bottom of the contextual menu, select More, and choose Configure Folder Actions. When the Folder Actions Setup dialog opens, be sure the Enable Folder Actions checkbox is turned on, then click the plus sign (+) button in the bottom left-hand corner of the dialog. A standard Open dialog will appear; navigate your way to the person's folder and click Open. When you do this, a dialog will pop down prompting you to Choose a Script to Attach. Choose the script "open—show comments in dialog.scpt" and click the Attach button. Now sit back and let the fun begin.

   CREATE AN EVEN MORE TERRIFYING FAKE DIALOG

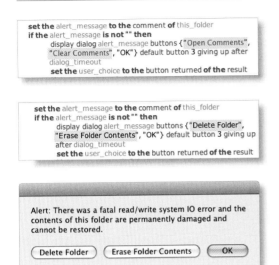

Annoyance Factor: 10+
Difficulty to Fix: 10+
If you are a truly evil person, you can take the last prank up a few notches by adding one more line to the Spotlight Comments field. Do everything just the same as the previous tip, but after you click Attach Script, click on the script name and click the Edit Script button (don't let this scare you: no scripting experience is required to do this). When the Script Editor window opens, scroll down past the comments until you see the actual script. All you have to do now is find the line that says "display dialog alert_message buttons" and change the text that will appear on the buttons in the fake dialog. When you've entered the new panic-enhancing options (such as Delete Folder and Erase Folder Contents, as shown here), press Command-S to save the script, then close the Script Editor window and the Folder Actions Setup windows. You might want to make sure there are no young children around when your co-worker opens the folder. I have a feeling some short, but expressive, words might start flying. *Note:* In case you're wondering what happens when they press one of the buttons—nothing.

HIDING, WELL...EVERYTHING!

Annoyance Factor: 5   Difficulty to Fix: 4

This is a great trick to pull on people who keep lots of stuff on their desktops. First, hide all open windows, then press Command-Shift-3 to take a screen shot of their entire desktop. Because Leopard has a semi-transparent menu bar, you will need to open the screen shot in Preview (or Photoshop) and crop it to remove the menu bar (if you don't, it shows through the real menu bar and makes the text look funky). Now, choose System Preferences from the Apple menu and click on the Desktop & Screen Saver icon. Click the Desktop tab, then drag your screen capture into the preview window at the top left of the pane (as shown here) to make the screen capture the new desktop background, and then close the System Preferences. Next, create a folder on their desktop and drag everything on the desktop into that folder, and drag this folder into their Home folder (for safekeeping). Then, go to the Finder menu, choose Preferences, and click on the General icon. Where it says Show These Items on the Desktop, turn off the Hard Disks, CDs, DVDs, iPods, and Connected Servers checkbox. Now go to the Apple menu, under Dock, and choose Turn Hiding On and change the position of the Dock to the Left or Right side of the screen to prevent it from "unhiding" if they move their cursor to the bottom of the screen. That's it. When they return, nothing they click on will work (except the menu bar)—all the icons, folders, hard disks, etc., appear frozen because they're seeing the desktop capture. Even if they figure out that it's a desktop background, when they change it, their drives are still missing and the Dock is still hidden and in a different spot than usual. This is one sweet prank.

   LOCKING SOMEONE OUT OF THEIR OWN MACHINE

Annoyance Factor: 4   Difficulty to Fix: 2

This is a good one to pull on someone who is a single user (they're not sharing their machine with other users), thus they're not used to logging in each day with a username and password. Choose System Preferences from the Apple menu, click the Desktop & Screen Saver icon, click the Screen Saver tab, and slide the Start Screen Saver slider to, say, three minutes. Now (this is the key to the whole thing), click the Show All button, go to the Security preference pane, and turn on the checkbox next to Require Password to Wake This Computer from Sleep or Screen Saver. Now, every time their computer sits idle for three minutes, it will require them to enter their password—if they can even remember what it is. Ahh, it's the simple things in life.

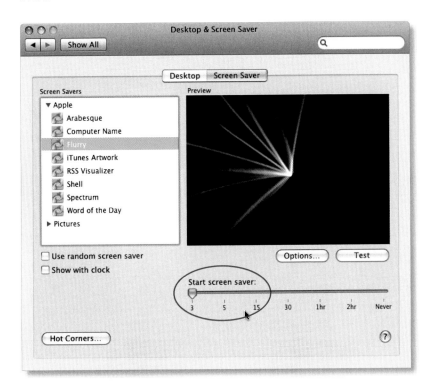

   UNCOLOR THEIR WORLD

Annoyance Factor: 4–7   Difficulty to Fix: 5

This has a variable amount of annoyance—from mild to strong—because you have options. Start by going under the Apple menu and choosing System Preferences, then click on the Universal Access icon, and click the Seeing tab. In the Display section, click the White on Black radio button, which gives their entire computer the "negative" look. Perhaps even better is the checkbox to the right of that—Use Grayscale—which removes all color from everything. Very effective, as shown here, and Universal Access is the last place they'll look—they'll spend hours looking in Display preferences.

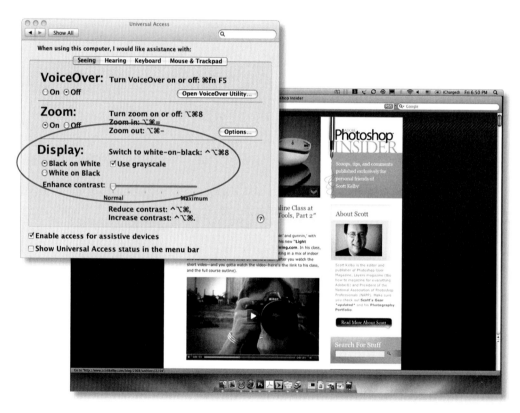

   JAM THEIR DOCK

Annoyance Factor: 8   Difficulty to Fix: 9

This is just one of those things that makes people crazy, because without getting your hands dirty, there's really no quick way to undo the damage, and it takes a long time and a lot of clicking to get things back to the way they were. Start by looking through the victim's hard drive until you find a folder with lots of items from one application (for example, any folder with 50 or more files qualifies, but think, "The more, the merrier!"). Shift-click to select files in groups of ten, and then drag them to the Dock. Repeat this with as many files as you like, until your victim has countless items in the Dock. Not only will this make their Dock microscopic in size, but there's also only one way (short of some serious under-the-hood system tweaks) to get these items back out of the Dock—clicking-and-dragging them out one by one. A full reinstall is probably faster. This is something you should probably save for your last day at your current job, for obvious reasons.

UNEXPLAINED LAUNCH MYSTERIES

Annoyance Factor: 8   Difficulty to Fix: 7

If you know which types of files your victim uses most (images, text, PDF, etc.), find one of them on their drive and get ready because the fun is about to begin. Click on the file you found (here, I chose a PDF), then press Command-I to open the file's info. Now go down to the Open With section and, if it's not already expanded, click the gray right-facing triangle. You should see a pop-up menu with the name of the application that is currently set as the default to open this type of file—but that's about to change. Click the pop-up menu and select a new default application from the list. This is the application that will be used from now on (or at least until they figure out what's going on) when they open a file of the same type. Remember, your purpose is to drive someone nuts, so pick something that just seems crazy. In the example here, I clicked the Change All button so any PDF document they open will open using Mail instead of Preview. If you want just this particular document to open in Mail, just ignore the Change All button. It might actually drive them crazier trying to figure out what is causing just this one document to open with Mail. There's just no limit to the fun you can have.

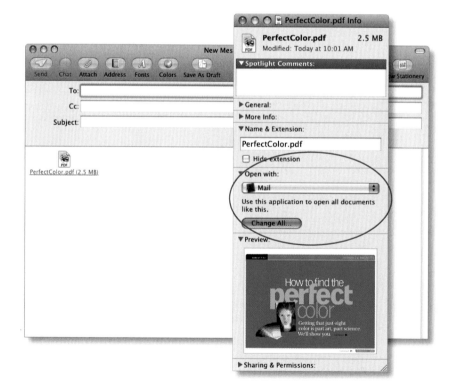

   APPLICATION ICON MADNESS

Panic Factor: 10+   **Difficulty to Fix: 2**

Imagine if you clicked on an application and, instead of launching the application, it just opened an empty Finder window. This would get mighty frustrating, wouldn't it? This type of thing would basically bring a person's work to a halt, wouldn't it? Sound good? Here's what to do:

STEP ONE: Press Command-Shift-N to create a new blank folder on the desktop and name it "Gotcha!" Now create a second blank folder (you don't need to give it a name yet) and press Command-I to open an information window.

STEP TWO: Go to your friend's Applications folder, click the icon for one of their major applications (something like Photoshop CS3) to select it, and then drag this icon and drop it on top of the blank folder's icon in the top-left corner of the Info window you just opened.

STEP THREE: Now go back to the Applications folder and click-and-drag the Adobe Photoshop CS3 application icon into your Gotcha! folder. Click-and-drag the blank folder, now sporting the Adobe Photoshop CS3 icon, into the Applications folder, and rename the folder "Adobe Photoshop CS3." If they have an icon for Photoshop in the Dock, you'll need to replace it with one for the "new" Photoshop folder.

You can repeat this process for as many of their apps as you want, keeping in mind their breaking point. Now every time they click on one of these apps, all they'll get is an empty Finder window. After they've been curled up in a ball whimpering and sucking their thumb for awhile, you can lead them to the Gotcha! folder—for a small fee.

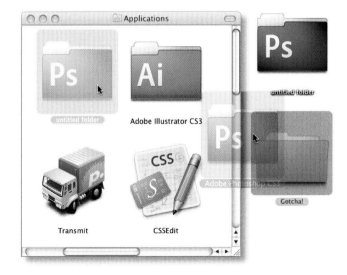

MAKE THEIR FONTS ALL JAGGY

Annoyance Factor: 4   Difficulty to Fix: 4

I gave this one a fairly low annoyance factor, because some people won't really notice it, but some people (like designers) will and it will irk them just a little every single day. Not enough to reinstall, not enough to call the IT department, but just enough to make them cringe on a daily basis. Go to the Apple menu, select System Preferences, and click on the Appearance icon. When the pane appears, where it says Turn Off Text Smoothing for Font Size *X* and Smaller, change the size to 12 from the pop-up menu. If you want to be a bit more subtle (which will increase the annoyance factor), use 9 or 10 instead of 12. What this does is remove the anti-aliasing from any text smaller than the point size you just selected. What that means is anytime they use a font that is, say, 10 point or smaller, it will look really jaggy and awful. It's still readable, but it's painful to look at. Again and again, day after day, week after week, month after…well, you get the idea. In fact, this one is so subtle, it's just plain mean. Or bold mean, or italic mean.

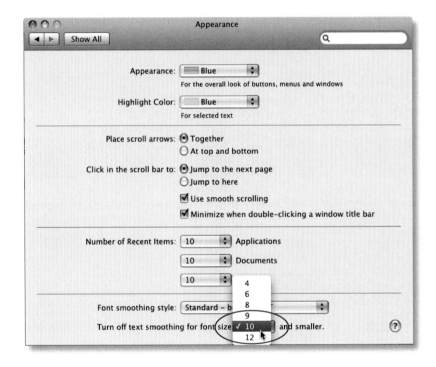

   BLOW UP THEIR CURSOR

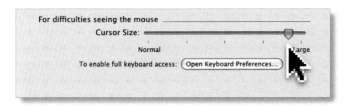

Annoyance Factor: 3
Difficulty to Fix: 3
If the standard-size cursors seem a bit too small for you, now you can make that cursor huge. Just go to the System Preferences (in the

Apple menu), click on the Universal Access icon, then click the Mouse tab. Near the bottom of the pane, you'll see a slider for Cursor Size. Just click-and-drag the slider to the right, and as you do you'll see the new size. This is great to use when you're doing presentations projected onto a big screen, so people don't lose track of the cursor while you're working. But it's also great for a quick prank.

  MAKE THEM THINK THEIR SCREEN IS TRASHED

Annoyance Factor: 4
Difficulty to Fix: 3
This will take you like two seconds to do, which means you can do it while they're in their office, which makes it seem like it must not be a trick. Who could do something this bad this fast? You, that's who. Just press Command-Option-Control-8. The colors on their display will invert. Even better—if you can have access to their machine to enable screen sharing, you can do it to them from anywhere in the world. They'll never suspect you.

   BLOW OUT THEIR SCREEN

Annoyance Factor: 8   Difficulty to Fix: 7

This is the perfect kind of prank: It has a high annoyance factor, and it has a very high satisfaction level (for you) because it is so easy to do, and you can literally do it while they turn their back for 10 seconds to pick up a cup of coffee or answer a phone call. What you're going to do is increase their screen's contrast and remove the anti-aliasing, making it pretty much unusable for much of anything. Here's how you do it: Press Command-Option-Control-. (period) repeatedly until the screen looks as bad as you want it to be. The first few times you press, it won't look like anything is happening. Keep going (the screen shots here are normal, five levels, 10 levels, and 15 levels) and it will start to go downhill. The antidote is the same shortcut, except use a comma at the end instead of the period. This is one of those pranks that's fun to stretch out for awhile. Make a subtle change the first time, just enough to make them wonder if they're imagining it. Then put it back to normal for a day or two, then boost it a bit more. As soon as they get ready to call in IT, put it back to normal. Do it to your screen one day so they'll think it's contagious or something. High annoyance, high satisfaction, loads of fun. Ahhhhh.

STRIP DOWN SAFARI WINDOWS

Annoyance Factor: 6   Difficulty to Fix: 2
They'll probably figure this one out pretty quickly, but it will still be good for a few yuks. Launch Safari, go to the View menu, and then start hiding all the things you need to be able to see in order to do much of anything with Safari. The example here shows what you're left with when you hide the Bookmarks Bar, Status Bar, Tab Bar, and toolbar. Not much!

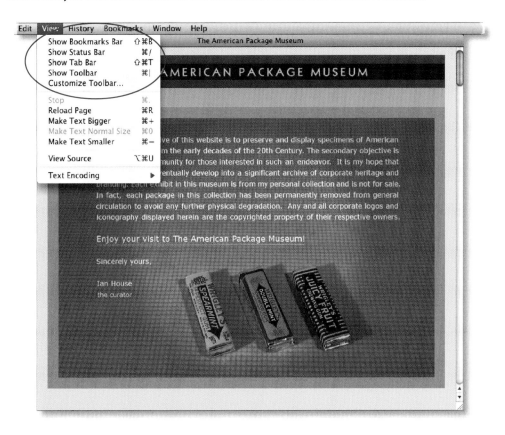

Index

Trash, emptying, 327
tuner, GarageBand, 339
Tuning Fork icon, 339
two-button mouse
    changing primary button on, 261
    Exposé functions and, 28
    replacing Control-click with, 48
type. *See* fonts; text

U

Universal Access icon, 394, 402, 407
updates, software, 326

V

vCards, 102–105
    hiding info on, 102
    importing, 104
    making your own, 102
    Notes sent with, 104
    sending other people's, 105
    sharing with friends, 103
    updating for groups, 296
Vector Smart Objects, 252
video chats
    hiding yourself during, 320
    one-way, 135
    recording, 142
    sharing files via, 147
videos
    importing into iMovie, 351
    merging clips from, 352
    options for watching, 206
    Playhead Info option, 350
    playing in floating window, 209
    resizing in QuickTime, 207
    scrubbing through, 206, 306
    selection options for, 354–355
    skimming through, 210, 349
    splitting into separate days, 350
    storage space conservation, 353
    See also DVDs; movies

viewing
    spaces, 34
    stacks, 62
    See also displaying
views
    Column, 11–12
    Cover Flow, 8–9
    Finder, 300
    Icon, 10
    List, 9
    setting, 13, 14
Visualizer, iTunes, 203
VoiceOver tool, 396
volume controls
    silencing beeps in, 323
    speaker volume, 279
    warning beep volume, 303

W

warnings
    beep volume for, 303
    Empty Trash, 327
    file extension change, 328
Weather widget, 388
Web Archive, 174
Web browser. *See* Safari Web browser
Web Gallery, 371–373
    controlling access to, 373
    options for adding photos to, 372
    publishing albums to, 371
    subscriptions to, 373
webpages
    adding photos to iPhoto from, 267
    bookmarking links to, 159
    emailing links to, 168, 315
    making widgets from, 175
    Parental Controls for, 176
    saving as Web Archive, 174
    searching words on, 172
    sending from Safari, 170
    text links to, 315
White, Terry, 293

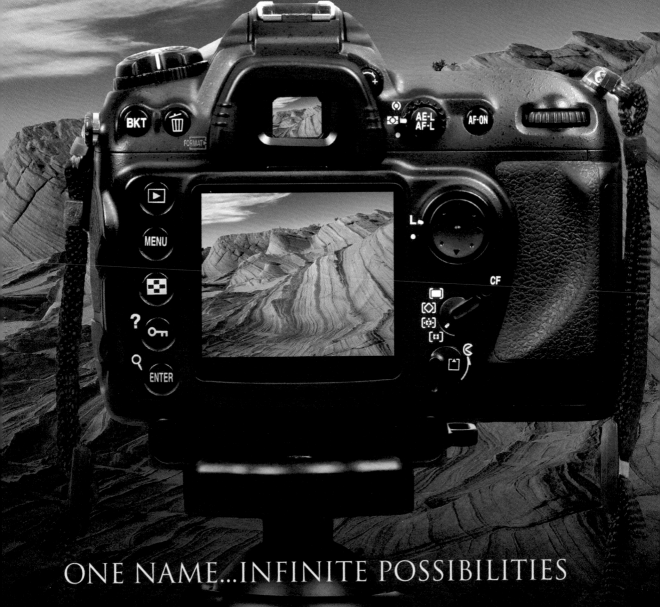

ONE NAME...INFINITE POSSIBILITIES

AT KELBY TRAINING WE SHARE YOUR PASSION FOR PHOTOGRAPHY AND CREATIVITY.

THAT'S WHY WE'RE YOUR PREMIER SOURCE FOR INSTRUCTIONAL

DVDS, BOOKS, ONLINE TRAINING AND LIVE TRAINING EVENTS THAT WILL

BOOST YOUR SKILLS AND TAKE YOUR WORK TO THAT NEXT LEVEL.

Kelbytraining
EDUCATION FOR CREATIVES

BOOKS • DVDS • ONLINE TRAINING • LIVE SEMINARS

WWW.KELBYTRAINING.COM OR CALL 800-201-7323

Log on & Learn
WORLD CLASS ONLINE TRAINING

The Best Teachers on The Planet—Online—All in One Place

Scott**KELBY** Katrin**EISMANN** Bert**MONROY** Corey**BARKER** Dan**MARGULIS**
KLOSKOWSKI Tov**SIRKIS** Dave**CROSS** Ben**WILLMORE** Eddie**TAPP**
WHITE Moose**PETERSON** Joe**MCNALLY** Rich**HARR**
NIGRO **KELBY** Dave**ZISER** RC**CONCEPCION**
KLOSKOWSKI Vincent**VERSACE**

Mastering Adobe Photoshop®, digital photography,
and the entire Adobe Creative Suite®
has never been easier or more affordable.

$199
OR
$19⁹⁹
PER YEAR   ## A MONTH

NAPP Members $179 a year or $17.99 a month.

Our Classes. Your Schedule.

Kelby Training offers two simple ways to subscribe. Either way you get 24 hour a day access to everything.
All courses, all lessons, and all accompanying exercise files. **No strings attached.**

Log on to www.KelbyTraining.com for your 24 Hour Free Trial.

Adobe, Photoshop, and Creative Suite are trademarks of Adobe Systems Incorporated. All rights reserved.

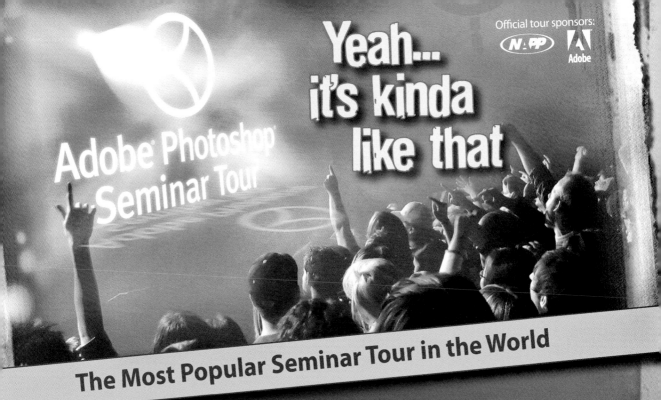

Official tour sponsors: N·PP Adobe

Yeah... it's kinda like that

Adobe Photoshop Seminar Tour

The Most Popular Seminar Tour in the World

It's time to get excited about Photoshop® all over again!
Don't miss your chance to get up close and personal with the world's most renowned Photoshop® authors, teachers, and creative gurus. Ask questions, get your favorite Photoshop® books autographed, or just hang out between sessions and talk Photoshop® one-on-one. The Adobe® Photoshop® Seminar Tour provides a rare opportunity to see the best on the planet teaching the absolute hottest and latest tips, tricks, and techniques that are sure to keep your creativity on the cutting edge. **Welcome to the Show!**

Adobe Photoshop Seminar Tour

Produced by

EDUCATION FOR CREATIVES

For only **$99**   NAPP members pay only **$79**

Your one-day seminar also includes a detailed seminar workbook, keyboard shortcut guide, issue of *Photoshop User* and *Layers* magazines, and a bonus Kelby Training DVD ($29.95 value).
To register visit www.KelbyTraining.com/seminars

Coming to a City Near You!

SCOTT KELBY   DAVE CROSS   BERT MONROY   BEN WILLMORE

**Call 800.201.7323 or visit www.KelbyTraining.com/seminars
for upcoming tour dates and cities.**

Adobe, Photoshop, Illustrator, InDesign and Photoshop Lightroom are registered trademarks of Adobe Systems Incorporated.

Get free online access to this book!

And sign up for a free trial to Safari Books Online to get access to thousands more!

With the purchase of this book you have instant online, searchable access to it on Safari Books Online! And while you're there, be sure to check out the Safari on-demand digital library and its Free Trial Offer (a separate sign-up process)—where you can access thousands of technical and inspirational books, instructional videos, and articles from the world's leading creative professionals with a Safari Books Online subscription.

Simply visit www.peachpit.com/safarienabled and enter code 2TH4-B4MH-XVKZ-2BHD-7V1M to try it today.